THE D.A.R.

An Informal History

THE D.A.R.

An Informal History

MARTHA STRAYER

Public Affairs Press, Washington, D. C.

ABOUT THE AUTHOR

Former president of the Women's National Press Club and one of Washington's most outstanding newspaper women, Martha Strayer probably knows the DAR better than any other American journalist.

A native of Jefferson County, Ohio, she can trace her ancestors way back to Colonial and Revolutionary days. After earning her spurs on an Ohio newspaper, she came to the District of Columbia in 1920. She has been a member of the staff of the *Washington Daily News* since 1921.

Miss Strayer is one of the few newspaper women to win the "Big Story" radio award. In 1955 the National Education Association honored her for "noteworthy contributions and services to education".

She is an associate member of Theta Sigma Phi, national women's journalistic sorority; a member of the Women's National Press Club; and a member of the American Newspaper Guild.

Copyright, 1958, by Public Affairs Press
419 New Jersey Ave., S.E., Washington 3, D. C.

Printed in the United States of America
Library of Congress Catalog Card No. 57-6902

PREFACE

My interest in the Daughters of the American Revolution is primarily that of a newspaper woman who has "covered" the organization since the 1920's.

Although my colonial and Revolutionary ancestors were considerate enough—and patriotic enough—to establish amply my eligibility for membership in the DAR, I've never taken advantage of this opportunity. I'm just not a joiner. Moreover, I have made it a point not to become personally associated with any organization or activity which I have to deal with objectively, as a journalist must.

However, it has been my good fortune to come to know the DAR as well as any member. I believe I've "covered" the organization for a longer period than any other American journalist. I say this not boastfully but for the sake of the record. I think the reader ought to know my credentials.

I was present at the famous 1929 session when Mrs. Helen Bailie was denied a hearing of her appeal from expulsion; I wrote a story about her heated comments and those of Mrs. Alfred Brosseau, then President-General. When Marian Anderson was barred from the DAR's Constitution Hall, I stood on the greensward near the Lincoln Memorial and heard her give her concert almost at the feet of the Great Emancipator.

I remember many leading ladies of the DAR—for instance, Mrs. George Thatcher Guernsey, the "plain woman from Kansas", and Mrs. George Maynard Minor, the spiritual New Englander. I can even remember, dimly, Mrs. William Cumming Story, that lovely lady from New York, in what must have been her last appearance at a DAR Congress.

I have seen the Daughters do many wonderful things in connection with historical projects, their schools for mountain children, and Americanization of the foreign born. And I have also seen them do some silly things.

With this background, I set out to write an informal history. Unfortunately, I was able to get no official cooperation from the organization; I asked for permission to use DAR official records as source material for research, but my requests were denied. So I went to the great Library of Congress, which fortunately has voluminous files on the Society.

I am grateful to certain individual Daughters for invaluable assistance. Mrs. Rex Hays Rhoades, who directed the Daughters' last building project, loaned me a copy of the Lockwood-Regan "Early History" and many volumes of Congress proceedings. Mrs. Vylla Poe Wilson, a DAR authority, searched her memory to recall some of the things I didn't know or couldn't remember. Mrs. William Sherman Walker, whom I had known only from a distance through watching her when she was the DAR's national defense leader, gave me material I could have obtained from no other source.

I am also indebted to some former DAR genealogists for aid on genealogy and to Mrs. Cecil Norton Broy, first DAR museum curator, for authentic information about the planning of the Society's beautiful museum and the collection of its priceless relics.

Editors of the Public Affairs Press have helped improved the text considerably. Yet, in spite of their efforts and mine, the book isn't everything I would have liked it to be. Needless to say, it is in no sense a definitive study.

Over the years, I have seen the Daughters pursue their objectives with single-minded firmness. I have watched them make mistakes and sometimes over-rate the importance of their organization. But I have never under-rated their loyalty and devotion and sincerity and my admiration for many of them as individuals, has never faltered.

MARTHA STRAYER

Washington, D. C.

CONTENTS

TO THE TRUE SPIRIT OF
THE AMERICAN REVOLUTION

CHAPTER I

THE FOUNDERS

A pure white memorial to the founders of the DAR stands in a sheltered spot on a close-clipped lawn at the Daughters' national headquarters in Washington. The memorial is a feminine figure whose outstretched hands seem symbolically to welcome to the organization the thousands of women who continue to swell its membership.

Each year a wreath is laid at the base of this memorial in honor of the four Victorian ladies—Eugenia Washington, Mary Desha, Mrs. Helen H. Walworth, and Mrs. Mary S. Lockwood—who founded the society in 1890. Two of these women were government clerks, one a great grand niece of George Washington; the other two were Washington widows, one a woman of means and the other a boarding house keeper whose rooms rented for $1.25 single, $1.50 double, per day.

Each of these ladies was a distinct personality, stamped with many of the sturdy qualities of her forefathers. Eugenia Washington was a clerk in the Dead Letter Office of the Post Office Department; Mary Desha, descendant of a Kentucky Revolutionary colonel, a clerk in the Pension Bureau; Mrs. Ellen H. Walworth divided her time between literature and the family estate at Saratoga Springs, New York; Mrs. Mary S. Lockwood ran a private hotel in downtown Washington. A fifth lady, who became a storm center in the young society, was Mrs. Flora Adams Darling, dynamic widow of a Civil War general, author of Victorian romances, prolific letter-writer and busy magazine editor. A handsome woman, in no way a feminist, Mrs. Darling professed to "believe in men for offices—women for pleasure."

Who indeed did found the new organization? Mrs. Darling claimed the honor exclusively for herself, but her claim was hotly

1

disputed. Recriminations flew, petticoats bristled. Elected second in command among the initial group of top officers, Mrs. Darling functioned for nearly eight months as Vice President in charge of organization, established chapters and recruited wealthy and prominent women as chapter regents and organizers.

Official records fail to provide a clear-cut story of the origin of the DAR; long forgotten volumes at the Library of Congress contain at least four different versions of its beginnings.

Despite many dissensions and difficulties the early Daughters held steadfast to their goal and created an organization which has had a continuous, vigorous, and often controversial existence since its founding in 1890.

Mrs. Darling was undoubtedly a thorn in the flesh of some of her fellow members, Also undoubted, however, is that she made a very tangible contribution to the founding of the society, although that contribution is not officially recognized today.

Mrs. Darling's side of the story may be found in a book published in 1901. This book was an elaboration of an earlier account printed in the *Adams Magazine*, a small periodical of which she was editor and chief contributor. For six months, from January to July, 1891, the *Adams Magazine* was the "official exponent" of the newly founded DAR; one section of the publication was devoted entirely to news about the organization. When Mrs. Darling was removed from office, however, the magazine ceased to be the official mouthpiece and in a few months it ceased to appear.

Mrs. Darling's own account of the founding is inconsistent as to many details. Another version, written with the vitriolic pen of Mary Desha, was published in pamphlet form in July, 1891. Miss Desha challenged Mrs. Darling's claims. Numerous inquiries led to the publication of an official account in 1908. While more objective than Miss Desha's pamphlet, this account denied Mrs. Darling's claim as sole founder, but admitted her connection with the early organization. All accounts agree that it was the older Sons of the American Revolution who inspired the ladies to unite on the basis of their common Revolutionary heredity and that a meeting held on October 11, 1890, led to the founding of the DAR.

The official DAR version of the early history of the organization includes the October 11th date as one of three associated with founding. This version carefully points out that the society was founded on August 9, that organizational details were developed on October 11, and that organization plans were completed on October 18.

Although the Sons of the American Revolution excluded women, some "daughters" were considered auxiliary or unofficial members. However, certain of the Sons objected to the idea of any woman having any status in their organization. In the spring of 1890 the Sons held a national convention at which they took formal action flatly excluding women descendants of Revolutionary ancestors from their society.

The ladies simmered in silence for several months, but in the heat of the summer of 1890, the indignation of Mary S. Lockwood erupted in a letter to the editor of the *Washington Post*. It was a good letter. Mrs. Lockwood had a flair for writing and her protest was so effective that it aroused widespread interest—so much interest that it is considered to have been basically responsible for bringing the DAR organization into existence. The *Post*, then a small but influential paper, published the letter not on its editorial page, but as a news story.

Mrs. Lockwood's letter told the story of Hannah Arnett, an unsung Revolutionary heroine. Wife of a wavering patriot residing in Elizabethtown, New Jersey, Mrs. Arnett heard her husband, Isaac, and some of his friends, meeting in the Arnett home, discuss the idea of deserting the Revolutionary cause and accepting amnesty from the British. It was December, 1776, and not even the signing of the Declaration of Independence concealed the fact that the Revolutionary tide was at low ebb. As a typical wife of the time, Mrs. Arnett was given no part in the male discussion; she sat listening in the next room.

"Picture a large room with a low ceiling, furnished with the heavily carved furniture of those days, dimly lighted by wax candles and a fire in the huge fireplace," Mrs. Lockwood wrote. "Around the table sat a group of anxious, disheartened, discouraged looking men . . . Into this room came Hannah Arnett, throwing open the parlor door and in her womanly majesty confronting the group of councillors.

"Consternation for the moment ruled supreme. Mrs. Arnett's husband advanced towards her, shocked and chagrined that his wife had so forgotten herself that she should come into the midst of a meeting where politics and the questions of the hour were being discussed. He would shield her now. The reproof he would give her later on; and so he was quickly at her side, and, whispering, said to her. 'Hannah! Hannah! This is no place for you. We do not want you here just now.' He would have led her from the room.

"She was a mild, amiable woman and was never known to do aught against her husband's wishes, and if she saw him now she made no sign, but turned upon the astounded group. 'Have you made your decision, gentlemen?' she asked. 'I stand before you to know; have you chosen the part of men or traitors?'

"The group replied that the case was hopeless; the Revolutionary army was starving, half clothed and undisciplined, repulsed everywhere . . .'We are ruined and can stand out no longer against England and her unlimited resources.'

"Hannah Arnett listened and spoke in a strangely sweet voice. 'Brothers,' she said, 'you have forgotten one thing which England has not and which we have—one thing which outweighs all England's treasures, and that is the right. God is on our side, and every volley of our muskets is an echo of His voice. We are poor, and weak, and few, but God is fighting for us; we entered into this struggle with pure hearts and prayerful lips; we had counted the cost and were willing to pay the price, were it in our heart's blood. And now—now because for a time the day is going against us, you would give up all, and sneak back like cravens to kiss the feet that

have trampled upon us. And you call yourselves men—the sons
of those who gave up home and fortune and fatherland to make
for themselves and for dear liberty a resting place in the wilderness! Oh, shame upon you cowards!' "

Mrs. Arnett's husband still tried to silence her, but, according
to Mrs. Lockwood's account, "Her words already had begun to
rouse the little manhood remaining in the bosoms of the men,
though not a word was spoken. She had turned the light of her
soul upon them, and in the reflection they saw photographed their
own littleness of purpose or want of manly resolve.

"Hannah Arnett talked on: 'Take your protection if you will;
proclaim yourselves traitors and cowards, false to your God. But
horrible will be the judgment you will bring upon your heads and
the heads of those that love you. I tell you that England will never
conquer . . . For me, I stay with my country, and my hand shall
never touch the hand nor my heart cleave to the heart of him who
shames her . . .' She turned to her husband and gave him a
withering look that sent a shock through every fibre of his body.
Continuing she said: 'Isaac, we have lived together for twenty
years, and through all of them I have been to you a true and loving
wife; but I am the child of God and my country, and if you do this
shameful thing I will never own you again as my husband.'

"The scornful words uttered in such earnestness; the pathetic
tones in which they were spoken; the tears that dimmed Hannah
Arnett's blue eyes, appealed to the heart of every man before her.
They were not cowards all through, but the panic sweeping over
the land had caught them also. A latent courage put on a new
activity; manliness renewed its strength in strong resolution.
Before these men left the house of Hannah Arnett that night, every
one had resolved to spurn the proffered amnesty and had taken a
solemn oath to stand by their country through good days and bad,
until freedom was written over the face of the fair land.

"There are names of men who fought for their country and
won distinction afterward, who were in this secret council, but the
name of Hannah Arnett figures on no roll of honor.

"Where will the Sons of the American Revolution place Hannah Arnett?" Mrs. Lockwood challenged, in conclusion.

Inspired by this dramatic appeal, William O. McDowell, great grandson of Hannah Arnett and member of the Sons of the American Revolution in New Jersey, also wrote a letter to the *Post*. Mr. McDowell thanked Mrs. Lockwood for recalling the name of his ancestor, expressed his interest in the establishment of a society for women like her, and offered his cooperation. After suggesting the DAR name, he promised to help draft the organization's constitution and by-laws, and called upon interested women of Revolutionary ancestry to communicate with him. All versions of the early history agree that Mrs. Lockwood and Mr. McDowell thus jointly provided the initial inspiration for the DAR, but from this point on there is considerable disagreement about the sequence of events.

Mary Desha was the first prospective Daughter to reply to Mrs. Lockwood's letter of July 13th. Even before Mr. McDowell made his offer of help, she had written Mrs. Lockwood and volunteered to cooperate with her in organizing a society of Daughters of the American Revolution. Within a week the two ladies met, talked over the possibilities of organization, and began to project plans. At their second conference, Mrs. Lockwood was ready with names of several of her friends who were eligible for such a society and who she felt sure would join it. Seven of the ladies on her list were among the 818 who signed up as charter members within the first year. Mary Desha suggested the names of two women and proposed to broach the idea of the organization to them—Miss Eugenia Washington and Mrs. Ellen H. Walworth, both of whom eventually became founders.

Miss Washington, a great granddaughter of Colonel Samuel Washington, brother of George Washington, was to be honored by being listed as No. 1 on the roster of DAR members.

Personal descriptions of three of the founders are given by a lady who knew them and saw them in action. Mrs. Adlai Stevenson, second President-General of the organization and grandmother of the later Presidential candidate, Adlai E. Stevenson, says of the first Daughter in the *Early History of the DAR:* "Miss Washington would gladly have sacrificed life and all that she held most dear, for a settled principle. The whole history of her brief stay among us proved her fidelity to friends and the cause she loved."

A description offered by the contentious Mrs. Darling is less charitable. Remarking briefly that Miss Washington "had been so long in the Dead Letter Office, she had, in fact become a dead letter," Mrs. Darling claimed that she had been completely overlooked in 1889 when New York celebrated the anniversary of George Washington's oath of office as first President of the United States, until Mrs. Darling herself appealed to a prominent New Yorker, the Honorable Hamilton Fish, to give Washington's grandniece a place on the program. "She was an unclaimed memory of departed glory," wrote Mrs. Darling.

Mrs. Walworth, the third official founder, is described by Mrs. Stevenson as a woman of "unusual beauty and attractiveness in person and manner, a writer of many charming works upon historical and patriotic subjects." Living in Washington during the early years of growing pains, Mrs. Walworth later returned to her ancestral home in Saratoga Springs, New York, but continued to make faithful appearances at annual DAR Continental Congresses.

Of aggressive Mary Desha, Mrs. Stevenson writes that she was "a forceful and emphatic speaker, of striking and handsome appearance, with the intellectual power and marked personality of her ancestors."

Ironically enough, although Mrs. Lockwood was the author of the Hannah Arnett letter which helped to launch the DAR, she was not called one of its founders. Her name is on the founders' white marble monument at DAR headquarters, but early Daughters withheld the official title of founder because a summer storm kept her—and other interested ladies—away from a meeting at Mrs. Walworth's apartment on August 9, 1890, when Miss Desha, Miss Washington and Mrs. Walworth met and established their claim to go down in history as official founders of the DAR. This, according to official records, was the first organization meeting.

In a *Washington Post* feature story of April 17, 1955, on the organization's founding, Mrs. Lockwood was reported to have been passed over in the original list of top officers because she ran a boarding house in the District of Columbia. Her address was the Strathmore Arms and there is disagreement in the early records about the exact location of this now vanished landmark where the Daughters' second organization meeting was held in October, 1890. One reported location, 810 Twelfth Street, N.W., now is a parking lot. Another, 1101 K Street, N. W., is occupied by a three-story building remodelled for offices and storerooms.

There is clear indication in an 1891 issue of the *Adams Magazine* that Mrs. Lockwood herself mentioned in her book on Washington houses that she had combined literary work with her duties as "head of a private hotel." Later, in 1896, the Strathmore Arms at 1101 K Street, N.W., was listed among boarding houses available to delegates coming from out of town to the DAR Congress. Mrs. Lockwood does indeed seem to have run a boarding house, and we can only speculate as to whether this fact kept her off the founders' list.

Mrs. Stevenson's early history reports that Mrs. Lockwood occupied several key DAR positions. She served "most acceptably" as DAR representative on the board of the General Federation of Women's Clubs; was second editor of the magazine, from 1894 to 1900; was honored at an official groundbreaking ceremony for Memorial Continental Hall in 1902; and named Honorary Vice-President-General in 1905. Regardless of her services, however, Mrs. Lockwood's name was missing from the roster of officers elected at the meeting of October 11, 1890, which the DAR regards as its formal organization meeting.

On the October 11th list appeared Mrs. Darling's name, second from the top and next to that of Mrs. Caroline Scott Harrison, who was the wife of President Benjamin Harrison and who became the first President-General. At that time there was no hint that Mrs.

Darling was out of favor. The assignment given her was of prime importance—to go out and recruit members for a new and unknown society; organize chapters; give the organization recognized standing; chart a course on an uncharted sea. The only New Yorker in the original group, worldly and enterprising, Mrs. Darling must have seemed peculiarly fitted for this responsibility; and the record shows that she did indeed bring in members, organize chapters and give the organization standing.

A friendly biography, appearing in the periodical she edited, the *Adams Magazine* for October, 1891, tells Mrs. Darling's personal history. She was married in 1860 to General Edward Irving Darling, an officer in the Confederate Army who was killed while fighting in November, 1863, leaving his young widow with a two-year-old son behind Confederate lines.

"Desiring to return to her father's household in New Hampshire," the magazine explained, "she was granted a passport by federal authorities but was subsequently arrested and sent to prison, in direct violation of the flag of truce. While in the custody of New Orleans officials, her trunks were robbed of a casket of jewels and $25,000 worth of bonds. These she never recovered . . .

"Upon her return north she called upon President Lincoln and stated her case, and he recognized it as a just one and manifested his intention to see it righted. His untimely death prevented this, however, and for the past twenty years the case has been in litigation, supported by eminent counsel who have no doubt that she will ultimately succeed in recovering not only principal and interest, but compensation for the hardships to which she was subjected.

"She is a favorite writer, a good speaker, a true friend and always an agreeable companion . . . She has all of her life been in the social atmosphere of the great men and women closely associated with national affairs. President Franklin Pierce was one of her childhood friends and his affection continued through his life. He visited her father after his election and corresponded regularly with her. She has been a voluminous and successful writer. Her most widely known and popular work, *The Social Diplomat*, was called a 'novel of great merit'."

Mrs. Darling may or may not have had other sources of income than her writings; the record does not say. Of some social prominence, her acquaintance was broader than that of the Washington ladies. The embittered Mary Desha is authority for the statement that Mrs. Darling felt her social contacts would be more valuable to the new organization than those of a "mere government clerk." Mrs. Darling's contacts would certainly be no handicap.

Starred as the one and only founder in her own book, Flora Darling is assailed in Mary Desha's pamphlet; she is given credit as a member of the group and first chapter organizer in a DAR history written by Mrs. Lockwood and a collaborator, Mrs. Emily Sherwood Regan; and she is mentioned briefly in the official DAR version of 1908. This last publication admits that Mrs. Darling had talked to Miss Eugenia Washington in the summer of 1890 about organizing such a society, but put off taking any action until the fall because "everybody" likely to be eligible had left Washington for the summer.

In one of her own two conflicting versions, Mrs. Darling relates that she was first inspired to initiate the DAR when she heard a speech at an official meeting of Sons of the American Revolution in New York. In another version she says she talked to a Son in Washington about the idea, which had occurred to her while she was visiting in Virginia. Omitting all mention of Mrs. Lockwood's letter to the *Washington Post*, Mrs. Darling's account quotes at length from a letter received from members and describes in great detail her own activities and organizing technique. That technique was based on the selection of an important lady as the nucleus for a chapter, appointing her chapter regent and allowing her a free hand in recruiting other eligibles.

Mrs. Stevenson, whose husband was Vice President in President Grover Cleveland's second administration, and Mrs. Lockwood and her collaborator, wrote ladylike and restrained stories of the founding and early history. Not so Mrs. Darling and Miss Desha, those ancient enemies. Miss Desha charged that Mrs. Darling, having decided that the new organization was a good thing, came to Washington, announced that she had been appointed by Mr. McDowell to organize, and took over. Mrs. Darling countercharged. She said Miss Desha was appointed "by me" as Chairman of the Executive Board of the DAR at the October 11th meeting. Then, Mrs. Darling continued, "when I was obliged to remove her (Miss Desha) because of Mrs. Harrison's objection, Miss Desha became an insurgent. Not until then was there a word of discord."

The "Mrs. Harrison" is, of course, the wife of President Benjamin Harrison, first President-General of the DAR. Accounts differ as to how Mrs. Harrison's election came about. Mrs. Lockwood reports that three hours before the October meeting Mrs. Harrison's carriage stopped at Mrs. Lockwood's door, and Mrs. Harrison's niece appeared with Mrs. Harrison's genealogy, inquiring how much of it would be needed for membership application papers. According to Mrs. Lockwood, she urged the First Lady to accept the Presidency, but did so at first without success; then, when Mrs. Harrison was assured that some one else would be elected to relieve her of arduous duties, she consented to let her name be put in nomination but exacted a promise from Mrs. Lockwood that if there was one dissenting vote her name would be withdrawn.

Mrs. Darling states, on the other hand, that it was she, as DAR organizer, who first talked to Mrs. Harrison about naming a second-string officer to substitute for the First lady. Feeling that Mary Desha's loyalty and early efforts deserved recognition, Mrs. Darling claims to have included her name in the list of top officers submitted to Mrs. Harrison for approval. The First Lady approved all except the Pension Bureau clerk. According to Mrs. Darling, "Mrs. Harrison stated that in the capacity of chairman of the Executive Board Miss Desha would be in close official touch with her, and represent her officially at many places and on most occa-

sions. For that reason Mrs. Harrison thought that a married
woman, one who had social prominence and a residence of some
pretension in Washington, should be chosen for the office.

"I realized instantly that in endeavoring to give Miss Desha a
place of such prominence I had committed an error of judgment.
I suggested the name of Mrs. William D. Cabell. The suggestion
was agreeable to Mrs. Harrison. I wrote to Miss Desha that she
must be sacrificed for the 'good of the cause'."

Whether or not Mrs. Darling's version is the true one, Mary
Desha was eliminated and consequently became bitter in her antag-
onism towards Mrs. Darling. She was made one of seven Vice
Presidents General and dropped two levels below Mrs. Harrison
on the first officer list. The two ladies who were named Vice
Presidents General Presiding, serving as substitutes for Mrs. Harrison after she made brief official appearances, are unmentioned
in the earliest stages of the founding, but did have the necessary
social qualifications. Lending credence to Mrs. Darling's report
of Mrs. Harrison's ultimatum, Mrs. William D. Cabell, the lady
who actually served as Vice President presiding during the First
Lady's incumbency, claimed both social prominence and a "residence of some pretension in Washington".

Mrs. Cabell, who, with her husband, ran a fashionable girls'
school in Washington for daughters of prominent public figures,
lived in a "spacious residence" on Massachusetts Avenue. Although
she had no part in the organization's origin, Mrs. Cabell became
one of its most prominent early figures, while Miss Desha apparently nursed her wrath and blamed Mrs. Darling for the unfortunate turn of events. The two Daughters continued to feud and
play their separate roles. Miss Desha lost her chance to head
the organization, but was finally victorious in her minor official
capacity.

In a book written in 1901, Mrs. Darling heaps further fuel on
Mary Desha's smoldering fires. She states that Miss Desha originally had an entirely different organization in mind. Unmentioned in Miss Desha's own history, it was to be comprised of all

the women in the country, to "work for the advancement of woman-
kind," with stock issued at $5 a share, and with the unwieldy if
descriptive name of "Wimodaughsis."

Mrs. Stevenson's "Early History" supports Miss Desha rather
than Mrs. Darling in this early scrimmage. Mrs. Stevenson observed that no one who had not felt the depressing, wilting heat of
a summer day in Washington, can "realize the courage it took to
call a meeting of any kind in August, in the almost forsaken Capital." But, she reported, the three founders who met on August
9, 1890—Miss Washington, Miss Desha and Mrs. Walworth—
were undaunted by the absence of all other invited guests and
proceeded to appoint a board of management with Miss Desha as
chairman, Mrs. Walworth as secretary and Miss Washington as
registrar. These three founders, Mrs. Stevenson comments," from
that date never faltered in their work of completing the organization thus happily launched".

William McDowell, the New Jersey Son who had promised his
assistance, waited while Washington's wilting summer wore to an
end. Meanwhile, application blanks were distributed, letters
written, friends approached and notices put in all the newspapers
that applications should be sent to Miss Washington as Registrar.
With preparations under way for a large meeting to be held in
the early fall, on October 7, 1890 Miss Desha and Mrs. Walworth
received a letter from Mrs. Darling informing them that she and
Mr. McDowell would be at a Washington hotel on October 11 at
2 p.m. "to organize the national society, Daughters of the American Revolution".

Mr. McDowell had emerged to become an important factor in
the Darling-Desha feud. Miss Desha reported that the Washington ladies were "perfectly astounded at their sudden decapita-
tion" by Mrs. Darling's letter of October 7. However, Mary
Desha continued, they thought Mr. McDowell must have good
reason for such a seemingly discourteous proceeding and felt it
was more important that the society be launched harmoniously
than that they should be recognized as leaders. They were de-

termined to support Mr. McDowell but, Miss Desha caustically informed Mrs. Darling, it would be impossible for her to organize the society, inasmuch as that already had been accomplished. Miss Desha added "no doubt the officers already named would be glad to resign, as they had accepted the positions, not for self-aggrandizement but to help on the work".

Mrs. Darling was not to be undone by such self-abnegation. In her reply, she calmly claimed she had not known there was a temporary organization, insisted she was "only acting for Mr. McDowell" and suggested "the election might be delayed . . . This can be decided upon by Mr. McDowell, who is the 'pope' for one year.' The Washington ladies, who later scoffed at her suggestion that the new society should be headed by a "pope", were grateful to have the experienced Mr. McDowell preside at the October 11th meeting and prepare the motions adopted by the group membership. Mr. McDowell's experience in this connection was to serve him well.

Mrs. Lockwood, writer of the Hannah Arnett letter, refrained from taking sides in l'affaire Desha-Darling. In her book she reported that Mary Desha was the first to answer her letter in the *Post* and that together they recruited the initial group of eligibles. Later, she confirmed part of Mrs. Darling's story, reporting that early in September, 1890, Mrs. Darling wrote from Culpeper, Virginia, where she was visiting, to ask if Mrs. Lockwood would come to her home and help organize the National Society, Daughters of the American Revolution. Mrs. Lockwood countered with an invitation for Mrs. Darling to come to her apartment, where for "six weeks the work went efficiently forward . . . By correspondence and personal visits, Mrs. Darling enthused many in the new enterprise . . . [and] sent out invitations to the organization meeting of October 11."

On the question of a policy later to assume considerable significance, that of limiting eligibility for membership to the direct descendants of Revolutionary ancestors, Mrs. Darling's judgment proved better than Miss Desha's. The organization's early policy of admitting descendants of "mothers of patriots", that is, collateral descendants, was subsequently abandoned.

Responsibility for this policy was laid to Mary Desha, who moved, just as a meeting was about to adjourn, that a "mothers of patriots" clause be added to the society's constitution. It was late, nobody was paying much attention, the motion carried and the constitution was revised. Protesting vigorously as soon as she learned of the action, Mrs. Darling warned that, with the allegiance of some Revolutionary families divided between the British Crown and the ragged rebels, women eligible for membership as mothers of patriots might also be mothers of Tories and thus objectionable. The admission of collateral descendants did in fact prove an embarrassment to the society's genealogists.

In one instance, a Virginia lady descended from a "mother of patriots," was found by genealogists to be the descendant of a Tory son of the same mother. In Pennsylvania, descendants of a young woman of the Revolution, whose brothers went to war while she stayed at home taking care of their parents, were held eligible through her own mother under the "mother of patriots" clause, though she had no Revolutionary service. Mrs. Darling, who opposed the idea from the start, admitted that she crossed out the "mother of patriots" wording from membership applications distributed by her as Vice President General in Charge of Organization. Her judgment was vindicated years after she herself was out of the Society, when this clause was eliminated from the constitution.

The two adversaries also clashed on the origin of the idea for the design of the DAR seal, showing a Colonial costumed woman sitting at a spinning wheel, a "fit companion for the 'Minute Man at the Plow' " in the Sons of the American Revolution insignia. For the woman at the spinning wheel, Mrs. Darling found an apt quotation from Abigail Adams, wife of President John Adams and first mistress of the White House, who, when her husband was absent on one of his many trips as chief emissary for his country, wrote him these words: "I will seek wool and flax and work willingly with my hands; there is indeed occasion for all our industry and economy." Admitting that Mrs. Darling had found the quotation, Miss Desha nonetheless insisted that she was the originator of the "woman at the spinning wheel" idea, and her claim is supported by Mrs. Lockwood.

Another admitted contribution by Mrs. Darling is the "Home and Country" motto which appears on the DAR seal below the seated figure of the Colonial dame. A Latin motto, "Amor patriae," proposed by Mrs. Walworth and officially adopted, was later replaced by the simpler "Home and Country."

After the October 11th meeting, Mrs. Darling returned to New York and for eight months was a dominant figure in the DAR organization, while Mrs. Desha fumed in the obscurity of the Pension Office. In featuring the Vice President General in charge of organization, the *Adams Magazine* reported: "Mrs. Darling and Mrs. Grover Cleveland were elected honorary life members of a Harlem chapter . . . Frances E. Willard sat in the front row at a New York chapter meeting at which Mrs. Darling also was present; Mrs. Darling called this chapter meeting to order and introduced Mrs. Cabell." In words that were soon to have new import, Mrs. Darling stated: 'In the organization of our Society [Mrs. Cabell] was to me what John Hancock was to Sam Adams, and I hope our long and trusted friendship will end only when one of the two of us crosses the river to join the patriots and tell of the DAR . . .' "

Miss Desha's pamphlet gives vent to her feelings: "With every issue of the *Adams Magazine*, Mrs. Darling became bolder and bolder in her false assertions, more and more positive in her assumption of power. All this was quietly endured, the ladies believing that peace and harmony should be preserved at almost any cost; until, intoxicated by her success and emboldened by their silence, she falsified history and made the pedigree of the society of doubtful origin".

In July, 1891, the "ladies who had believed in peace and harmony" removed Mrs. Darling from her position as Vice President in charge of organization. In reporting this development the *Washington Post* carried a two-column story on the front page of the July 28 issue. Quoting from a membership letter of which it had somehow gained possession, the *Post* revealed that ruling Daughters on the Board of Management charged that Mrs. Darling had been insubordinate, refused to make reports or to submit to organization rules, accused her fellow officers of conspiring against her, and in general was no longer acceptable to the society. In a later issue of the *Adams Magazine*, then shorn of its DAR section, Mrs. Darling said there was proof beyond doubt that a few members of the board of the DAR in Washington conspired early in April against her, socially and officially, and destroyed any influence she might have had . . ."Jealousy was the cause . . . False impressions, rumor, calumny, public announcement of my removal from office, under color of authority. But the truth shows I had tendered my resignation before July 27, when the plot was consummated . . ."

The supreme irony of the removal is that it was Mrs. W. D. Cabell who signed the Board of Management resolution providing that as "Mrs. Darling does not see fit to resign, she is removed." According to Mrs. Darling, Mrs. Cabell owed her appointment as Vice President Presiding in Mrs. Benjamin Harrison's administration, to her sponsorship. The "John Hancock-Sam Adams friendship" was over. Bitter about her removal from office, Mrs. Darling was through with the DAR, though she declared she had been elected to life membership on account of her services in the founding. She was "stunned by the force of the storm," but she had her loyal supporters. "Women were furious at the assault, men thunderstruck, at the recklessness and audacity of the action . . . My deeds and words confirm the fact that I founded the Society of the Daughters of the American Revolution, and as it is written so it must stand."

A few months earlier the *New York World* had carried an account of a glowing interview with Mrs. Darling, calling her a "woman with an idea" and giving her full credit as founder. On

July 30, 1891, both the *World* and *New York Times* reported Mrs. Darling's downfall but with no statement from the lady usually so ready with words about her work, now off to Europe without presenting her case. It is obvious from the space devoted to Mrs. Darling's removal, in those days of small newspapers and few news stories, that she had become a public personality and that the DAR was already good copy. Later she organized two new patriotic societies, the Daughters of 1812 and the Daughters of the Revolution, the latter making unsuccessful overtures to unite with the DAR, which apparently wanted no more of their self-styled originator. Although Flora Darling had left her mark on the society, she is one of the casualties of the early years. Her name is missing from the founders' memorial at Constitution Hall and most members probably have never heard of her.

CHAPTER II

EARLY GROWTH AND DEVELOPMENT

The DAR was wise enough to profit from the mistakes made by the Sons of the American Revolution. Once launched with the assistance of the Sons, the Daughters made steady progress on their own. Fervently devoted to their ideals and objectives, with a keen eye for publicity and having the good fortune to avoid major organizational pitfalls, they became what the Sons never became; a large and nationally influential society.

One of their first sound decisions was to follow the advice of a New York Son, Wilson L. Gill, to organize not as the men had done —into individual state societies—but as a national group including state societies. It is to the constitution written by Gill—the original draft of which is still in existence—that the Daughters owe their "phenomenal success," according to Mrs. Mary S. Lockwood.

The establishment of the organization's headquarters in the nation's capital also proved well-advised. New York had been suggested by maverick Mrs. Flora Adams Darling but the Washington ladies thought otherwise. On the day when their constitution was adopted, Mrs. Lockwood reported, "It was determined that the society should not only be national but its headquarters should be in Washington and the head of the organization should be a woman of national repute."

In actuality, however, the infant organization had no "headquarters", few members and a treasury with the grand total of $33 after initiation fees and dues had been paid. "Headquarters" were Mrs. Lockwood's "private hotel"—an historic spot which, strangely enough, the Daughters have failed to mark. It was years before they could afford office space, however modest.

Having written off their feud with Mrs. Darling, the Daughters, taking themselves with utmost seriousness, moved ahead. Not once did they sell their movement short. Resolving to choose a prominent woman as President-General, they managed a ten-strike by recruiting the First Lady. Mrs. Benjamin Harrison brought to the DAR more than the prestige of her official position. She is described by the newspapers of the period as a woman of political judgment and imagination in her own right. She certainly was aware of the potentialities of the new organization, and was perhaps not unpleased with the opportunity to extend her husband's political influence.

A White House reception in October, 1891, brought considerable favorable publicity, the "Daughters' first official recognition in Washington," according to Mrs. Stevenson's early DAR history.

One of Mrs. Harrison's last public appearances was at another White House reception for the Daughters in February, 1892, within months of her death. Wearing an "elegant pearl white satin gown," "very gracious and courteous," she received, with President Harrison, officers and delegates to the organization's first Continental Congress. Members revere Mrs. Harrison almost as a patron saint. They think of her as a gentle lady, failing in health at the tinme she accepted the top office, who gave the last of her strength to serving the cause. After her death, when they still had only a handful of members and a slim treasury, the grateful Daughters commissioned a life-size portrait of Mrs. Harrison and presented it to the White House. A copy now hangs in the President-General's reception room at Constitution Hall in Washington.

The post of President-General remained unfilled until February, 1893, when Mrs. Adlai Stevenson, wife of Grover Cleveland's second term Vice President began her enthusiastic and active administration. Youthful and energetic, the new President-General called the ladies "My Daughters", obviously enjoyed her four years of service, withdrawing only for the interim year of 1895-1896 because of illness and death in her family.

Mrs. Stevenson recalled years later: "The first Board meeting over which it was my privilege to preside in March, 1893, comes back to me like the memory of a pleasant dream. Had it not been for the kindly services of Mrs. Simon B. Buckner, State Regent of Kentucky, I doubt if I could have found my way to the little room on the second floor, over the old Riggs Bank, 1505 Pennsylvania Avenue. A dark, steep stairway led to the now historic little chamber. In it were gathered the active officers of the Board, a few State Regents, and a few Vice Presidents-General. The room was so narrow that there was barely seating room for the members of the Board around the long, plain table which filled the center of the room.

"I was at once impressed with the earnestness of the ladies, with their ability to plan and execute, and with their willingness to do whatever the cause demanded, whether in physical or intellectual effort. As I recall these and later days of those strenuous times in the society's life, I rejoice in the fact that to me it was given to have some share in the moulding and in the shaping of the character of the organization as it is today. Without hesitation it gives me satisfaction to state that it was then and under the auspices of these persevering, energetic and patriotic women, that the foundation was laid, deep and enduring, upon which the splendid superstructure now rests."

Not so friendly, at the outset, however, was public reaction to the new organization. Mrs. Stevenson concedes that "its objects were not understood and there was great doubt as to the necessity or advisability of founding a national patriotic society upon purely sentimental grounds." The counteraction of this sort of attitude, the early President-General reports, "was the main object of active officers—to disabuse doubting minds, to overcome prejudice and to start chapters in every state and territory under the leadership of state regents who were to inaugurate a campaign of education." Confirming the public skepticism Mrs. Lockwood writes that although the new society had caused considerable interest, "if not curiosity," such searching questions were being asked as—What is the society for? Is it intended to build up an aristocracy?" Mrs. Lockwood concludes: "Cynical observers prophesy its speedy dissolution."

These were fighting words. The ladies gathered their social artillery. Mrs. William D. Cabell, acting for Mrs. Harrison, proposed a large reception as the best way to provide "that social prestige so necessary to anything emanating from the City of Washington," and to demonstrate that the organization had "vitality and enthusiasm based upon American ideas of patriotism." The grand reception was held in February, 1891, at Mrs. Cabell's spacious residence, and "though Washington is noted for the magnificence with which such occasions are surrounded, none had surpassed this one in its personnel or the beauty of its appointments."

Mrs. Harrison received; Minute Men in Continental dress of buff and blue formed a double line through which guests passed to the receiving line; there were stirring speeches and patriotic music; in the supper room, the Society's colors (blue and white) were reproduced in flowers and decorations . . . Everything was done to arouse pride in heroic national ancestry, which alone gives the right of entrance to the new organization."

The occasion was not to pass unexploited. In Mrs. Lockwood's impassioned prose: "The story of this reception in Washington, marked by the spirit of patriotism in speech and song, reached to the farther ends of the country, and success was assured. Soon the beacon lights of patriotism were saluting each other from hilltop to hill-top—the fire caught in the valleys and crossed the rivers until the Nation was awakened with a new light. Newspapers took up the cry and sent the intelligence over the land. Application papers began to pour in. American women were awakened by this revelation, and now 'What is it for?' was answered. It is not for an aristocracy but to honor the men who carried the muskets and the boys who beat the drums and fifed 'Yankee Doodle' for liberty; for the honor of women who served the country in keeping the home fires burning while their men were on the battle lines."

On Washington's birthday in 1892 the Daughters reached

another great milestone when they held their first Continental Congress, a rather small gathering at what was then the Universalist Church of Our Father in downtown Washington.

Held on a clear, cold day, the event packed the galleries with visitors; members filled the small reserved area on the main floor. According to Mrs. Lockwood's account a "vast audience" was in attendance.

In 1955, the *Washington Star* quoted a lone survivor—an impressionable young page at the 1892 Continental Congress—as recalling that the meeting proceeded very smoothly. However, Mrs. Lockwood and her collaborator, Mrs. Emily Sherwood Regan, conceded that "it would be a trick of the most enthusiastic imagination to represent the proceedings as 'quiet, orderly and dignified.' " Inexperienced at any meeting larger than a ladies' church auxiliary, drawn from the most conservative circles, with a handful of clubwomen among them, the delegates tried desperately to maintain order. Some later complained that they were unfairly made the targets of newspaper reporters quick "to satirize feminine organizations and activities."

Mrs. Lockwood goes on: "Many of the delegates wanted the floor at the same time, and to have to wait for recognition from the chair was considered almost an affront. They ignored parliamentary usage because they knew nothing about such rules. They would step out into the aisle and advance to the front to attract attention; while the presiding officer, equally inexperienced, had to be prompted constantly by the man at her elbow, armed with Robert's Rules . . ."

"It provided amusement for reporters and they passed it along to the public for their readers' entertainment," but Mrs. Lockwood scolds, "for the time ignoring the fact that other women's societies had had their days of trial also." She concludes triumphantly:

"Notwithstanding the chaotic aspect of the first DAR Congress, there was no reason for alarm. Splendid work had been done by the initial National Board of Management. The popularity of the movement had almost overwhelmed those executive officers

with work . . . Members of the Board gave not only days but
weeks and months to bringing 'Family Records' up to date. The
organization had adopted a good working Constitution. The
many Chapters already formed under it were represented by some
of the brainiest women the country afforded."

Only a year later the society had progressed so much that it
took part, although not without some initial fear and trembling, in
the Chicago World's Fair Columbian Exposition. Appointed by
President Harrison as a delegate-at-large on the Women's Board
of the Exposition, Mrs. Lockwood relayed to her own organization an invitation to be represented at the Exposition. Reaction
was immediate and Victorian; the ladies didn't want to move so
fast. "From all parts of the house arose objections, if not downright opposition," Mrs. Lockwood writes. "One lady feared it
would commit the society to the suffrage movement. Another said
the society might be placed in an embarrassing position as to
declarations regarding other societies and organizations. Other
ladies objected to the publicity such a gathering would draw DAR
members into. The very atmosphere was charged with a feeling
of conservatism which amounted to timidity."

Obviously the time was not ripe. To avoid defeat, the motion
was withdrawn. The leadership bided its time and when the same
resolution was presented later, participation was unanimously
approved.

The highlight of the Exposition's "splendid program", according to Mrs. Lockwood, was Mrs. Cabell's eloquent opening morning address on "The Ethical Influence of Women in Education"
which "held the rapt attention of the large audience."

The problem of a building site continued unsolved. Since the
fireproof headquarters building for the preservation of Revolutionary relics, approved when the organization was less than a day
old, had still not been found, Mrs. Stevenson brought to bear her
political influence as wife of the Vice President of the United
States. She appointed a committee to petition the Congress for a
grant of land on which to erect Memorial Continental Hall. In

1897, at long last, a bill was passed by both Houses, setting apart for the permanent use of the DAR a plot of land 200 feet square almost adjacent to the White House. Unfortunately, however, the plot turned out to be part of the Washington Monument grounds, which by statute had to remain perpetually a public reservation. The grant was revoked, and the ladies' hopes for a solution to the building site problem were dashed.

Undaunted, however, they made plans for a $700,000 structure and even chose a name for it—Memorial Continental Hall—at a time when their building fund had reached the grand total of $650. Seven years later they were still far from realizing their ambition, with only $11,231.98 on hand.

As long as the Democrats were in power, Mrs. Stevenson's influence continued and assurance was given that the House would vote a suitable new site. But with William McKinley's Republican victory over William Jennings Bryan, a "new King reigned." When the question of a substitute site came up before the new Congress, Mrs. Lockwood reports, it was defeated by "one man" who refused to recognize the maker of the bill. "This one man was the Speaker of the House, whose word was final."

Unfortunate in the matter of a headquarters building, Mrs. Stevenson's regime did accomplish the first major project of national importance, the building of a monument in memory of George Washington's mother. To this fund established by the Mary Washington Memorial Association, the DAR contributed about three-fourths of the necessary $11,000. The Memorial was dedicated in Fredericksburg, Virginia, in May, 1894, with President and Mrs. Grover Cleveland, Cabinet members, the Governor of Virginia, and his staff, and Mrs. Stevenson in attendance. Of this event, Mrs. Stevenson wrote:

"It was appropriate that the first great endeavor of the Daughters should have been in aiding another great women's organization to bring to a happy conclusion their purpose to erect a monument to the memory of a woman, by women."

Another woman of national prominence, Mrs. John W. Foster,

wife of President Harrison's second Secretary of State, was chosen
to succeed Mrs. Stevenson as President-General. Cosmopolitan
Mrs. Foster had lived in Mexico, Russia and Spain where her husband had held diplomatic posts. An unusually gifted linguist, she
was distinguished in her knowledge of protocol and social savoir-
faire. "Her perfect acquiesence in every requirement and the
fulfillment of each duty made her an honored representative of
the great American people," according to Mrs. Stevenson's glowing description. She was the unanimous choice for re-election
after her one year in office, but declined the honor.

Again Mrs. Stevenson—the only President-General who successfully ran for that office four times—returned to power.

A very prominent lady whose husband was Secretary of the
Treasury in Grover Cleveland's first administration, Mrs. Daniel
T. Manning, followed Mrs. Stevenson's second term. Biennial
elections were started at this time, and Mrs. Manning served a
one-year term followed by another of two years. Daughter of an
early merchant prince in Albany, New York, Mrs. Manning was
her husband's second wife and lived many years after his death in
1887. It was President-General Manning who directed the society's first war project.

Fast upon the declaration of war against Spain in April, 1898,
the DAR National Board of Management assured President
McKinley that its services were at his disposal. The organization's War Committee, along with Commodore Dewey's fleet, was
ready for action.

What at first appeared to be a flamboyant and not very useful
gesture turned out to be of some consequence when the Surgeon
General of the United States, Dr. George M. Sternberg, designated
a DAR committee as the official screening agency for war nurses.
Mrs. Lockwood proudly boasts that every Daughter, from the
highest to the humblest, "manifested an earnest desire to assist the
government in any and every possible way, to prosecute the war
and bring it to a speedy conclusion, thus proving herself worthy of

her noble ancestry, from whom she had inherited her patriotic sentiments."

Surgeon General Sternberg turned over to the DAR committee for processing some 4600 applications—a "regiment of women" in the Society's own words—and from this list 1000 nurses were sent out. "Fifty times he made a demand for nurses, and not once did it take more than 24 hours to fill," writes Mrs. Lockwood with satisfaction. The person in charge of the Spanish-American War nurse corps—named "Daughters of the American Revolution Hospital Corps" in honor of its organizers—relates: "Realizing as we fully did, that there was a great principle at stake, we exercised the greatest care in the preparation of our list of eligible women. First of all, the candidate must be of virtuous character and suitable age; second, she must possess good health; third, she must have the training which is essential to the successful prosecution of her work .... The only sure policy to follow, with the safety of sick soldiers, was to demand actual graduation from a training school."

To handle the volume of correspondence and personal inquiries, DAR officers followed an almost military regime, manning their posts daily from 8 a.m. until 11 p.m., from spring until fall, with all clerical work done by volunteers. In addition, $2500 was raised to buy for the hospital ship Missouri a steam launch christened "D.A.R." They sent gifts of lint, clothing of every description, delicacies, pamphlets, newspapers — "everything", according to Mrs. Stevenson, "that could be thought of to render less distressing the condition of the wounded soldiers and sailors."

This service paved the way, Mrs. Lockwood's history claims, for a permanent Army nurse corps. "All the work of those patriotic women was accomplished with such dispatch, every order so promptly executed, and administration of the nurses proved so valuable, that the Government has opened its official doors and the White Cap and Apron Brigade has become a permanent adjunct of the Army organization."

Two years after the Treaty of Paris, international luster was added when Mrs. Manning, appointed by President McKinley as the official delegate, represented the United States at two important functions of the Paris Exposition. On July 3, 1900, a statue of George Washington, financed by the DAR and presented by the American women to the French nation, was unveiled, and on the Fourth of July a plaster model of an unfinished statue of Lafayette, the gift of American children, with a tablet contributed by the organization, was dedicated. The *New York Times'* Paris edition reported of the Lafayette unveiling that Mrs. Manning "presented a charming picture as she stepped to the front of the platform. Her gown was of white crepe trimmed with old lace, and her white hat was trimmed with white feathers and roses. Across the front of her gown she wore a broad blue ribbon, a decoration of the Daughters of the American Revolution. Her voice, as she delivered her speech was perfect, and she could be heard from one side of the enclosure to the other. She talked possibly 15 minutes, proved herself to be a past mistress of the art of speechmaking, and was listened to with the greatest of attention."

Mrs. Manning was received by the French President, decorated as chevalier of the Legion of Honor, and the society's patriotic exhibit was awarded the "Grand Prix," having "excited much interest among those who still sympathize with Republican principles," Mrs. Lockwood notes, adding that, although the National Board of Management had appropriated $2000 for her trip, Mrs. Manning financed it from her own funds, returning to the treasury all the money except that spent in installing the Daughters' exhibit. The young organization grew in size and standing during Mrs. Manning's term as President-General. In 1893-94 some 1950 members had been admitted and in 1894-1895 the number rose to 3488. By 1898, when Mrs. Manning took over, the membership had grown to 23,097; when her administration ended in 1901 there were 35,092 persons in the society.

The first rebellion over uncontested elections for President-General came in 1901, when the name of Mrs. Donald McLean,

New York State regent, was placed in opposition to that of the
official choice, Mrs. Cornelia Otis Fairbanks. Mrs. McLean was
nominated from the floor with a dozen ladies rising, in quick succession, as enthusiastic seconders, but Mrs. Fairbanks won, 323
to 208. The youthfully handsome, plump wife of the bewhiskered
Senator Charles W. Fairbanks, later President Theodore Roosevelt's Vice President, headed an efficient two-year administration
and was then re-elected. Mrs. Fairbanks' "beautiful home on Massachusetts Avenue was a rallying place for Daughters . . . her
cordial hospitality won for her the regard and affection of members whose privilege it was to know her during those delightful
days. Nor was her hospitality confined to members of the National
Society. Her home, while Mr. Fairbanks was United States
Senator and later when he was Vice President of the United States,
was the scene of many brilliant gatherings of the notable people
who make Washington a city of unique interest," Mrs. Stevenson
recalls in 1911.

The flourishing organization began to play an active part in
public functions after the turn of the century. In 1904 the DAR
not only participated enthusiastically in the Louisiana Purchase
Exposition held at St. Louis, but also used the occasion for the
celebration of the organization's founding. That ceremony was
marked by a "well merited tribute to women as a factor in the
Exposition's success" by its President David R. Francis, and a
"beautiful address" of welcome by Mrs. Daniel Manning in her
role as President of the Exposition's Board of Lady Managers.
There were more speeches and "many charming receptions in the
afternoon and evening", Mrs. Stevenson writes, concluding: "With
happy hearts and pleasant memories of the beautiful hospitality of
the Daughters and of citizens of St. Louis, we returned to our
homes, imbued with higher ideals of our obligations as promoters
of a larger and broader patriotism.".

With the close of Mrs. Fairbank's administration in 1905 began
a new era of organizational politics. Multiple candidates were to
enter the race for President-General. The days of heated elections

were at hand. As the membership of the society rose and it at-
tained recognition from coast to coast, the positions occupied by
the principal officers were much sought after.

The new contenders gave sharp focus to the issues. Mrs.
George M. Sternberg, a Vice President-General and wife of the
former Surgeon-General, typified the wife of a Washington official,
up until now the prototype of the successful candidate. Mrs.
Donald McLean, the wife of a wealthy New York lawyer, emphasized the need for country-wide representation, as apparently did
the third candidate, Mrs. Charles Warren Lippett, Rhode Island
State Regent.

Undaunted by her failure in the previous election, Mrs. McLean,
according to the newspapers, reached her goal "after a struggle
of eight long years". She became President-General on the second
ballot by the narrow majority of forty of the total of 684 votes.
Mrs. McLean was good copy and newspaper reporters besieged
her carriage as she came out of the DAR meetings. Not only
had she worked hard for the organization and stumped the country
for the election. She had glamour and political flair. A surviving
photograph shows her in a floor-length black velvet gown with
a squirrel and ermine stole sweeping almost to her hemline, while
an 1897 issue of the DAR magazine had reported that she carried
with her at all times a small silk American flag. A full scale
campaign had been required to turn the vote from automatic
selection of a Washington official's wife. While that policy had
served very well—starting the infant society off on the right political foot— a change was due. In her acceptance speech, Mrs.
McLean, claiming to be the first President-General elected from
the country at large, promised: "I shall try to see that the influence
of the organization is felt in the upbuilding of every chapter
throughout the country."

While the early historians have minimized the heat of this 1905
election, strong partisan feeling existed regarding the candidates.
Stating that the election "had been the subject of discussion and
agitation throughout the land for months", Mrs. Lockwood's book,

dedicated to the Daughters as a "labor of love", reveals obvious distaste for the new President-General: "The election of Mrs. McLean as sixth President-General marks a line of departure from the official position of former candidates to one of pure personality. Mrs. McLean has persistently cherished an ambition to fill this high office, and has been encouraged by a large following of those delegates who were inclined to revolt from the constitutional method of selecting candidates from official circles." Mrs. Lockwood concedes in conclusion: "The success of Mrs. McLean after such a long siege proves her staying qualities once she has put her hand to the plow. . . ."

Mrs. Stevenson, on the other hand, seems to have been a supporter of Mrs. McLean. "In looking back over the vista of years," she writes, "there comes the memory of a scene never to be forgotten; the center of the scene, one radiant in the glow of youth, health and enthusiasm. . . . . I need not tell you to whom I refer; her name has been a household word and is interwoven with the warp and woof of the history of the organization. She was a charter member of the National Society and she has attended every meeting of the Continental Congress since the beginning, I believe, and is known from the Great Lakes to the Gulf that bounds the Southern States, from the rock ribbed Atlantic Coast to the smooth waters of the faraway Pacific. Do you know her, Mrs. Donald McLean?"

Personalities and even principles changed, but the organization's growth went steadily forward, reaching the milestone figure of 50,000 members in 1906.

CHAPTER III

HISTORICAL PROJECTS

"It is a reasonable assumption," Mrs. Mary S. Lockwood asserted in 1906, "that if the Daughters of the American Revolution had been born a quarter of a century later, the historic records that have been rescued by this society never could have been collected." The organization has always been at its best when engaged in such projects as the restoration of historic buildings, the erection of tablets to commemorate historic events, the collection of Revolutionary relics, the painstaking assembling of genealogical records, and the marking of long forgotten graves of Revolutionary soldiers.

The DAR is one of two organizations—the American Historical Association is the other—required by the charter granted by the Congress to make annual reports to the Smithsonian Institution in Washington. These annual reports, transmitted to the Congress and printed at government expense, describe in detail the historical projects undertaken during the year as part of the society's function of patriotic education. Each report lists the graves of Revolutionary soldiers marked during the previous year, a requirement under the society's semi-official status. As early as 1906 Mrs. Lockwood reported "thousands of Revolutionary soldiers' graves have been marked and burial places sunk into decrepitude restored and made places of interest."

The first grave marked was that of Abigail Adams, wife of President John Adams, in Quincy, Massachusetts, and on it the Abigail Adams chapter of Boston, Massachusetts, "lovingly placed a stone tablet." In describing the appropriateness of this action, Mrs. Lockwood notes that Mrs. Adams had "experienced all the danger and vicissitudes of war; while her husband was absent in Congress and in foreign courts, representing his government,

Abigail cared for the family, and managed the farm, waiting upon seed time and harvest. Her incomparable letters to her husband in his long absences give insight into the home life of a true woman patriot and mother of the Revolution. A product of the Colonial struggle for liberty, while her husband was away, Mrs. Adams practiced the virtues of industry and frugality, trying to remedy the financial disasters which had overtaken Mr. Adams, and of which he had complained."

A Plymouth, Massachusetts, chapter inaugurated the "gracious service of decorating the neglected and forgotten graves of Revolutionary heroes, whose very headstones were weary of telling the simple story of those who lay beneath the sod; whose headstones were broken, cracked and disintegrated by the heat and frost of a hundred summers and winters gone." This "gracious service," which according to Mrs. Lockwood prevailed "wherever a Revolutionary soldier is buried," was not, judging by the lack of further records, continued.

But meanwhile other work went on. A Connecticut chapter took charge of a cemetery containing graves of a number of Revolutionary soldiers: other Connecticut Daughters rescued names of hundreds of Revolutionary soldiers from oblivion and enrolled them in the national society's lineage books. A Vermont chapter marked 22 Revolutionary soldiers' graves in its town cemetery and compiled each soldier's military history; in another Vermont town a memorial was erected to "Soldiers of the American Revolution buried in unknown graves". A Maine chapter named after a Revolutionary heroine, carved her name on her tombstone, thus recalling the heroine's identity, which had been lost through a second marriage. In New York a circus and baseball game raised $400 for the restoration of an old cemetery and the marking of its historic graves. A Georgia chapter raised money to erect a monument to the Revolutionary hero for whom it was named, and whose body lay far from home, in an unmarked grave in Philadelphia.

There was a great variety of other projects. The Colonel

Bigelow Chapter of Worcester, Massachusetts erected a bronze tablet to mark the site of Worcester's first school house in which John Adams taught from 1755 to 1758, and searched for the graves of 400 soldiers from their town who served in the Revollution. The Hannah Winthrop Chapter, Cambridge, (named for the wife of distinguished scientist John Winthrop, and stepmother of a soldier wounded at Bunker Hill) restored a Revolutionary War fort. The Deborah Sampson Chapter, Plymouth, marked the birthplace of the Revolutionary heroine for whom it was named— a twenty-year old country school teacher who put on men's clothes and fought for three years before she was wounded, taken to the hospital, and her identity discovered. She was discharged from service by George Washington himself, without reproach for her three years of misrepresentation. "One word of condemnation from General Washington would have crushed my heart," said the girl who fought like a man.

Another Massachusetts chapter, in Medford, bought and restored the headquarters of General John Stark, who commanded a regiment quartered at Medford before the battle of Bunker Hill. This chapter was named for Sarah Bradlee Fulton, who carried dispatches from George Washington, behind the enemy's lines. Because her husband was too ill to accept this patriotic assignment, Mrs. Fulton walked by night to the water side of nearby Charlestown, found a boat and rowed across the river, delivered her dispatches and returned as she went, getting home at dawn. General Washington called upon her in person to thank her for this service.

A Hartford, Connecticut chapter restored tombstones of Revolutionary heroes in an old church burying ground, and aroused such a spirit of patriotism that the town spent $100,000 tearing down an adjoining tenement section and replacing it with a fine boulevard. Another Connecticut chapter erected a beautiful gateway to a cemetery in which forty-two Revolutionary soldiers are buried; another marked Revolutionary graves of twenty French soldiers of Lafayette's army in a Norwich cemetary. A fountain memorializing Nathan Hale was built by a Norwalk, Connecticut, chapter; a Winstead, Connecticut, chapter marked the site of its first meeting house.

In New Hampshire, Keene Daughters placed a granite boulder on the road over which patriots of the town set forth for Concord and Lexington, on the day of the battle of Lexington. The Exeter house where Continental money was kept during the Revolution was marked by the local chapter, which also placed a marker on a house where George Washington breakfasted one morning in 1781. Maine Chapters induced the state legislature to appropriate $1500—the first money ever given in that state for historical purposes—as the nucleus of a fund to restore an old stone castle which was part of a British fort at Bangor. In this forgotten spot, two ladies discovered a curious underground storage place, believed to have been a "safe deposit" in war time.

Stirring stories of Revolutionary heroes and heroines fired the Daughters' enthusiasm for paying homage to the memory of their forbears. Some of the stories were already famous; others were little known and only given currency by the organization's work. The stories are legion. There was Molly Stark, who turned her house into a hospital for the smallpox patients among the troops commanded by her husband, General John Stark, and who served as both nurse and doctor, saving men and boys, including her own young children. There was General Israel Putnam of Plainfield, Connecticut, who rode his horse down a steep declivity, cleared 100 steps, and the pursuing British dragoons did not dare to follow. Captain Jonathan Oliphant of Trenton, New Jersey, not only spent his personal fortune in equipping and maintaining his militia company; his wife, with women servants and farm tenants, kept grain mills running day and night while he was away to provide food for every living thing on the place.

Another heroine was Lydia Darrah of White Marsh, Pennsylvania, who overheard Lord Howe in a council of war at her house, planning to march against Washington's troops. Managing to get a passport from Lord Howe on the pretense of going to the mill, she rode instead to the American lines and sent the information to

Washington, who thus was ready for the British when they appeared. Still another heroine, Rebecca Motte of South Carolina, whose beautiful home on the Congaree River had been taken over by the British, provided Revolutionary soldiers with bows and arrows which had been sent her from the East Indies, so that they could fire the roof of her home and capture the invaders. Emily Geiger was a young South Carolina girl who rode fifty miles as a messenger for General Green and, when captured by the British, chewed up and swallowed the message he had entrusted to her and finally delivered it in person from memory.

Thus the Daughters were discovering many untapped sources of historic interest. In Brooklyn they raised $200,000 for a monument on Long Island to the thousands of Revolutionary prisoners of war who were the victims of a cruelty hardly surpassed in ancient or modern times. These men were on ships of the Royal British Navy anchored just off shore near the site of the present-day Brooklyn Navy Yard. On one of these prison ships 11,000 men are said to have died of disease and hardships. Portholes in the old sailing vessels were sealed and four 20-inch iron barred airholes were pierced in each side. There, between decks, unfortunate prisoners were confined in space so small that they slept with legs and arms over each others' bodies, able to move only en masse. The food was horrible and insufficient; and the prisoners had no heat, no fire, no medical attention and only scant clothing.

Each morning, as long as they could walk, they were brought on deck and given a glimpse of the green shores of their native land and a taste of sunshine; then they were offered their freedom if they would enlist under the British flag. Only one yielded to this temptation, according to the Lockwood-Regan volume, "and he was said to have been a foreigner." The DAR biographers fail to explain what they mean by a "foreigner;" but they report that among the prisoners who refused to betray their country the casualties were as many as on all battlefields of the Revolution.

The new organization's mission was not limited to uncovering historical material. The Daughters found that they could provide a common ground for women all over the country, including many of those whose loyalties had been torn asunder by the bitter struggle between the States. By the turn of the twentieth century, only a few "real daughters" of Revolutionary heroes survived; but there were countless thousands of survivors of Civil War Soldiers. These had formed the United Daughters of the Confederacy and Daughters of Union Veterans. Bitterness of conflict still separated these post-Civil War organizations.

But the War of the Revolution had no "North" and "South", no "damyankees", no Dixie. No Mason and Dixon line divided its heroes. The Revolutionary South had General Nathanael Greene, who led a brilliant Southern campaign; the North had Ethan Allen, who with eighty-three Green Mountain Boys surprised and captured Fort Ticonderoga, calling for surrender by its British Commandant "in the name of the Great Jehovah and the Continental Congress." Virginia produced George Washington, Massachusetts John Adams and the Boston Tea Party.

In those early years, history was revived in a thousand different spots. Had it not been for the Daughters, it is unlikely that anyone would have erected a liberty pole where Revolutionary wives and mothers, dressed in men's clothing, defended a bridge; or petitioned President Roosevelt for a memorial park on the site of Revolutionary forts; or marked the site of a mansion at 37th Street and Park Avenue, New York City, where a Quaker lady entertained Sir Henry Clinton and his staff with a glass of wine, to give Washington's army time to pass a danger point. Would anyone else have built a memorial in Frederick, Maryland, to the 12 judges who were the first to declare the British Stamp Act unconstitutional and void; or travelled 30 miles over mountain roads to care for the needs of an old lady whose father had fought in the Revolution; or inspired the descendants of Connecticut's Oliver Ellsworth, one of the framers of the Constitution and Chief Justice of the Supreme Court under George Washington, to present his home to the Connecticut Chapter as a historical museum?

Inheritors of a tradition, the Daughters created for themselves a special mission. Although some skeptics predicted the time would come when neither Daughters nor Children of the American Revolution, having marked all graves and other historic places "by monument, table,or wayside stone," would have anything left to do, Mrs. Lockwood gently reminds them: "That can never be, so long as we cherish American ideals, for those places we have marked will have become shrines, and those who cherish the past will find expression for their abiding reverence and faith through annual pilgrimages in remembrance."

Mrs. Lockwood's prophecy has come to pass. Historic restorations attract hordes of visitors each year. Many of these have been described in *Historic Restorations of the Daughters of the American Revolution,* written for the organization by Lewis Barrington in 1941. In her foreword to the book, Mrs. Henry M. Robert, Jr., then President-General, states that historic buildings "speak more forcibly than the human voice of the struggle for existence, the courage in face of danger, the ingenuity, initiative and steadfastness of an accomplishment. To the extent that historic buildings remain a demonstration of the spirit which has made a people, to that extent their restoration is justified."

The photographs in the profusely illustrated Barrington book— many of which were taken with WPA project funds—show restorations from New England to Arizona and Florida, bringing history to life for all to see. Not only Revolutionary history is set forth, but the stories of the Pioneer West, of the generations of Indian fighting and the less spectacular conquest of the farm lands of the great mid-western states.

Paul Revere's two-story home in Boston was restored partly with the help of DAR contributions. This hero of the ride immortalized in Longfellow's poem was a silversmith, and some of his work is preserved in the beautiful modern museum at Washington headquarters. The hero of another DAR restoration, Fort Churchill in

Nevada, by contrast, was Captain Charles C. Churchill of the Fourth U. S. Army, who led the settlers in the last phase of their long struggle against the Indians.

Fort Churchill, writes Mr. Barrington, was headquarters for the blue-uniformed U.S. Cavalry in Nevada and terminus for western telegraph lines. From there messages had to be sent by pony express to Fort Kearney, Nevada, terminus of eastern telegraph lines. The Indian threat was so great that it was necessary to send twenty soldiers with each pony express rider, to give him sufficient protection. In 1870 the fort had been abandoned and was offered for sale; everything in it that was movable was sold for $750. In 1931 the land was transferred to the state, through the efforts of Nevada's Sagebrush DAR chapter, and the chapter was made custodian of the fort, now a public museum. One of the old buildings was later restored by the Civil Works Administration of President Franklin D. Roosevelt's administration.

Since so many of the Daughters are housewives, it is natural that historic homes should have been among their chief interests. They have restored or helped to restore many of these, including Mississippi's famous mansion, "Rosalie".

"Rosalie" was originally a fort built in 1716 by the French— at a time when France still had high hopes of successful American colonization—to protect the town of Natchez from the Indians. Named after the Duchesse de Pontchartrain, whose first name was Rosalie, the fort survived until 1729, when it was abandoned after Indians attacked and murdered its garrison. For nearly 100 years Rosalie was only a tradition, until in 1820 it was bought by a lumber magnate and built into a mansion. With thick walls made of brick baked on the site by slave labor, the rooms were 21 feet square and the ceilings 14 feet high. Adorned with marble mantels and ornate mirrors, Rosalie became perhaps the finest example of early Mississippi architecture. By the time of the Civil War, the mansion was owned by strong supporters of the Confederacy, who were hosts there to Jefferson Davis. Then Vicksburg fell and Rosalie became headquarters for General

Grant and his Union soldiers. In 1938 Mississippi DARs acquired the mansion, and it has been restored to look just as it did in 1858, with the same rugs on the floors, the same rosewood furniture in the drawing rooms, and ornaments, mirrors, and fireplace sets duplicated. It is now a public museum.

Rockingham, Washington's headquarters at Rocky Hill, New Jersey, is a vastly different restoration; it was originated in 1897, when the organization had not yet celebrated its tenth birthday. Built in 1760, Rockingham was the home of John Berrien, surveyor, who later became a judge of New Jersey's Supreme Court. The harried Continental Congress of 1783, meeting in Princeton, New Jersey, eleven miles from Rockingham, was faced with the grim necessity of finding money for army payrolls, long overdue. Needing George Washington close at hand for consultation, Rockingham was a convenient headquarters. It was here, in an upstairs sitting room, that he wrote his farewell orders to the Armies of the infant United States.

During the next century Rockingham changed hands a number of times. Its ancient walls were endangered by blasting from a nearby stone quarry. Creating an association to save this historic mansion, the founder of the Princeton DAR chapter bought the old house, and had it moved to a better site and restored, the work ending in 1897. Years later it was deeded to New Jersey and is now in the custody of the state's Commission on Historical Sites.

The two and one-half story house of General Nathanael Greene in Anthony, Rhode Island, was restored by the General Nathanael Greene Homestead Association. Washington's right-hand man at Valley Forge, General Greene performed his best service for the Revolution as commander of American troops in the South. Contributing to the reputation of the home during Revolutionary War years were many pleasant entertainments given by Mrs. Greene for French officers stationed at nearby Newport. Rhode Island DAR's have two trustees on the board of the Association.

Halfway across the continent, in Yanktown, South Dakota, is a pioneer restoration which tells the story of the state as a territory. In 1861 President Lincoln named his family doctor, Dr. William Jayne, as governor of the vast South Dakota territory, and Dr. Jayne chose Yanktown as the capital of the territory. The first territorial legislature had nine members in the upper house and thirteen in the lower house—a membership so small that it met in the home of William Tripp, a Yanktown lawyer who later became captain of a volunteer company during the Civil War. In 1936 this small story and a half frame house was given to a DAR chapter, was moved to City Park and restored to its original condition. The chapter keeps historical relics there and opens the house to the public on special occasions.

The one-room log cabin of Nancy Hart, a rough and ready, illiterate, cross-eyed and smallpox-pitted Georgia Revolutionary heroine, disappeared long before Daughters of the American Revolution came into existence. Early "Daughters" loved to tell Nancy's rustic saga. Later the Georgia Society built a replica of her cabin, furnished it with copies of Nancy's crude home-made household belongings, and managed to include an old clay pipe which she once smoked.

According to DAR stories, Nancy was a crack shot, an expert cook and housewife, and a bee fancier. She had plenty of children and a husband who ran and hid in a nearby swamp to avoid fighting for his country when the Revolutionaries were looking for volunteers, and also to avoid "King's Men" who occasionally swooped down on the place. One day a group of "King's Men" appeared and ordered a meal. Nancy cooked her last turkey for them, drank with them, and at the height of the party, grabbed "Old Bessie", her gun, and dared them to move. The first who did was killed with a load of buckshot. Another tried to escape and met the same fate. Then Nancy ordered one of her children to run to the swamp for her husband, and when he arrived with reinforcements she turned over the captive group with orders to string them up . . . "hanging is too good for them," she said. And in due course they were strung up on Nancy's own trees.

One of Pennsylvania's few remaining toll houses at Addison,

on U. S. Route 40, has been an official base for a DAR chapter since the early 1900's. Carefully inscribed on a weather-worn board is a list of toll charges in the 1800's—6c for every score of sheep; 3c for every led or "drove" horse, mule or ass; 2c for every coach, phaeton or chaise with two horses and four wheels.

A relic of Pennsylvania's past, the quaint structure is a one-story stone building of hexagonal shape, with shingle roof.

Gadsby's Tavern in Alexandria, Virginia, where Lafayette slept when he visited the United States long after the Revolution, has been restored through the combined efforts of the American Legion, DAR, four local chapters of Children of the American Revolution, and Virginia Colonial Dames. The Mt. Vernon DAR Chapter restored the doorway and the front steps where Washington stood and reviewed his troops and where he gave his last military command. John Alexander Chapter restored and furnished the room known at the "Female Stranger's Room," so named because it once was occupied by a mystery woman, apparently the victim of personal tragedy, whose identity never has been known. Kate Waller Barrett Chapter furnished the room occupied by Lafayette, and Children of the American Revolution restored and furnished two rooms. A hall and stairway were done over with the help of funds provided by a former member of the Mt. Vernon Chapter in memory of her father.

Wakefield near Fredericksburg, Virginia, birthplace of Washington, was destroyed by fire in 1780 but has been duplicated by the Wakefield Association, assisted by Virginia DAR chapters, the Federal government and John D. Rockefeller, Jr. Maintained and administered by the National Park Service, it is open to the public daily.

The pride of Minnesota Daughters is Sibley House on Sibley Memorial Highway, Mendota. Sibley House was the home of Henry H. Sibley, first governor of Minnesota, who came up the Mississippi in 1834, as a young man of 23, and took charge of trading between Sioux Indians and the American Fur Company. He decided to make his headquarters at the confluence of the

Minnesota and Mississippi Rivers and there built a two-story native stone house, employing more than 100 hunters, traders, and Indians of both sexes as builders. The house had hand-split shingles, hand-hewn timbers, and river mud smeared over hay-wrapped willow shoots as a pioneer substitute for plaster and lath.

Governor Sibley sold the house in 1902. It became successively a parochial school, a summer art school, a storehouse, and finally, an abandoned building. In 1909 the St. Paul DAR chapter succeeded in getting possession of the building with the understanding that it would be restored. Since 1910 it has been open as a museum, featuring personal belongings of the Sibley family.

The Creek National Council House in Okmulgee, Oklahoma, was the seat of government for Creek Indians when they made their last stand in the Indian Territory. There they held their tribal councils, with 38 tribes represented at one time. In 1919 the council house was purchased by the city of Okmulgee and the Okmulgee DAR chapter raised money for its restoration.

The Young Cabin at Sunset Park, Washington, Iowa, was built by Alexander Young in 1840, occupied by the Young family for 36 years and was the center for church, school, and social affairs of the neighborhood. By 1912 there were only two surviving members of the family left in the country, and they were persuaded to give the cabin to Washington DAR Chapter as a memorial to the pioneers. The cabin was carefully removed to a new site and furnished in pioneer style.

Thus the work of restoration has been carried on from coast to coast and from Maine to Florida. Most of the historic restorations have been done by chapters, but the national organization has had its projects too. Perhaps the chief of these is the 114 feet high, $500,000 bell tower at Valley Forge, Pennsylvania. Dedicated in 1953, this was one project which the society almost abandoned before the last dollar was in hand and the last bill paid.

The project originated in 1941, and the cost was estimated at $75,000. For ten years funds were solicited at annual meetings and construction was finally begun in 1952. By that year the Daughters had become more interested in a much larger project—remodelling and rebuilding their offices in Washington, at a cost of $1,250,000. Mrs. James B. Patton, then President-General, appealed to the 1952 Congress to complete the Vally Forge bell tower, "as we have completed all other projects ever started by our Society." The Congress ordered a new money drive in order to obtain $1 per member. The Andrew W. Mellon Trust added $25,000. With this financial encouragement the tower was finished and paid for. As a final touch, however, three great carved stone eagles had been added near the top of the tower; the DAR seem to have been somewhat reluctant to pay for this part of the project until General Douglas MacArthur thrilled them with an appearance at their 1951 Congress upon his return home from Tokyo on President Truman's orders. As a tribute to the deposed General and Mrs. MacArthur, money to pay for the eagles was reportedly raised without difficulty.

In a memorial room in the Valley Forge Bell Tower there is a statue of Washington which was originally designed without a hat. "Because of a motherly concern lest the Father of his Country look cold around the ears," according to the Schenectady, New York, *Union Star* of April 14, 1955, a hat was added. On the walls of the memorial room four bas-relief panels symbolize the American colonists' struggle for freedom. Stained glass windows, one of which alone cost $10,000, picture Washington at prayer, events in the Revolutionary alliance of America with France and the spirit of Valley Forge. A carillon of 56 bells plays hymns, patriotic airs, and folk songs daily throughout the year.

What a magnificent contrast with the first modest DAR project described by Mrs. Stephenson: "The Continental Congress of 1896 appropriated $100 for the restoration of the embankment at Jamestown, Virginia, thus rescuing from the encroaching waters the first colonial settlement on the American continent."

CHAPTER IV

GENEALOGY

Genealogy is the lifeblood of the DAR. The organization is built upon family trees and a relentless search for Revolutionary forbears. And the accusation of ancestor worship, often levied, leaves the Daughters unmoved. Therefore it is not surprising that over the years a great amount of effort has gone into perfecting the process of investigating, verifying and, of course, many times rejecting membership claims based upon Revolutionary descent. As of the beginning of 1956, 445,000 membership applications had been put through the geneological process and approved for eligibility, and probably hundreds of thousands had failed to receive the stamp of approval. According to a 1955 article in *Reporter* Magazine, only one out of five applications is approved.

In the words of the organization's constitution, membership is open to any woman 18 or older, "descended from a man or woman who with unfailing loyalty to the cause of American independence, served as a sailor, a soldier or civil officer in one of the several Colonies or States, or in the United Colonies or States, or as a recognized patriot, or rendered material aid thereto; provided the applicant is personally acceptable to the Society."

For years before their own organization was founded in 1890, the lineage conscious Daughters had been working with the Sons of the American Revolution. Many of the early members required little or no genealogical digging to prove their eligibility; for example, there was no need for Eugenia Washington, great grand-niece of George Washington, to establish a fact so generally known. Likewise, a descendant of Revolutionary General Lighthorse Harry Lee, the father of Civil War General Robert E. Lee, required no

Daughters' voluminous file at the Library of Congress. Early members were separated by only three generations from the Revolution, which genealogically speaking, is actually only one generation. Since it is assumed that applicants can remember their parents and grandparents, genealogical research begins with the great grandparents. With less necessity for genealogical proof only a century after the Revolution, some of the early applicants prepared their papers so badly that, according to a former DAR genealogist, they would not have passed later entrance requirements. Even the 818 charter members, admitted during its first year, had sketchy proof of their ancestry.

If the proof was sketchy, so were the means of checking applications. A DAR lineage book revision reported in 1908 that in the early years, with "facilities for acquiring data . . . meager and difficult of attainment" the first registrars and Historian-Generals labored under great difficulties.

The admission of collateral descendants, under the controversial "Mothers of Patriots" provision, was discontinued after a few years of unsatisfactory operation. The reason for the provision is unclear. It is said to have been introduced to admit Miss Eugenia Washington, who otherwise would not have been eligible, since she was only a great grandniece of George Washington. This theory seems to be wrong, however, as records show that her great grandfather, Colonel Samuel Washington, had Revolutionary service.

Another explanation for the rule is that it was introduced to swell the organization's revenue by relaxing the eligibility provision. Whatever the explanation, apparently no permanent injury has been done by Tory invasion of the Revolutionary ranks since the bulk of the members admitted as collateral descendants have subsequently proved their eligibility through direct descent.

Information about unsuccessful applicants is supposedly kept confidential. Occasionally, however, a story gets out—for example, one which is told freely by some members and illustrates the organization's attitude toward the admission of Negro eligibles.

On March 22, 1894, the Corresponding Secretary General received a letter from a lady asking if "personally acceptable" in the eligibility requirements meant that no Negro would be admitted. The answer was an unequivocal "Yes."

The following story is probably also credible: the applicant, a mid-westerner, submitted the name of a Revolutionary ancestor which genealogical search failed to identify except as a Negro slave who had accompanied his master to war. The applicant was rejected, apparently without consideration as to the amount of "material aid" the slave might have rendered "the cause of American independence."

Quoting a qualified DAR genealogist, a *Washington Daily News* story of 1955 has some stark overtones of what may have been a family tragedy of long ago. An applicant for membership based her claim on descent from the son of a Revolutionary "patriot." Genealogical search revealed that the son had been disowned by his patriot father, in whose will he was referred to as a "supposed son." "We can't honestly admit the descendants of that 'supposed son'," the DAR genealogist decided, cautioning that mistakes of identity made by Society genealogists in the early days resulted in the admission of members who, although they have "never been questioned" may be of doubtful eligibility.

The subject of still another story is a doughty Revolutionary ancestor with many descendants who despite their reported "stack" of applications have failed to establish eligibility. This old boy, with a first wife and family in a southern border state, travelled north, stayed for years on a land-grant in the Northwest Territory, and produced another family. His potential fortune in land was turned over to the second family whose descendants prospered and became excellent material for DAR membership. But proof of marriage in each generation has always been required and the worthy ancestor had never taken the trouble to legitimize his second family.

Other genealogical problems were reported by the DAR Registrar-General as recently as 1942. Imploring chapter registrars to catch "glaring mistakes before the papers are sent to Washington" the lady moaned: "I have seen papers in which two fathers are claimed for one person in the ancestral line, in which a child's marriage is given as two years after the marriage of his parents, in which a child is claimed to have been born six years after the mother's death."

Additional observations on the scope and difficulties of genealogical research in the early years are given by Mrs. Lockwood in her history. She reports that the careful screening of applicants makes it necessary to compare the lineage, vital statistics and service of ancestors claimed by applicants with the papers already approved for other members of the same family. "Some idea of the labor involved may be realized when it is understood that for each member there is now an average of fifteen DAR members —some of the more prominent ancestors are represented by as many as forty-two members," Mrs. Lockwood writes.

Mrs. Lockwood further notes that a wife's name is often the critical one genealogically because in many instances it is the only name by which papers can be verified. There might be many husbands of the same name, but not husband-wife combinations. For example, Revolutionary Joe Z. Smith might have had a wife Emily and Tory Joe Z. Smith might have had a wife Jane. The two Joes might be confused with obvious disastrous results, except for Emily and Jane. Even President John Adams might have had a pretty thin time in DAR circles were it not for Abigail. "Without his wife's name, John Adams would have stood for naught in Massachusetts genealogy," wrote Mrs. Lockwood. "There were forty-nine John Adamses who fought in the Revolution."

Along with its matriarchal emphasis, the DAR has been accused, by the ousted Mrs. Flora Darling, for one, of attempting to establish an aristocracy based on ancestry, and to welcome as members only descendants of officers or other well-placed Revolutionists. This has been strenuously denied, but it must have had wide circulation among the early Daughters, because Mrs.

Lockwood reported that at the first Continental Congress in February, 1892, "more than one delegate went on record against any such idea." An Alabama delegate said: "Let no one suppose that we are organizing to make social or national distinctions or castes. The blood of the private soldier is just as noble as that of the General in command." Mrs. Eugenia Washington declared, "We want a patriotic society founded on service. I will never have a part in a society which is founded on rank."

On the other hand, Mrs. Darling based her charge on the fact that a "Committee of Safety" had been appointed by early DAR leaders to "keep out" plain people by the "blackball method." The problem came to a head in New York City where Mrs. Darling founded a rival chapter in Harlem (then predominantly a white residential area) in competition with the regular New York City chapter headed by the socially snobbish Mrs. Roger Pryor. Although the use of the "blackball method" in Mrs. Pryor's chapter is not verified and official histories make no mention of it, it is given some credence by the fact that the New York chapter held its meetings at the famous Sherry's rendezvous for the city's Four Hundred.

The Daughters hotly deny accusations of social snobbishness and point out that their most famous recent recruit, Mrs. Dwight D. Eisenhower, is a descendant of a private soldier of the Revolution. It is a little hard to see this as "letting down the bars," however.

Lacking genealogical research materials and the money to buy them in the early days, the Daughters proceeded to employ their devoted womanpower to compile them. They pored over dusty, disintegrating records in county courthouses. They scraped moss off tombstones in old graveyards, read and copied names of Revolutionary patriots buried there, searched family Bibles, copied marriage licenses of the Revolutionary period, and sent voluminous genealogical material to the society's national headquarters. Early issues of the DAR magazine had a Genealogical Records Department which provided detailed pertinent data—including, for example, a list of all Revolutionary war pensioners in Alabama as of 1840.

At the first Continental Congress, in 1892, the Historian-General told the delegates: "Now is the time to search for family letters, data and memoranda in old chests and trunks of your ancestors." An initial project of the New York chapter was the preservation of historical records.

An ardent Connecticut member who had copied the complete Revolutionary records of her home town was congratulated by the national officer to whom she presented them in these words: "To rescue from oblivion and secure from the inroads of time the records of a community, is a work of importance which can not be too highly estimated. The difficulties to be overcome in the deciphering of nearly illegible papers, the time consumed, the absolute accuracy demanded, all combined to make the task of the transcriber no easy one."

The members themselves had painfully gathered up the nucleus, and now other materials were being collected to start a library. The first 126 reference books came as a gift at a time when the organization had no place to store them. Since then, a genealogical library has been built up which is rated along with the Library of Congress and the Newberry Library in Chicago as among the top three in the country. There are even some Daughters who insist—perhaps with an overdose of organizational pride—that it surpasses the genealogical material and facilities of the Library of Congress.

Impressively housed in what was once the auditorium of Memorial Continental Hall, the genealogical library is open five days a week to outside researchers—except in April during the Continental Congress when it is reserved for the use of members—and has its own staff of genealogists to verify application papers.

An attractive room, the library has American and state flags suspended from ivory-white wood-panelled walls at ceiling height, and, looking down over an auditorium stage now converted into a card index center, a $20,000 portrait of George Washington.

The card catalogue is as simple as possible, for the benefit of beginners in ancestry research. There is no book borrowing and the Society furnishes no genealogical service to aspiring prospective members; they must ferret out their own ancestors or employ a genealogist to do this for them. However, the library staff is glad to make helpful suggestions.

Non-members must pay a fee of $1 a day and an extra 25 cents per hour is charged for the use of a machine which enlarges microfilms of ancestor rolls and copies of the U. S. Census records for 1850, 1860, 1870 and 1880. (Census records earlier than 1850 are of little genealogical value, because they list only the heads of families, which means the father in most cases.)

Centering largely around the organization and its excellent library, genealogy is a thriving but highly competitive business in Washington. Genealogists advertise in the DAR magazine, and library staff members will provide the names of genealogists to inquirers, carefully refraining from recommending any particular one.

By 1906 the library had a carefully-documented card catalogue of 20,000 titles, and was operating an active exchange system. Thrifty as always, the organization appropriated $50 each year to be spent exclusively for the purchase of Revolutionary records. For most accessions to its collections of histories, biographies and genealogies, it depended on gifts and exchanges from chapters and individuals, authors and friends of the Society.

Consolidating a great deal of previous research, the first lineage book was published in 1891. It listed the names of members in the order in which they joined the Society, together with the name and service of the Revolutionary ancestor from whom each was descended. Providing a complete family tree for each member through great grandparents, the listings were in the best feminine tradition—no birthdates given. Writing as the compiler of that first lineage book, Mrs. Lockwood predicted that lineage books would "relieve the generations who come after us from the task of delving through dusty archives of the past to prove their lineage, and never will the record of their ancestors be in danger of being lost."

A 1905 leaflet, "How to Become a Member"—tattered and torn, but still readable—may be found in the Library of Congress; it offered practical hints to aspiring candidates about where they could get material to verify service of their Revolutionary ancestors. Old letters and verified copies of pension, state, town or county records would be acceptable as verification. Extracts of material from rare historical volumes not available in the organization's own library had to be attested. If original Revolutionary War pension certificates had been lost, certified copies could be had. Sons of the American Revolution in Maine had published a roster of Revolutionary soldiers of that state; Connecticut's roster, also a state publication, was "very fine"; it was hard to find Virginia Revolutionary records, owing to destruction of papers during the Civil War; New York's Revolutionary archives were good, as were South Carolina records.

More than fifty years later, with 45,500 volumes and 20,000 manuscripts in their genealogical library, records are still being collected through the unceasing efforts of women all over the country. The 1956 Continental Congress was told that 7,000 pages of Bible records and 13,000 pages of cemetery records, collected by chapters and members under the direction of 710 Genealogical Records Committee chairmen, at the nominal cost of $2897.69, had been received by the National Genealogical Records Committe chairman. Only such records as these could in many cases answer the hundreds of requests that women send in each year for information about the records of their forbears. To meet this demand and replenish its stock in trade, the organization has set for its members the ambitious goal of collecting all unpublished genealogical material pertaining to the entire nation prior to 1900.

As a stimulus to the state societies to continue their good efforts, small prizes are awarded annually for the societies which amass the greatest collection of genealogical records. The winner in

1956 was North Carolina's DAR, with 4481 pages copied and turned in; second place went to Ohio, with 2369 pages; third place to New York, with 1445 pages. A total of 66,833 pages of unpublished records had been added to the DAR library during the year, and there also was reported progress on another painstaking project of the Daughters—the repairing of old documents. With assistance from the Association for Virginia Antiquities and County Boards of Supervisors, a Virginia DAR Committee on the Restoration of Records had repaired masses of old and worn documents covering the period from 1743 to 1842. More committees of this type were needed, the Congress was told, "since old, worn records become illegible."

With an almost prissy meticulousness, the Daughters require a standardized preparation of the records submitted to the National Genealogical Committee for library use. They must be copied on standard size, 8½x11 inch, 16-pound paper, with the three carbon copies on lighter weight paper. Each chapter retains a carbon copy and sends the others to the State Chairman of its Genealogical Records Committee. Original copies intended for the DAR's Washington library, must be bound and sent to the National Genealogical Records Committee along with two carbon copies to be used in exchanges with other libraries that furnish unpublished genealogical material.

There is a personal incentive for members to collect genealogical records—the right to wear in addition to the membership pin a gold bar with the name of each verified supplemental ancestor. "Supplementals" have been so popular lately that the price of verifying them has been increased to $17.50: $10 for verifying the supplemental paper and $7.50 for the ancestral bar. "When we're educating our families, we have to save money and we can't afford luxuries like supplementals at this price," mourned a member at a recent Continental Congress. She might have added that the society keeps the $10 fee if the claim is not established.

The organization's monthly magazine also has a Genealogical

Department, which lists records compiled by members and other items of interest. A 1956 issue devoted three pages to the marriage records of Maryland's Baltimore City and County from 1777 to 1779. These had been copied and compiled by the Maryland State Regent, and constituted only the first phase of an ambitious project. A glance at the list proves again that it is the woman's name that swings the weight genealogically speaking. In 1796, two William Pembertons of Baltimore were married, one to Mary Maxwell and the other to Sarah Odle. Likewise, two John Prices were married in 1799, and could be differentiated only by the names of their wives.

Genealogical tidbits make interesting reading for lineage-concious Daughters, to judge by the space the magazine devotes to them. There is even a column in which readers request information needed to track down elusive ancestors, the question being abbreviated like money-saving want ads in daily newspapers. For example, Mrs. Waldon A. McBridge of 483 South Main Street, Crown Point, Indiana, ran this item: "Des inf. on pars. other data on Henry Gillespie (1793-1863); res. Chillicothe, Ohio, 1850; d. Benton Co., Ind.: fa. bel. to be Rev. sol." Interpreted, this means that the lady would like to know something about the parents and relatives of Henry Gillespie, who lived in Chillicothe, Ohio, in 1850, died in Benton County, Indiana, and whose father was believed to be a Revolutionary soldier.

For the critical procedure of making membership application, the applicant sets to work filling out a four-page document sold by the society at ten cents per set. Library genealogists do no original research but leave the applicant to fill in the empty spaces of a family tree going all the way back to the Revolution. Genealogists urge telling all, through great great great grandparents if possible, since if one line fails to produce a Revolutionary ancestor, another may be more fruitful.

A search may bog down at one point or another, either because documentation is not available or the cost of reproducing records becomes prohibitive. Proof of Revolutionary residence as well as proof of patriotic service is required for a successful application, and references as to where the proofs can be found should be clearly given. In dealing with early records, this is often quite impossible. A typical case is one where the nearest thing to a proof of Revolutionary residence was an undated will on file in a little courthouse on the Eastern Shore of Maryland. Here the DAR library came to the rescue. The library card index revealed the ancestor's name in a history of the state of Delaware. Moreover, the family line had already been established by another member, a Delaware minister, and so the search was over and library facilities had made it inexpensive.

Properly filled out, the application blank is sent to the Registrar-General at DAR headquarters. There the genealogical process begins. From the Registrar-General's office the application is sent to the "book room," where "old" papers of established lines are bound and ancestor catalogs filed. Trained staff members check to see if the new applicant belongs to a family whose line is already established or if the Revolutionary ancestor she claims is listed in ancestral catalogs. If so, the applicant is "in", unless the trained checkers find discrepancies between her family tree and old records. If her line is new and must be verified, the application papers are sent to the head DAR genealogist, and the second step in verification begins.

The applicant's papers are then handed to a staff genealogist— in a busy period such as from 1953 to 1956 all staff genealogists were kept engaged on applications alone—and the library facilities are turned over to assist in the search. The applicant's word is taken as to the identity, marriage and birth of her parents and grandparents, of whom she has personal memory; but for previous generations she must furnish proof of vital statistics by certified or attested copies of wills, deeds, Bible, church and cemetery data, and census and Revolutionary records.

The popular view tends to be that only active Revolutionary soldiers or sailors qualify as ancestors for DAR purposes. As a matter of fact, however, there is a long list of non-combatant services which are also acceptable. Eligibles may be descended from signers of the Declaration of Independence; from civil officers serving between 1775 and 1783, including Town Clerk, selectman, juror, town treasurer, sheriff, constable, highway surveyors, justice of the peace and even jailer; from those who served six months on committees made necessary by the war—Correspondence, Inspection and Safety, Care for Soldiers' Families; from signers of oaths of allegiance and oaths of fidelity and support; from participants in the Boston Tea Party and aid to Boston in 1774; from Ministers who preached patriotic sermons and encouraged patriotic service; from women who performed patriotic deeds or served as nurses; from patriots who furnished supplies (with or without pay) or loaned money for the Revolution; from defenders of forts and frontiers; from signers of several colonial declarations defying the British government; and from prisoners on British prison ships; and finally, even from munition makers and gunsmiths.

Nor is genealogy merely a matter of the dear dead past. Its current political potentialities were demonstrated in 1956 when, with President Eisenhower's health a campaign issue, a search was made through DAR records of five generations of his male and female forbears. The resulting average 74-year life span was publicized as indicative of the President's own life expectancy.

CHAPTER V

IMMIGRATION

The DAR takes an almost proprietary interest in the kind of immigrants who enter this Republic and what happens to them once they get here. Despite its good works in the past on behalf of the Americanization of the foreign-born, it now gives signs of keeping America safe for the natives and Western Europeans.

The prevailing viewpoint of the society on the McCarran-Walter Act which closely limits immigration by fixed quotas for different countries, was summarized by a former National Defense Committee Chairman at the 1956 Continental Congress in these words:

"We went into this question very carefully with the drafters of the immigration law.

"We studied it from all points of view. I had the feeling—and those who were with me at the time and have since studied it feel exactly the same way—that there is no idea of undue restrictions. We must recognize, while our ancestors were all immigrants originally, quite a few of them were immigrants who came to this country with a very definite set of ideas which vary greatly from many of the ideas of the present immigrants who are trying to tear down the quotas, trying to change the ideals and ideas brought here by our ancestors. We are simply agreeing with those authorities who feel that it is only possible to assimilate a certain number of alien elements. If we take in too many of a varying philosophy, we will be entirely lost. America as we know it will be gone. Since we are descendants of the men who established our country, and of the men and women who through generations have kept it as it is, free and ideal like no other country, we feel we have a perfect right to think as they did when our country was founded."

Loud applause greeted this clear statement of the immigration policy which the DAR has steadfastly championed for the past thirty years. When the applause had subsided, another delegate stepped to the microphone, and newsmen waited for a voice in opposition to the resolution affirming support for restricted immigration. But no, the delegate solemnly advised the assembly that the word "principle" in this resolution had been misspelled! The misspelled word was solemnly corrected and the resolution passed. The DAR had reiterated one of its prime inconsistencies—opposition to increased immigration and great pride in its record of aid to immigrants in the past.

The immigration law of 1924, fixing the total annual immigration at 154,000 and starting the great swing in the curtailment of immigration from central and eastern Europe, was strongly endorsed.

President-General Mrs. Anthony Wayne Cook told the organization in April, 1924: "Even while this speech is being delivered the United States Congress is considering immigration on the floors of the House and Senate. The present restrictive immigration law will expire in June. The inherent characteristic of our national life shall be in danger of extinction unless Congress again provides a restrictive measure. The Census of 1920 shows that of 14,000,000 white persons of foreign birth in the United States, less than half are naturalized citizens. If our present legislation lapses in June, we shall be submerged by millions of south Europeans from the war torn countries of the Old World, whose predecessors already here, herding in our congested centers of population, constitute the American naturalization problem as well as the danger spot in our body politic." Mrs. Cook pointedly concluded: "A two per cent quota of admission, based upon the naturalization of alien immigrants during 1890, would prove a mighty bulwark to stem the flood of foreign immigrants."

The way had been carefully paved by the author of the 1924 Immigration Act, Representative Albert Johnson of the state of Washington, who was vigorously applauded when he told the organization: "Our right to say who shall live among us and be one of us has been challenged. Our nation has been threatened with gravest consequences from this immigration act. I say to you that no nation can or will compromise its sovereignty. This nation, born of the deeds of your ancestors, will never do that. To do so is to invite wars. Not to compromise is to prevent war."

With its political ear to the ground, the DAR carefully notes the considerable opposition to the restrictive immigration, but it seems to be unmoved. In 1956 Attorney General Brownell urged Congress to liberalize the Act, by substituting the 1950 census as the basis for arriving at quotas, thus increasing annual admissions to 219,461. And President Eisenhower, in February, 1956, made an unsuccessful attempt to persuade the Congress to enact more liberal legislation. Nevertheless the DAR persists in its view that restricted immigration is necessary to national security, maintaining that the "vigorous attack" upon it has been led by "Communists and other left-wing groups." A National Defense Committee leaflet printed in 1956 states: "These groups have been joined by others who doubtless with good motives have been misled by the barrage of propaganda which has been unleashed against this law. One of the frightful things about the attack on the McCarran-Walter Immigration Act is the extent to which so-called humanitarian, uplift, do-good groups have been misled by the catch-phrases 'second-class citizens', 'discriminations', 'racious', and the like. Pressure is being exercised by those who seek to solicit the so-called minority bloc votes of the Nationality groups. . . . It has been proposed that the National Origins Quota System be scrapped and that in its place there be created a commission which would allocate quotas among the various countries of the world. This method would actually invite political pressures. Our immigration system would be at the mercy of politicians and special interest groups."

Since 1956 brought revolt in Hungary against Soviet Russia and thousands of Hungarian refugees to the United States, the Daughters might have been expected to join with other Americans in condemning Russia for its merciless action against Hungary.

But there were the complications of emergency admissions of refugees and the organization's equally long standing opposition to unrestricted immigration and support of the McCarran-Walter Immigration and Nationality Act.

However the Daughters didn't feel they were torn between the horns of any dilemma. At the 1957 Congress there was no resolution of sympathy for the Hungarians or condemnation for the Soviet action. President-General Groves made the only reference to the Hungarian revolt when she reported rent-free use of Constitution Hall for a Hungarian relief program.

At the same time, in the lobby of Constitution Hall a mimeographed leaflet entitled "Hungarian Refugees" was on sale with other National Defense Committee literature. After quoting members of Congress on the dangers of Communist infiltration among Hungarian refugees, this publication added: "At President Eisenhower's order, more than 20,000 refugees have been admitted to the United States since the October revolution in Hungary. . . Our security officers are deeply concerned over the potential dangers involved, and certainly their fears are justified." Concerning the McCarran-Walter Immigration and Nationality Act, the leaflet stated: "The finest law we have ever had, if protection of the United States is the goal!"

The delegates to the 1957 meeting heard a fiery speech by Richard Arens, Director of the House Communittee on un-American Activities, who told them that "The Number 1 target of the Communist conspiracy in the United States today is destruction of the McCarran-Walter Immigration and Nationality Act." They applauded loudly when Mrs. T.B. Throckmorton of Des Moines, Resolutions Committee Chairman, read a resolution reiterating the Daughters' support of the McCarran-Walter Act. The resolution was passed unanimously.

Against the background of a controversial immigration policy which has been the subject of severe criticism in some quarters, there is a long history of concern for the welfare of the individual immigrant and his family. For more than a generation, the society's "Americanism" program has been one of the most effective and worthy causes.

In 1922 Miss Alice Louise McDuffee of Michigan, American-ism Committee Vice-Chairman, prefaced her report with this little sermon: "The alien cannot speak our language, important as that is as a means of affording mutual understanding. His desire must be roused and only through genuine interest will he respond. The harm done by calling a Hungarian a 'Hunkie', a Jew a 'Sheenie', or an Italian a 'Dago', cannot be overcome merely by a change in phrasing. The withering glance of race prejudice or class scorn, if we are to have a real appreciation of American spirit and ideals, must be replaced by a sympathetic understanding . . .on the part of the native born."

Then Miss McDuffee described the program which was putting into practice the philosophy she preached. She noted that in thirty-two states helpful assistance had been rendered for the foreign-born naturalization courts; forty states were helping teach foreign-born men and women. The District of Columbia, and some states—Idaho, Illinois, Michigan, Minnesota, New York, Tennessee, Texas, Ohio, Oregon, Washington, West Virginia and Wyoming—had chapters that were giving financial help to high schools or summer schools for the foreign-born or were furnishing volunteer teachers from their membership for such schools. Louisiana had classes in domestic science for immigrant wives and daughters. A small chapter in Michigan had established and was supporting a night school with two paid teachers and sixty-two foreign-born pupils. Another Michigan chapter fur-nished twelve teachers each week for a community school. A teacher from one of the Minnesota chapters gave many extra hours to her students for their extra-curricula needs, for which she received no compensation.

California and Oregon led in the work of educating foreign-born women in their homes. California had classes for mothers and nearly all California chapters reported they were helping

teach foreign-born women. Oregon had employed the first home
teacher under a new law passed in 1922 at the instigation of the
DAR State Regent. Indiana chapters gave two large parties for
foreign-born men and women in a high school gymnasium, and
also conducted sewing classes interspersed with frequent picnics
in local parks. In New Jersey stories about George Washington
and early America were told at afternoon parties where foreign-
born women came with their families. Arizona reported that the
DAR helped teach large classes of Mexicans, and cooperated actively with parent-teachers associations.

Another marked contribution was the Ellis Island Immigrant
Aid Committee set up in 1923 with Mrs. Alfred J. Brosseau as
chairman. With the permission of the United States Immigration
Service the Committee directed the work of occupational therapy
in the women's detention room at Ellis Island, chief point of entry
for immigrants. Mrs. Brosseau rosily described the Committee's
work: "A year ago I came before you with little more than a
dream and a prophecy. Today I feel that the realization is yours.
Your gifts of money and of materials, your never-ceasing interest
and your splendid cooperation, have won the day and now the
Daughters of the American Revolution are recognized on Ellis
Island as an indispensable factor for good and for the kind of
service that . . .asks nothing in return. . . . We are now serving
75 women daily and during the past year approximately 9000
have applied to us for work materials. Nearly every nation on
the globe has been represented among these women, but in numbers
the English, Russian, Polish, Armenian, Greek, German, Yiddish
and Italian immigrants have predominated. As I have often told
you, the character of the work done by these women is excellent—
sometimes most extraordinary—and the pride and joy with
which they display finished articles is really very touching."

Ellis Island was one of the Daughters' most cherished projects
and was continued until the Island's crowds of waiting immigrants
became a memory and there was no further need for it.

The education of immigrants continued and in 1921 a compact, factual, and common sense manual was published for new arrivals on these shores. Mrs. John Laidlaw Buel of Connecticut compiled it, with the aid of government experts, and it was eventually translated into eighteen languages and distributed annually by the hundreds of thousands. Paid for by small assessments, state quotas were established on the basis of 25c per member. In the first year of publication, chapters contributed $12,375 for this project.

The contents of this 1921 booklet indicate that the authors combined practicality with idealism, helpful hints with a dash of early American history and a "Message to the Immigrant" which can stir the blood of any American. "Since the discovery of America," the Message began, "more than 33,000,000 immigrants have been welcomed to the United States. Most of these were of European stock. They came because they were poor and sought to make a home for themselves and family. They came because of religious persecution. They came to escape tyrannical governments. The poverty, unhappiness and oppression which caused many of them to migrate have become a memory. They have found peace and happiness and have prospered. America expects that those who come here shall accept its institutions, obey its laws and be peaceful, honest, industrious naturalized citizens. America expects them to respect and defend the flag that protects them; to love, honor and pay loyalty to the country that gives them this peace, happiness and prosperity; to make themselves worthy to receive the great gift of American citizenship; to become true Americans in heart and soul."

Also included in the 1921 manual was a simply-worded story of "The Beginning of America." In short sentences, as in a first-grade reader, the immigrant was told the history and hardships of the earliest foreign-born who came to the New World, among them the small group of colonists who settled in 1607 at Jamestown, Virginia, where the English set up their first small American outpost.—"They sailed across the Atlantic in midwinter, in three little ships. They came hoping to find gold and pearls. No gold or pearls were here. They soon learned that only by hard labor could they live. They must cut down trees, clear the land, till the soil and raise corn. They soon used up the food they had brought over from England. They did not at first grow enough corn to live on. Then came a time of terrible starvation and famine. Many died. Many others were killed by Indians. In despair the colonists were about to return home. They set sail down the James River. At its mouth they met a supply ship from England, sailing up. They were saved and Jamestown prospered from that time on. Other settlements soon were made.

In 1928 the Manual was revised and expanded but the same "Message" and the "The Beginning of America" were retained. A 1954 revision replaced the "Message" with a new "Greetings" written by Miss Gertrude S. Carraway, 1953-56 President-General. This new feature reflects a different approach on the part of the Daughters to the problem of helping in the Americanization of immigrants. Considerably more emphasis is placed upon the responsibilities and opportunities inherent in citizenship and in a more sophisticated world of expanded communication, less upon the textbook-type of advice for the new arrival. Miss Carraway wrote: "New as well as older residents should keep fully informed on our past history, present legislaion and future trends. . . .Our Way of Life is seriously threatened. To save it, it is essential that we understand the dangers, stay alert to our opportunities for service, and strive to do our part for greater progress through devoted American and patriotic education. No Republic can be stronger or better than its constituents. Every citizen, accordingly, should be ever mindful of his or her obligations as well as rights under our representative form of government. . . . May this DAR Manual for Citizenship encourage you to be so proud of your advantages and blessings in our great nation that you will accept its Constitutional responsibilities and work to become a Good Citizen of whom we may all be justly proud."

By contrast, the earlier Manuals of the 1920's specialized in practical information on such subjects as "Finding Work" which referred the immigrant to "licensed" employment agencies "with a good reputation for honesty and reliability." Under the heading "Labor Laws," the immigrant was told, among other things, that forty states made wages the first claim against an employer, who must pay his workmen before paying any other debts; that usually children were not allowed to work before they were fourteen; that many laws required healthful and sanitary working conditions; and that workmen could get compensation from their employers for injuries. The immigrant was also encouraged to learn English as a help in obtaining employment, and was told that, if English classes for immigrants were not offered in his town, "the government will try to get the public schools to start one for you . . . America believes in education . . . All the states have excellent school systems with free tuition."

In case of "Sickness in Your Family," the immigrant was advised to go to the city or county health officer or to the Associated Charities . . . "The Town Clerk can tell you where to find the Health Officer. If you are hurt at work, report to your employer at once." But to help him stay well, the new arrival was told to keep his home well ventilated and in a clean and tidy condition. "Do not allow garbage, trash or manure to accumulate in your home."

The manual also contained a section entitled "Helpful Hints". If arrested and put in jail, the immigrant was informed he could get out on bond and had the right to hire a lawyer; but he was advised not to hire a lawyer "who has come to see you in jail, unless you have sent for him. Good lawyers don't go to jails looking for cases . . . There are many good lawyers and some bad ones."

For non-English speaking immigrants there was a warning against dishonest interpreters and advice to take along an interpreter if called into court, "so you will be sure the court knows what you mean. Many times boys of your own race who are attending high school make good interpreters." If served with legal or court papers, the immigrant was advised to take them to the county clerk or local Americanization teacher, "to find out at once what they are. You may get into serious trouble if you wait." And "don't", the Manual warned, "sign your name to any paper until you know what it says. If you do, you may suffer a great loss."

The newcomer was informed that the laws of the United States require marriage licenses and the support of children. He was advised to go to his Americanization teacher or a community organization in case of trouble between husband and wife or any kind of family difficulty. He was told of the importance of carrying insurance for family protection and advised to place his money in a bank for safekeeping. "Checks are as good as money, so long as there is money in the bank," the manual explained.

By 1954, the manual reflected a consolidation of the organization's immigration policy and was published only in English, Spanish, French, and German. The tone is decidedly less homey than the earlier editions with their helpful hints. The "Manual for Citizenship" has become an objective political pamphlet, reproducing the Constitution, Declaration of Independence, and "The Beginning of America" as did its predecessors, but adding a marked sample voter's ballot, the story and photograph of the Statue of Liberty, a map of the United States, a diagram of the organization of Federal Government, and addresses of the Immigration and Naturalization Service in most large cities. The age of the DAR's maternal immigration policy had come to a close.

After its years of work in Americanization, the DAR had the choice of continuing to play its Statue of Liberty role supporting an immigration policy admitting the oppressed from all countries, and breaking through all quota barriers, or of becoming rather a fraternity house mother with a sharp eye out for "desirables." In the name of national security and national defense it has chosen the fraternity house mother role.

CHAPTER VI

EDUCATION

On April 10, 1929, *The Nation*, the nationally known liberal weekly, told the story of young Pat O'Brien and the DAR.

Joseph Patrick O'Brien, a student at Tucson High School in Tucson, Arizona, read a notice posted in the school that the local DAR would award a prize of $7 for the best essay written about American policies and ideals. Pat decided to enter the competition and chose for his subject the policy of the United States in Nicaragua. His entry was selected by the judge, a visiting teacher from New Jersey, as the best of the 500 papers submitted.

But, *The Nation* reported, when the local chapter took a look at Pat's essay, "they shrank back in horror. Never, they said, would the DAR touch a thing like that, for Pat had said a number of things that good little Americans never say, if they are to win prizes from the DAR." His prize was withheld and *The Nation* quoted at length from his essay which acknowledged that "American capital" had "developed the natural resources" of Nicaragua but condemned the "inconceivably un-American attitude of President Coolidge and the U. S. State Department" in "violating the sacred character of the ballot" and attempting to control the Nicaraguan elections.

Pat concluded: "Perhaps some day the people of the United States will forbid their government to perform acts contrary to the principles of democracy for which the nation stands, and the Stars and Stripes, free from the blemishes of imperialism, will stand once more as the symbol of liberty and democracy for all."

The Nation, already allergic to the DAR because of its superpatriotic activities of the late 20's, gleefully pounced upon Pat O'Brien's brush with the Tucson chapter. It publicized the incident in the magazine's customary style and rewarded Pat for his literary effort by sending him a check for the $7 he had been denied by the DAR sponsors of the essay contest. "Never, we believe," wrote the *Nation's* editor, "has a gift of $7 given the giver a more sublime sense of downright virtue."

This oversimplified incident points up the problem of academic freedom which is as old as education itself and in which the DAR has played an active and often much criticized role. The issue centers about such questions as: How should history be written and taught? Should teachers be forced to take loyalty oaths? How should controversial subjects like Communism be presented to young minds? History and civics textbooks dealing frankly with past and current problems have felt the iron hand of censorship. Adopted by state after state, teacher loyalty oaths have irked professional educators whose philosophy was well expressed by Chairman H. B. Allman of the National Education Association's Commission on teacher Tenure and Academic Freedom in 1945. Dr. Allman said that, while most teachers have no objection to taking a loyalty oath, they do "object to the use of laws requiring such oaths as threats against the right of children to learn the truth and the freedom of teachers to speak the truth."

The DAR's philosophy of education apparently causes them no embarrassment in regard to these issues. They have insisted on teacher loyalty oaths and have unshamefacedly censored history textbooks. An objective of the society, as expressed in its national by-laws, is the "encouragement of historical research in relation to the Revolution and the publication of its results." During their early years, they accomplished this objective through the extensive restoration and preservation of historic landmarks. Otherwise, they have showed only slight interest in history. A series of history lectures was given in Memorial Continental Hall shortly after it was opened in 1905, but created so little stir that it was never repeated. The Daughters apparently did not get excited about the teaching and writing of history until the 1920's, when they joined other patriotic groups in battling pacifists and pacifism, in urging strong national defense (called militarism by their opponents), and in promoting the first "Red scare". Their initial warning about "insidious pacifist dogma" in the classroom came from Mrs. Anthony Wayne Cook, President-General from 1923 to 1926, when she announced that the organization should "see that our school boards are not allowing our public school system to be used for the dissemination of propaganda, which under the guise of so-called peace literature, is in reality dangerous and insidious pacifist dogma." Reporting that too much of that sort of thing was already in active circulation, she warned that "it is cleverly prepared, so that it might insidiously stir up unrest and discontent in the minds of both pupils and teachers concerning the use of time-tested governmental institutions." Four years later an impressive lady from Cincinnati, Ohio, Mrs. Lowell Fletcher Hobart, President-General from 1929 to 1932, cautioned: "Un-American tendencies are rampant."

In 1934 the American Historical Association reported that Professor David E. Muzzey's *American History* had been frequently denounced by the ladies because "they feel it gives to military history insufficient emphasis to make good soldiers out of children." The volume, the American Historical Association revealed, had been removed from North Carolina's official textbook list because some local DAR members felt that Professor Muzzey slighted their state and "unjustly called slavery the chief cause of the Civil War." In 1937 *The Nation* commented: "If any textbook views America's past at all realistically, its author is immediately accused of everything but treason and sometimes even that."

The magazine reported that of hundreds of American histories only two seemed to "meet DAR prejudices." These two were *The Story of Our American People* by Professor Charles F. Horne, and *The American Government Today* by Frederick J. Haskin, head of Haskin's Information Bureau in Washington. *The Story of Our American People* frankly stated that its object was to "tell the truth optimistically and to speak chiefly of success," according to *The Nation*. Strongly sponsored by the Daughters who brought

it to the attention of local school boards and urged its adoption
as a textbook, Professor Horne's volume described the survivors
of pioneer hardships in America as a "chosen race" of Europeans.
Admitting that the "great leaders of Europe, her chief scholars,
artists, and scientists remained of course at home," the book lauds
the immigrants by piously declaring that "strong and clever folk,
resolute and earnest ones, were established in America and received stern training in its wilderness. They were built up into
a sturdy company indeed, well fit to be the ancestors of a new race,
the 'Americans.' " Devoting much space to Revolutionary and
Colonial history, the two-volume work described the problem of
disbanding the "ragged, penniless Revolutionary soldiers," some
of whom even declared that America would only be safe as a
monarchy, with Washington as its king: "With sternest reproof
Washington forbade his friends even to think of restoring the
old British system of inequality, wherein one man was perm-
anently set above another. . . . He made an earnest effort to gather
money for the troops from Congress or from any source, but
failed. So with a final splendid heroism of endurance, the Con-
tinentals disbanded quietly. . . . They scattered, as their great
leader wrote in bitter indignation for their wrongs, 'without a
farthing in their pockets.' "

Professor Horne's "truthfully optimistic" history apparently
never made much headway as a standard textbook in the nation's
public schools, despite the fact that the DAR itself actually distributed thousands of copies of his book. One annual report states
that "the author" had given them 12,000 copies for distribution to
schools, CCC camps, and so forth.

Meanwhile, realizing their limited success in sponsoring or
distributing history texts, the Daughters concentrated on efforts to
censor established texts such as Dr. Muzzey's and urged the adoption of teacher oaths, a campaign which was to involve them in a
prolonged controversy with the National Education Association.
The two organizations are worthy of each others' steel. The DAR is
big, but the NEA is bigger; the DAR is proud that it is still

growing after two generations, but the NEA is growing faster. When the DAR reported a membership of nearly 185,000 in April, 1957, the NEA more than tripled that with 614,000. In the previous year, when Daughters added almost no net increase in members, the NEA added 43,000. As real estate owners, too, the contestants are well matched. DAR headquarters property is valued variously at $7,500,000 to $11,000,000; expanded and modernized NEA headquarters will be worth an estimated $6,-000,000 when additional new buildings are completed.

It was twenty years earlier, in 1936, when the organization began a real crusade for teachers' oaths. Formal announcement came from pretty President-General Mrs. William A. Becker of New Jersey, elected in 1935 over a scholarly and dignified lady educator from Tennessee, Dr. Flora Myers Gillentine, who might well have steered a more moderate course. A sidelight on the campaign was a newspaper photograph of Speaker of the House James Byrnes warmly shaking Mrs. Becker's hand although he was a dinner guest of the Gillentine supporters. The Gillentine faction charged "Foul!" when the picture appeared in a newspaper the next morning, but Mrs. Becker was elected, two to one, and a year later led the DAR into a campaign for teacher oaths. Mrs. Becker declared that the organization would "check closely in states requiring oaths" to see that the laws were enforced; in others they would urge enactment of such laws. "We are not trying to raise a Red scare," she maintained. "Our one purpose in insisting on this pledge is to weed out as far as possible the un-American teacher engaging in planting subversive doctrines in the minds of future citizens. . . . It is not true that the DAR is attempting to create the alarming impression that America's public schools are packed with Communistic teachers."

Her words of assurance apparently failed to convince the professional educators. On August 19, 1936, Louis M. Hacker, Columbia University lecturer, told the American Federation of Teachers, in convention at Philadelphia: "The DAR's are busy-bodies and witch hunters. It is time this organization stopped its witch hunting and terrorizing of teachers by campaigning for loyalty oaths."

Even before the DAR launched its campaign for teacher oaths, its attitude had begun to disturb many educators. In February, 1936, Dr. George S. Counts of Teachers' College, Columbia University, addressing 1000 school administrators in St. Louis, just before the opening of the National Education Association's annual convention, denounced the organization along with newspaper publisher William Randolph Hearst and Detroit radio priest Father Coughlin. Dr. Counts warned that Mr. Hearst was trying to "control the curriculum of our schools," and that Father Coughlin used his "sacred office to spread confusion, misunderstanding and falsehoods among the people;" as for the DAR— "most of them are too ignorant of American history and American ideals to know what they are doing. Their patriotism is a combination of thinly veiled snobbery and the protection of privilege."

All this followed a controversy in Massachusetts the year before, when that state passed a teacher's oath law and Dr. Kirtley F. Mather, professor of geology at Harvard, refused to take the oath and urged other liberals on Harvard's 1800-member faculty to do the same. Shortly thereafter Mrs. Becker, speaking at Pittsfield, Massachusetts, criticized Professor Mather for his stand and said,"If anyone teaching in public schools or institutions cannot take the oath of allegiance to the constitution of his state and country, he should not be instructing American youth." Most Massachusetts educators complied with the law, but Harvard announced it would take no steps to punish faculty members who, like Dr. Mather, balked at the compulsory pledge.

According to *The Nation* a year later the organization was determined to "oust teachers opposed to its conception of American government. . . . Charging but not proving they had evidence that many educators were selling themselves out to the Communists, the Daughters went on record as favoring dismissal of any and all who, in their opinion, revealed Moscow connections through aver-- sion to DAR loyalty oaths."

Children of the American Revolution—the youth organization sponsored by the DAR—reflected the views of the parent body in expressing a decided distrust of their teachers on several occasions. Even before the parent organization opened its drive on teacher oaths, the "Children" precociously on two occasions voted that "Whereas there are sinister influences being used in schools to undermine love of the flag and our country, be it resolved that the CAR formulate a bill and present it to the United States Congress, making it necessary for all teachers to subscribe to the oath of allegiance to our country, or resign the certificate to teach." Clearly the children were on the alert.

Alarmed by increasing pressure against the teaching profession, the National Education Association set up a Committee on Teacher Tenure and Academic Freedom, and in 1937 this Committee began sending out trained people in response to appeals for investigations of alleged unfair dismissals of teachers. Investigating the history of loyalty oaths, the Committee discovered that some states had required teacher oaths soon after the Civil War and that the number had slowly increased even before the hysterical furor of the 1920's. A flood of new teacher oath laws followed in the 30's—five states passed them in 1931, one in 1933, and six in 1935; all this before the Daughters entered the fray.

The movement continued through 1941, with three more states joining the procession in that year; then it died away until after World War II. New and more drastic "anti-disloyalty" oaths were adopted by five states between 1950 and 1952; while in some other states teacher associations were able to beat down efforts to get such stern laws through state legislatures. Oklahoma passed a loyalty law so drastic that it made membership in any Communist front or subversive organization automatic grounds for a teacher's dismissal without trial or hearing, but it was thrown out as unconstitutional by the United States Supreme Court in 1952. Justice Hugo Black called this Oklahoma statute "but one manifestation of a national network of laws aimed at coercing and controlling the minds of men. Test oaths are notorious tools of tyranny. When used to shackle the mind they are, or at least should be, unspeakably odious to a free people."

In the face of more serious attacks on public schools, the National Education Association again rose to the defense and in 1941 established a National Commission for the Defense of Democracy Through Education, whose first task was to investigate conditions in a number of cities where schools were under attack —notably Pasadena, Houston, Chicago, and Kansas City, Missouri.

Dr. Robert A. Skaife, National Commission field secretary, addressing the Connecticut Education Association in 1951, described the post-war technique used in attacks on schools. He said "patriots" operating under respectable sounding slogans, were coming forward with proposals to "restore our Constitutional rights, drive the 'Reds' out of our schools, and above all, drive out progressive education." The word "progressive", he said, was being used as a "smear word" to discredit many educational practices which level-headed educators considered sound. And, he added, one of the dangers of this situation came from the fact that "certain conservative organizations had jumped on the bandwagon" in the new atack.

The DAR was certainly on that bandwagon. One of its National Defense Committee brochures described progressive education as a "plan of collectivists at Columbia Teachers' College, New York City, to propagate alien ideologies through the public schools from coast to coast."

A particular post-war target was a publication called *Building America,* published about eight times a year by NEA's Association for Supervision and Curricular Development. This publication had been used as supplemental material in U. S. classrooms since 1935. In 1948 the DAR Continental Congress was told that California Daughters had spent $500 the previous year to help suppress, through action of the state legislature, an edition of this publication, which they called "a series of subversive textbooks." In the opposite corner, coming to the publication's defense was the California State Superintendent of Schools, who said he would stake his professional reputation that it was not subversive. The California Parent-Teacher Association also studied the publication and said that it was "neither subversive nor Communistic" in approach; and the California Library Association's Committee on Intellectual Freedom defended *Building America* in a pamphlet answering charges by local patriot groups that the NEA publication was a "subtle attack on our American institutions." The Library Association committee said this NEA educational material "provided valuable extension of the basic textbooks in social science used by California public schools," and declared the critics "seem to have an aversion to unpleasant facts and pictures, even though they may be true. The publication on the other hand, has shown bad as well as good conditions, especially for the purpose of indicating progress."

The organization's approach to the development of controversial issues in the public schools is illustrated by its post-war campaign against the twenty-five year-old text by Dr. Frank A. Magruder, entitled *American Government.* A Tennessee DAR Americanization Committee chairman attacked this book in 1953, but the attack was effectively opposed by the *Nashville Tennesseean,* an outspoken daily newspaper.

As a result of the pressure exerted by Mrs. Julius Talmadge, former DAR President-General and a member of the Georgia State Board of Education, Dr. Magruder's text was removed from the state's school list twice from 1950 until 1952, when the State Board firmly reinstated it. Excitement seems to have centered around certain passages relating to the Soviet Union. According to Senator James E. Murray, Montana Democrat, speaking on the floor of the United States Senate in 1951, the problem was one of misquotations which made Dr. Magruder appear to have placed Russia in a more favorable light than in fact he had. The Montana Senator pointed out that the Magruder book was on the recommended book lists of all forty-eight states, and had been a classic in its field for twenty-five years.

In Texas a post-war state-wide DAR committee, commissioned

to "evaluate public school texts," sent a questionaire to Lone Star Daughters, asking such questions as, "Did they feel that their school had 'swung to the left' "?? How many "One-World" texts were being used in it? Had they checked their school libraries, and did their local newspaper and radio station cooperate in alerting the public to "subversive" educational trends? Going still farther, the statewide committee rated a list of seventy publications, including textbooks, as "bad," "very bad," "not good," "not satisfactory," "fair," "not recommended" "really a bad one." Only two of the 70 were called "good", one "fairly good", and one "very good". Four encyclopedias failed to make the DAR grade and were criticized or damned with faint praise for their sections on Soviet Russia; the *Americana* was "bad," the *Britannica* "not satisfactory", *Collier's* "fairly good", and the *World Book* "not satisfactory."

In 1950, the Continental Congress was told that 691 chapter members had made "surveys" of history books used in their local schools; an Indiana chapter induced its local school board to appoint a committee of three men to inspect history books; through the efforts of "Sons" and "Daughters" in West Virginia, "certain history books were replaced;' fifty Texas chapters read history books and in one city "action was taken and books changed." In 1951, a similar report said that "in order to ascertain if our children are being taught the principles embraced by our forefathers, we have asked that American history textbooks now being used in the schools be checked by our members; 393 members have read textbooks and 1695 have visited history classes."

The effect of such surveillance, according to the National Education Association, is a voluntary self censorship imposed by teachers who have preferred to observe what is locally orthodox rather than to express their own ideas and thereby risk dismissal on the grounds of disloyalty. On the basis of a 1951 questionaire sent to approximately 400 members of its advisory group composed of professional educators, the NEA committee on Teacher

Tenure and Academic Freedom concluded that such surveillance, with its consequent self censorship by teachers, "was today's most critical danger to the right of students to learn. If such conditions prevail, the injustice to students is that they will know nothing of the evils or dangers of Communism, and will grow up in a hot house environment that ill equips them to think for themselves." The same committee quoted President Dwight D. Eisenhower (then General Eisenhower) as having said that ignorance of Communism, fascism or any other police state philosophy is far more "dangerous than ignorance of the most virulent disease. . . . Who can doubt the choice of Americans between statism and freedom, if the truth concerning each be held before their eyes?" Here were words worth heeding.

In 1956 Dr. Richard B. Kennan, secretary of the NEA's Commission for the Defense of Democracy Through Education, reported that there seemed to be a lessening of attacks on public schools. This observation seems borne out by the annual DAR reports, which in recent years have emphasized a new history project instead of censorship of existing textbooks. The new project encourages the study of American history in the fifth through the eighth grades, and as incentives, prizes are awarded to the winners of essay contests and to those who get top grades in history. In 1954 it was announced by the society that 1654 medals had been awarded, 1857 gifts, $665 in cash and 100 certificates for top winners of essay contests, top grades or both.

In 1956 the organization resolved that "plans be formulated by the membership to continue an even more aggressive campaign to promote the study of true and factual American history in all our schools from grades to colleges and universities, to the end that it may become a required subject in high schools, colleges and universities, either state supported or privately endowed."

Disapproving Federal aid to education, the Daughters for many years have sponsored a "national aid to education" program of their own in which they take great pride. The aim of this program, to which members all over the country contribute, is the education of underprivileged children in remote areas. The keynote for the project was sounded by forward-looking Mrs. Matthew T. Scott, President-General from 1909-1913, when she made an appeal for the education of children, many of them descendants of Revolutionary heroes, who live in the mountain areas of Alabama, South Carolina, North Carolina, and Georgia.

It is to the society's credit that it has founded and supported two mountain schools: The Tamassee School at Tamassee, South Carolina, and the Kate Duncan Smith School at Grant, Alabama, both serving the joint purpose of the practical education of young people and as a community center. The national organization gives each school only $2000 a year in actual cash, but local chapters all over the country have literally built the two institutions, brick by brick. For example, the 1956 DAR Congress was told that Michigan Daughters had built a craft center at the Alabama school, costing about $15,000; Texas had donated $2000 for a hay baler; New York, $5,454.55 for tools; Pennsylvania, $500 for a concrete play area. Year after year, various state chapters take on such projects in behalf of both schools. They also send tons of used clothing to students and families in the mountain communities. One story Daughters like to tell deals with the comment of a member visiting one of the schools, who said she was surprised to see the students looking so well dressed. "They ought to be— they're wearing your clothes," replied a school employee.

A pamphlet recently published by the society reports with manifest satisfaction that the Tamassee school "reaches to the remote corners of the mountains of South Carolina, Georgia and North Carolina, for the forgotten and neglected children of the hills. . . . So far as is known not a single graduate of Tamassee has committed a crime or an offense unbecoming to a good citizen. The graduates occupy positions of leadership in their communities, take pride in having good homes and are making sure that their children have a good education." The booklet also quotes warm words of praise in the *Birmingham News,* for the Alabama school: "high atop picturesque Gunter Mountain, almost as

close to heaven as to earth . . . a place where the C's of Citizenship
and Character are taught along with the three R's. . . . In its
almost three decades of existence, this school has made a lasting
mark on the life of Marshall County as well as the state of Alabama. It has carried the torch of education to greater heights
by serving the entire mountain area."

Eleven other schools and colleges are approved by the organization as recipients of scholarships and other financial aid.
These schools either educate boys and girls who otherwise might
not have an opportunity for education, or instruct foreign born
students or students of foreign parentage in the American way
of life. After World War II the Daughters split up the balance
of a war fund, giving $25,000 to each of its own two schools and
$2100 to each school on the approved list.

On the issue of federal aid to education, the DAR and the
educational profession probably never will agree. The DAR is
against it, and the National Education Association, for one,
strongly supports it, pointing out that federal aid over the past
150 years has encouraged state effort and not resulted in the
feared federal control. The society's handbook urges members
to "explain the dangers of socialized medicine and federal aid
to education." It flatly states: "Either of these under any name is
socialism." In 1946 a resolution against federal aid to schools
warned it "would tend toward the further regimentation and
centralization of government and the removal of state control."

In 1947 another argument was added against proposed Federal
aid: it would not provide true equalization of educational
opportunity. In 1951 the organization was alarmed by "new
bills" for federal aid, and reasserted its opposition to legislation
that would, in whatever guise, place control of education under
any department or bureau of the national government, since any
increase in the federal bureaucracy "would advance socialism."
In 1956 a National Defense Committee mimeographed publication, on sale at the Continental Congress, warned against letting
"our schools become part of the socialistic scheme that has our

government building roads, setting the wage rate, buying surplus crops, and erecting hospitals." Another went still farther, with a dire prediction that, "eventually Federal aid means socialism, State socialism can become communism."

In 1957 the Daughters brought up to date their anti-federal aid to education crusade. President Eisenhower had pledged the weight of his power and prestige in behalf of billion-dollar legislation for federal aid to school construction—something new in the long struggle to tap the federal treasury for a direct subsidy to public schools throughout the nation. The President had sent "greetings" to the delegates in a message to Mrs. Groves, President-General, read at the opening session of the 1957 Congress, in which the President told the Daughters "responsibility for progress belongs to us."

But the Daughters were no more friendly to his school construction plan than they had been to earlier federal aid to education proposals. They adopted a resolution opposing federal aid to education "in whatever guise" and specifically charged that professional educators who have lobbied for this objective over the past 30 years, were chief advocates of federal aid to school construction; that Congressional hearings had failed to prove any school district "too poor" to meet its own school construction needs with local "and/or state aid;" and that the weight of evidence showed states were taking care of their own school building problems and did not need or want federal aid. Inevitably, of course, the resolution ended with a warning about the "risk of control which would be unavoidable with so-called federal aid."

One courageous delegate rose in opposition to this resolution. But there was loud applause without murmur of dissent when the 1957 Congress harked back to a 20-year-old crusade by adopting another resolution which demands loyalty oaths for teachers, professors and school administrators. This resolution urged members to seek adoption of loyalty oath laws by their respective state legislatures.

Consistently the DAR has been in the midst of the educational fray. Prime inheritors of our past, they have tended to censor and suppress history, to shape it to their liking in ways that no doubt arouse their indignation when followed by totalitarian countries. Watchdogs of the Republic, they have pressed hard for teachers' loyalty oaths. Faint-hearted, they have feared the exposure of young minds to controversial ideas. Stalwart and energetic, they have urged the more adequate teaching of American history and have provided educational opportunities for children in the *Tobacco Road* regions of the southern mountains.

Chapter VII

DOMESTIC POLICIES

Throughout the years the DAR has been in the thick of major domestic problems affecting such varied matters as immigration, education, the home and the family, the Negro, the "New Deal", and the Bricker amendment. Frequently the policies adopted have involved the organization in dramatic controversies. Inevitably they have often resulted in unfavorable publicity.

At least twice—first in 1939 and again in 1946—the Daughters had their pudgy fingers badly burned on the race issue. These experiences possibly explain their non-participation in the public school desegregation controversy when it erupted in 1956. They remained quite silent when southern states balked at the U. S. Supreme Court's ruling on the unconstitutionality of segregated schools and again when a large bloc of Senators and Representatives signed a manifesto denouncing desegregation. Mrs. T. B. Throckmorton, chairman of the Resolutions Committee, told a press conference in 1956 that resolutions on this issue had been submitted to her committee, but none would be reported to the society's Congress. "I lived through the Marian Anderson case," she said. "I don't want anything more like that."

Marian Anderson was the focal point for the organization's first trouble on the race issue. The Philadelphia-born Negro contralto, who had skyrocketed to fame in a 1935 Salzburg concert, was at the height of her triumphant career. Arturo Toscanini had commented: "Yours is a voice such as one hears once in a hundred years." In January, 1939, her manager tried to book Constitution Hall, the only large concert hall in the nation's capital, for an April 9 concert; DAR officials said they were sorry but the hall was taken for that night; Miss Anderson's manager suggested April 8 or 10, but the answer was the same. Newspapers learned of the incident and immediately a storm of protest beat about the Daughters' heads.

Mrs. Franklin D. Roosevelt resigned her life membership in the organization over the incident. World famous violinist Jascha Heifetz, arriving in Washington for a concert, said he was "ashamed" to appear in Constitution Hall under the circumstances. A group including Conductor Walter Damrosch, critic-composer Deems Taylor and a number of other leading musicians, churchmen and journalists, expressed the hope that the ban against Marian Anderson "reflects the judgement of some irresponsible DAR official." A protest meeting in Washington drew a crowd of 1500. Dr. Elsie Mitchell, 67-year-old surgeon and one of two honorary DAR life members on the Pacific Coast, followed Mrs. Roosevelt's example. She resigned with this terse statement: "I do not care to belong to an organization which violates any of the principles I cherish, chief among them being no race prejudice."

President-General Mrs. Henry M. Robert, Jr., refrained from comment. Following the District of Columbia mass meeting, there was an attempt to open a public school auditorium for the Anderson concert; but the District School Board officials refused to take what they feared would be a precedent-setting action.

But Marian Anderson did sing in Washington on April 9, 1939. On that bright Easter Sunday, at the invitation of Secretary of the Interior Harold Ickes, Miss Anderson stood in the open portico of the Lincoln Memorial, on a platform with top government officials from the North and the South, and sang for the thousands of people who crowded the park.

Only four years later—during World War II—the DAR Daughters invited Miss Anderson to give a benefit performance in Constitution Hall, still, however, refusing to rent the auditorium to other Negro artists. In 1946 they turned down a concert booking for Negro pianist Hazel Scott. In the same year one of their most prominent members took up this cause and again the organization was embroiled in the race issue.

Two lovely ladies of vastly different backgrounds were the chief adversaries in the 1946 "white artists" battle. President-General of the Society and proponent of the "white artists only" policy was Mrs. Julius Y. Talmadge, "the Georgia peach." Her antagonist was Clare Boothe Luce, Connecticut Republican Member of Congress and later Ambassador to Italy—one of the most glamorous and successful women of her generation. In the center of the dispute was Tuskegee Institute, one of the country's oldest and most respected educational institutions for Negroes, founded by the great Booker T. Washington. In 1946 the famous Tuskegee Institute choir, en route back to Alabama following a New York University recital, wanted to give a concert in Constitution Hall for the benefit of the United Negro College Fund, a long-standing philanthropic project for the benefit of 33 Negro educational institutions.

Tuskegee's booking was refused. Again the refusal became public. This time it was Mrs. Luce who led the revolt within the organization. The fact that Mrs. Talmadge was the first southern lady ever elected President-General and bears the name of the famous Talmadge family of Georgia, although she is not the wife of Georgia's Governor as was often thought, added to the general interest of the controversy. Touching off Mrs. Luce's opposition was the Hazel Scott incident. When this concert pianist was denied the privilege of performing in Constitution Hall, the organization's Executive Committee—haunted by the Marian Anderson affair—issued a clarifying statement. The Committee explained that the rules of management for the auditorium were drawn up in accordance with the prevailing custom in the District of Columbia—complete segregation in schools, auditoriums, clubs, canteens, theaters, playgrounds, and so forth. One of these management rules, the Committee pointed out, clearly stipulated that the words "white artists only" must be added to leases for the use of Constution Hall. Mrs. Luce took to the radio in February, 1946, and delivered a powerful punch which the Daughters could not counter. A brilliant and witty speaker, Mrs. Luce outclassed her member competitors. With tongue in cheek, Mrs. Luce insisted she did not believe the patriotic ladies really intended to practice racial discrimination; she merely wanted to warn Mrs. Talmadge—demurely—that the continuance of the "white artists clause" would give the society a "couple of black eyes."

At first the Daughters reacted to the Congresswoman's attack as they had done when Mrs. Eleanor Roosevelt resigned in protest against the Marian Anderson banning. After all, the Anderson furor had subsided and they had ridden out the storm. At any rate, Mrs. Talmadge tried to imitate the successful precedent established by her predecessor, Mrs. Robert. The Daughters again sat tight.

A few months later Mrs. Luce struck again by organizing a DAR Committee Against Racial Discrimination in Constitution Hall, composed of nine members and a non-DAR secretary, who served the group as a sympathetic bystander. Urging chapters to vote opposition to the "white artists only" clause, the committee obviously hoped enough steam would be generated to force consideration of this question at the coming annual Continental Congress.

A few days after the organization of the committee, Mrs. Talmadge received a telegram from Mrs. Luce, urging that the Tuskegee choir be allowed to sing in Constitution Hall, "lest once more DAR's all over the country are forced to apologize." Having mulled over this new attack, Mrs. Talmadge tartly notified the Congresswoman that the "so-called DAR committee against racial discrimination in Constitution Hall was hindering rather than helping the Tuskegee choir in its attempt to give a Constitution Hall concert." Then as time passed and Continental Congress came closer, Mrs. Talmadge made a suprise announcement which sounded like capitulation to the Luce rebels. Her announcement informed the world and Mrs. Luce that the Tuskegee Choir would sing in Constitution Hall on June 3, with no charge for the hall or for services of DAR employees. . . ."This is a most worthy undertaking and we will help in every way to make it a splendid financial success," said the lady from Georgia

But the Luce Committee was not ready to quit so long as the "white artists" clause was still operative. The committee took a perfectly proper procedural step, which Mrs. Talmadge herself announced. It submitted a resolution to the DAR Resolutions Committee, proposing that the "white artists only" clause be stricken from Constitution Hall leases. Mrs. Talmadge, in making the announcement, added that the resolution would not be reported to the coming Congress; that no action was planned on the "white artists only" clause and that "we're not anticipating any trouble." Naturally, the Luce committee immediately countered with a promise to get the resolution before the Congress, over any or all opposition.

After this initial skirmish, the battle of words began in earnest. Mrs. Talmadge called the committee "unconstitutional and illegal", and said she thought its members "would like to know what we are going to do at the Congress." The committee reported that Mrs. Talmadge opened Constitution Hall to the Tuskegee choir only because committee members threatened to "take action" if the choir were banned, and because the organization "feared public opinion." It charged also that Mrs. Talmadge had dropped an iron curtain between the DAR and public opinion some months earlier, when she sent a letter to 3000 chapters asking them not to discuss the "white artists only" question in public.

As the 1946 Congress opened in Atlantic City on May 20, Mrs. Talmadge again made a surprise move when she announced that the National Board of Management had named a special committee to investigate the question of Constitution Hall leases and report its findings and recommendations to the board for final action. She declared that banned artists had reaped millions of dollars' worth of publicity from the controversy, that "politics and publicity have lurked behind every curtain in every attack on our management of Constitution Hall," and quoted the following paragraph from Mrs. Luce's February 21 broadcast: "See here, Mrs. Talmadge of Athens, Georgia, you are a fine woman and a gracious lady, but whether you will admit it or not, in your deep concern for white faces you are paradoxically enough giving our DAR a couple of black eyes by insisting on this clause in our

Constitution Hall contract." In reply, Mrs. Talmadge told the Atlantic City Congress: "This attack on me personally demonstrates to what length antagonists will go in order to create division within our ranks."

"Her soft southern voice" deceived no one, a New York reporter wrote of the President-General's denunciation of Mrs. Luce's committee. New York reporters had flocked to witness the Atlantic City battle. Mrs. Luce was not present, but her name was on every tongue. No one knew what was going to happen, but the issue was not long in doubt. The chairman of the 1946 Resolutions Committee was a formidable member of long experience in intra-mural controversy and a former President-General—Mrs. Grace Lincoln Hall Brosseau of Greenwich, Connecticut. At the first business session, Mrs. Brosseau wasted no time in annihilating the enemy by strictly parliamentary tactics. The DAR leaders had contended that Mrs. Luce's group could not set themselves up as a committee, because no organization committee could be established without the society's sanction. On this parliamentary ground, Mrs. Brosseau read a resolution dissolving the Luce committee as unconstitutional, and the delegates passed it with thunderous "ayes". Having tested the feeling of her fellow-members, the chairman offered another resolution expressing "implicit confidence" in the ability of the DAR's National Board of Management to reach a "wise solution" of any controversial question that might arise. Again there was a chorus of loud "ayes", this time followed by applause. Mrs. Talmadge was vindicated; her judgement of the society's temper was correct; Mrs. Luce had wrung a concession from the society, but nothing more.

Still, the battle was not over. The Congresswoman had promised to get her controversial resolution on the floor of the DAR meeting, and she, too, was a force not to be lightly regarded. After some backstage maneuvering, the resolution did get to the floor just before the Congress was ready to adjourn. A member of the Luce Committee, Mrs. Eugene Denny Vann of New Jersey, was permitted to appear on the platform and read the committee's

proposal to delete the "white artists only" clause from lease contracts. Greeted by jeers and laughter from the 4000 assembled
members, Mrs. Vann had the last word; she surprised and dis-
appointed the gathering by reading the resolution and immediately withdrawing it, so delegates missed the satisfaction of voting
it down. After the meeting, Mrs. Vann announced that she was
"completely satisfied" with her own performance. "I knew if
the delegates voted I would take a fearful licking," she admitted.
Delegates had laughed loudly when Mrs. Vann said her chapter
felt "the support and interest of our responsibility has been fully
met by Mrs. Talmadge's announcement of a committee to study
the matter—we had no intention to cause dissention in the DAR."
Obviously they had been unmoved by her earnest statement of her
chapter's motives in offering the resolution. "In the first place,"
said Mrs. Vann, "we are a Christian organization and this policy
is not according to the Golden Rule. In the second place, we are
a patriotic organization. We have endorsed the United Nations
preamble which contains a clause about racial equality. In the
third place, we must be consistent. We put no 'for whites only'
on our buddy bags (DAR gifts which had gone by the thousands
to World War II service men and women). We help educate
Indians. But no Indian could lease Constitution Hall."

In criticizing the Daughters for their 1947 resolutions, the
New Republic declared a year later, "The DAR Buildings and
Grounds Committee announced that its 'middle of the road' color
line would be maintained until the District of Columbia changes
city-wide racial policies—which was a little confusing, inasmuch
as the DAR's allow negroes to sit in the audience but will not
let them appear on the stage of Constitution Hall, whereas District
of Columbia theaters allow them on the stage but not in the
audience." Representative Frances Bolton, multi-millionaire Republican Congresswoman and herself a Daughter, likened her fellow Daughters to Lot's wife, standing in the middle of the desert.
"Unless," Mrs. Bolton stated, "the organization promotes active

work for better national and international conditions, then fiddle de doo with the DAR."

To a student of DAR history these spectacular examples of the organization's attitude on domestic issues could not be too surprising. The society had been founded with its face turned towards the past, and its concern with current affairs was long in coming. In 1913 Mrs. Matthew T. Scott, President-General from 1909 to 1913 and one of the organization's great ladies, tried to arouse in her fellow members a feeling of social consciousness, and had some initial success, but this is not the accomplishment for which Mrs. Scott is remembered. The society's handbook listing each President-General and the official appraisal of her administration reports of Mrs. Scott only that she established a conservation committee and completed Memorial Continental Hall.

This majestic lady—tall and commanding in appearance, but with no claim to beauty—was a sister of Mrs. Adlai E. Stevenson. The sisters were daughters of Lewis W. Green, President of Centre College, in Danville, Illinois. Here Adlai E. Stevenson had studied for two years before he was forced to leave school after his father's death. He then read law in an Illinois law office and eventually returned to marry one of the college president's daughters.

A woman of wealth, prestige, leisure and unquestionable ability, Mrs. Scott added distinction to the society. At "brilliant" receptions given by her in the newly completed Memorial Continental Hall, guests included outstanding figures of the Nation's capital. Among other accomplishments, she was the first President-General to induce a President of the United States—William Howard Taft—to attend the opening of a DAR Congress and address the Daughters. This precedent was set in 1909 and has been followed by many subsequent Presidents.

Up to that time the organization had been absorbed in its own affairs—membership, building program, historical projects, and genealogy. At the 1912 Continental Congress, before the end of her administration in 1913, Mrs. Scott told the Daughters there was other worthwhile work awaiting their attention. She said that people who still persisted in seeing them as a "mutual admiration society for the promotion of pink teas and ancestor worship" also looked upon their chapter meetings, state conferences and national Continental Congresses as "inconsequential gatherings of a semi-social nature for the purpose of reading the minutes of the last meeting and electing officers for forthcoming ones. To those people our patriotic principles and efforts are merely a cloak to hide our real purpose . . . for the alert among us to gain admission to the society of the elite."

Calling this interpretation of their objectives "fatuous and calumnious," the President-General urged upon members three objectives. She said there were "unrealized possibilities in American home life"; that while many American women were wonderfully successful homemakers, many others were extravagant, ignorant of household economy and inefficient both as housewives and homemakers. "It is commonplace among sociologists that in an average American family enough food is usually wasted in the kitchen alone to keep a French family in comfort," she told the gathering. She added that she would like to see the organization's education program enlarged and broadened "so our national society would enter the realm of education in its true sense." Thirdly, she deplored the bargain hunting of American women, because it led them to look for bargains from the output of sweat shops. They were involved, Mrs. Scott said, "in a mad scramble for cheapness at any cost of human degradation." Pointing out that a Consumers' League had been organized, she praised its objectives, hoped for better wages in business and industry, and laid at feminine doorsteps the blame for some of the conditions she deplored. "We cannot," she concluded, "avoid our economic and moral responsibility as family purveyors and budget makers."

A year later, at the end of her administration, Mrs. Scott added a postscript to the lecture on social consciousness she had read in 1912. The U. S. Children's Bureau had been established, with Julia Lathrop—destined to become famous through her work for children—as its first Director. Inviting Miss Lathrop to address the 1913 DAR Congress, Mrs. Scott commented that the Daughters were "proud to have had a part in establishing the Bureau." If they had continued along these lines of progressive social welfare, the Daughters' own history might have been different. A committee, set up by Mrs. Scott on the welfare of women and children, made in 1916 a series of liberal recommendations: the passage of federal child labor and compulsory education laws; tuberculosis control; the betterment of sanitary conditions in stores and factories; work permits and the limitation of working hours for children under 16; juvenile courts; uniform marriage and divorce laws; the prohibition of the sale of liquor, cigarettes and drugs to minors; the regulation of working hours for women; and a ban on new tenements without proper heat, ventilation and sanitary facilities. But two short years later this committee was merged with another, and its program abandoned.

Not that the Daughters became completely oblivious to national problems. In 1915 they favored the federal construction of "common roads" in the country as a means of contributing to the material, educational and spiritual welfare of the people; they urged the national government to establish parks in large areas recently acquired by the government in the White and Appalachian Mountains; and they favored the creation of a National Conservation Commission composed of Secretaries of Agriculture, War Navy and Interior. For years before and after World War I they promoted the federal construction of a transcontinental highway on the "Old Trails" route taken by pioneers in pushing forward to the Pacific, now U. S. Route 40. As early as 1912 they passed a resolution in favor of a memorial highway, which was built after World War I, from Washington to Mt. Vernon; they also supported the establishment of a National University, but on this project nothing has been accomplished.

Another constructive move in the domestic field was the establishment of a Committee on Legislation pending in the United States Congress. This committee advised the organization to concentrate on a few pieces of legislation each year, to study these bills in local chapters and to use their influence with senators and congressmen by letter-writing and personal contact. In 1921 the Committee recommended support of a proposed U. S. Department of Education, and federal aid to the states for physical education, Americanization of immigrants and better teacher training. Even though this proposed federal aid was to be subject to supervision by state and local authorities, DAR endorsement of it is interesting in view of their more recent blanket opposition to any form of federal aid to education.

In 1922 the committee recommended support for four bills calling for a Federal Department of Education with cabinet status, the purchase of Yorktown battleground as a national military park and the erection of a National Archives Building. The fourth item was a piece of legislation under which the states and Federal Government cooperated in reducing the mortality of mothers and babies, which had been appallingly high. This was the Sheppard-Towner Act, which provided for Federal aid to states in setting up clinics for mothers and infants, the enactment of which was one of the great steps forward in the development of a national social consciousness. Responsibility for distribution of funds and the supervision of these clinics was in the Children's Bureau. Sadly enough, however, when the Act expired in 1927, despite continued support by other women's organizations, the DAR withdrew its early and significant support and opposed its existence—because according to the *Christian Century* of September 11, 1929, Mrs. Brosseau, then President-General, suspected Julia Lathrop and Miss Lathrop's equally noted successor, Grace Abbott, of being allied with subversives.

The society also took positions on other issues of national importance not directly related to its own objectives. Frequently these positions were unusual or vacillating; sometimes they simply echoed the prevailing national attitude. In 1919 the DAR joined practically every other American women's organization in supporting President Woodrow Wilson's League of Nations, which the President hoped would bring permanent peace to the world.

Considerably before the ailing League had breathed its last with the rise of dictatorship in the 1930's, the Daughters had turned their faces from this great humanitarian venture. In 1929 the *New Republic* reported that the previous year the "responsible head" of the organization (Mrs. Brosseau was then President-General) had sent out to the membership over her own signature, a reprint from the *Pennsylvania Manufacturers' Journal* describing the League of Nations organization as the "bottomless pit of damnation."

During World War I the society supported a compulsory rather than a voluntary draft. After the war, it joined with other American Women's organizations in urging the Paris Peace Conference to rule that women in conquered areas who had been mistreated by conquering German troops should be ranked as war casualties. President Harding's 1921 disarmament conference was held in Memorial Continental Hall and again the Daughters were thrilled with a new idea of world cooperation; but their National Defense movement, beginning in 1926, led them far from this goal and made them suspicious of advocates of international peace. In 1930 President Herbert Hoover made a major speech at the DAR Congress, in favor of the World Court—which the members didn't like. President Hoover's sister-in-law, Mrs. Theodore Jesse Hoover of California, was defeated as candidate for Vice President-General at that 1930 Congress, and there were rumors that this was a slap at the President on account of his World Court address. "Too silly for words," Mrs. Lowell Fletcher Hobart, President-General, said of this rumor. "Absurd," Mrs. Brosseau added.

Depression set its mark on the organization but the great new national policies of President Franklin D. Roosevelt followed one another with such rapidity that the DAR was officially speechless. In the depression years annual meetings followed the established pattern—elections, reports, processionals and all the rest—but not without some reference to the hard facts of financial disaster then overwhelming the country. In 1931 Mrs. Brosseau called upon women to "preserve the national serenity, so badly shaken by the late unfortunate business depression." A typical comment from the National Defense Committee was added by its chairman, Mrs. William Sherman Walker, who said that women were rallying in large numbers that year to solve such problems as how to stop runs on banks. She charged that "Communists have been detected starting runs by whispering campaigns, thus breaking down the confidence of the people."

In 1932, two presidents were elected: Franklin D. Roosevelt and Mrs. Russell William Magna, President-General of the DAR. A tiny woman with reddish blond hair, Mrs. Magna was one of the organization's most popular members; she was elected in spite of reports that she would lead the society into more moderate paths than it had followed when it supported a strong military expansion program and sponsored vigorous attacks on peace groups and liberals. Mrs. Magna's more liberal policies did not extend, with one exception, to New Deal measures. In September, 1933, she wrote an unprecedented letter to the forty-eight state regents and issued an equally unprecedented call to the organization's 160,000 members, urging the support of the President's National Industrial Recovery Act. "Partisanship must be forgotten," Mrs. Magna declared. "We must accept this patriotic challenge, for the NIRA must not fail."

Later declared unconstitutional by the United States Supreme Court, the NIRA had primed the pump and given the needed push towards better times. Mrs. Magna's support of this key New Deal measure was not followed by similar support of other Roosevelt policies—though none was openly opposed. With the financial crisis over and better times lifting the nation's spirits, the DAR went back to its own devices and its own peculiar interests.

During her three-year administration Mrs. Magna was frank about the depression's effect on the society; she admitted it had posed many problems, not the least of which was the difficulty of maintaining membership during that tragic period. Under economic pressure members had resigned by the thousands.

Following World War II, the Daughters opposed much of President Truman's "Fair Deal". They were against federal aid to education and "socialized medicine"; they did not like reciprocal trade pacts, but they did like the Bricker amendment limiting Presidential powers in foreign affairs. Having heard that gold reserves were shrinking, they became suspicious about possible shortages in the gold at Fort Knox, Kentucky. This led to a suggestion that careful count be made of the stored gold bars. When apprised of the resolution, President Truman tartly commented: "Tell them to go out and count it themselves."

CHAPTER VIII

THE UNITED NATIONS

Increasingly since World War II the DAR has reaped public criticism for its attitude towards the United Nations. To some observers it has seemed the Daughters were on the brink of repudiating the international organization, as they repudiated the League of Nations in the late 1920's, under not entirely dissimilar circumstances. They first enthusiastically endorsed the League; then later, pursuing their own nationalist policies, they joined the ranks of its bitter opponents. But the League faced different hazards, chiefly because of the United States' refusal to become a party to the famous and vital Article 10. On the contrary, almost all Americans unite in supporting the United Nations, and in 1956 the Daughters indicated they had no intention of repudiating it. Actually, the DAR attitude towards the UN has been consistent with their nationalist policies, to which they have clung through the years.

Before the end of the war, the organization began talking of peace on its own terms—which meant peace with nationalism, peace with a strong preparedness, peace with assurance that there would be no tampering with the U. S. constitution or with U. S. independence of action. In 1944 Mrs. William H. Pouch, President-General, told the annual Congress that a Peace Planning Committee had kept "members of our organization fully informed about post-war problems. It has a program of study in regard to peace planning. . . . We are thinking of peace in terms of strength rather than in terms of disarmament. . . . However great the responsibility of this administration has been in the global war, the responsibility will be just as great in the plans for what we hope will be a global peace."

A year earlier Mrs. Pouch had said, "We must preserve our

independence of decision and above all we must avoid entangling alliances which might restrict our freedom of action in world events. We are fighting for the privilege of living our lives as we choose. We are fighting to keep inviolate the Constitution of the United States of America and the Bill of Rights, which give us privileges and opportunities for development such as no other nation possesses."

War in Europe ended in 1945, and in the same year representatives of 51 nations met in San Francisco, drew up and signed the Charter of the United Nations. Two DAR ladies were present among observers from 42 national U. S. organizations. Mrs. Julius Y. Talmadge, who had succeeded Mrs. Pouch as President General in 1944, attended the opening of the charter conference as an accredited observer, and then left to visit DAR organizations throughout the West. Mrs. William A. Becker of New Jersey, still as handsome as when she was elected President-General 10 years earlier, "observed" the entire three-month Charter drafting sessions, on invitation from the State Department, as chairman of the Daughters' National Defense Committee.

At the ensuing DAR Congress of 1946, both ladies spoke with enthusiasm about the San Francisco gathering. Mrs. Talmadge said it was one of her "satisfying experiences" of the previous year. . . "impressive and thrilling." Mrs. Becker added that she was "privileged" to be invited by the State Department. "This was a rare experience—one in a lifetime," she said. "Committee meetings were stimulative, for the discussion problems were thought provoking. Representatives of 51 nations met to work out, plan, and set up machinery for the maintenance of peace and the prevention of war. Our chapters have followed our suggestions in devoting study to the Charter meeting, the United Nations Charter itself, and the various international organizations which have been established."

This seemed an auspicious beginning for DAR support of the UN. But when the organization adopted its 1946 resolutions, they constituted a distinctly qualified approval—"recognizing the necessity for international machinery to make and keep the peace of the world through cooperation between national governments in a continuing Council of Nations" but "unalterably opposing any political union of the United States with other nations that would deprive this government of free and independent action." For some this seemed like double-talk.

Mrs. Becker had paved the way for this resolution with a National Defense Committee report which was prophetic of the subsequent attitude towards the UN. She made the first official DAR reference to a new world government movement then beginning to show strength among war-weary Americans seeking a formula for permanent peace.

Warning that many speakers "from the platform and over the radio" were advocating world government and many books and articles were stressing its importance for preservation of peace, Mrs. Becker said there was a distinction between the theories of world government and the purpose of the United Nations. "The DAR is opposed to any program of federal union and world government," she said. "The National Defense Committee chairman urges you not to join any such organization." The official DAR action echoed her words, declaring that the United Nations Charter "provided the first practical method of settling international disputes by means of investigation, arbitration, conciliation, judicial review, and as a last resort, application of enforcement rules." While the Daughters pledged cooperation and support for the UN program of justice and peace throughout the world, they placed themselves emphatically on record for more "affirmative education to prevent confusion of the United Nations plan for world responsibility with any plan for world government involving world citizenship, universal currency, free trade, and the dominance of the United States by any other nation."

This resolution is the keynote of the Daughters' policy on the UN. The policy began back in 1946 and continues to the present time. There has indeed been little or no deviation from the 1946 doctrine; on the contrary, it has been strengthened and broadened by determined and continuous opposition to certain UN affiliated agencies and conventions—chiefly UN's Educational, Scientific and Cultural Organization (UNESCO), the Genocide Treaty, the Status of Forces Treaty, and the Declaration of Human Rights.

The Daughters believe in the United Nations provided it does not lead us down the road of international friendship (read "entangling alliances"); they suspect that UNESCO wants to penetrate American public schools with a new doctrine of world citizenship as opposed to blind love of country and pride in national heroes; they fear the loss of rights guaranteed U. S. citizens through trial in foreign courts for offenses committed in foreign countries.

Post World War II interest in world government evidently was the source of DAR suspicions. There was talk of expanding the UN into world government; and UNESCO made some statements which its enemies seized upon as evidence that it aimed to indoctrinate school children of the United States with world citizenship ideas.

By the late 1940's the Daughters could hardly contain themselves when world federalist delegates from nineteen nations held an international conference at which they urged that the United Nations be transformed into a world federal government by increasing its authority and amending its charter. This sort of action triggered of all of the DAR's built-in nationalism and distrust of any extended internationalism.

The Daughters perceived the specter of world government looming over the U. S. They saw the imminent threat of world government when nothing could have been further from the minds of responsible U. S. and UN officials.

By 1949 the Daughters were almost hysterical. On August 8th of that year, Mrs. Roscoe C. O'Byrne, President-General, announced that Mrs. L. L. Bruington, executive secretary of the National Defense Comittee, would lead her own and other organizations opposing the world federalists and their plans. Mrs. O'Byrne did not name the "other organizations" nor make it clear by what right the Daughters had assumed this leadership. It soon became clear, however, they were acting pretty much on their own in this connection.

Mrs. Bruington was a magnetic, white-haired but youthful Florida real estate woman and an active DAR who had earned something of a reputation as a speaker. On a southern trip, Mrs. O'Byrne heard her speak and was so impressed that she gave Mrs. Bruington the Defense Committee assignment. Inexperienced on the national level, Mrs. Bruington sought advice on how she should put her anti-world government program before the public. She was advised to plunge in and work hard—and the war was on. The results were soon evident.

In view of the weakness of the world government movement it undoubtedly would have collapsed without what the DAR feels was its decisive opposition. In 1950 the White House came out unequivocally against any form of world government; the State Department asked a Senate Committee not to draft resolutions favoring it; and former secretary of State Cordell Hull was reported as among the opposition. At the same time, New York state legislative leaders reported the receipt of floods of letters and telegrams opposing a world government resolution then before the Albany legislature, and predicted that the resolution, which had been considered as having some chance of passing would be allowed to die in committee.

A year later the battle in the state legislatures was practically won. A 1951 DAR resolution commended the organization's "valiant work" in inducing legislatures in twenty-two states to turn the tide against world government insofar as the U. S. was concerned. Up to that time the Daughters were still on record in favor of the United Nations, but there were rumblings of discontent.

In 1948, they became distressed about attention being paid the United Nations flag. They passed a resolution proposing legislation that the American flag, of which the society considers itself chief custodian, continue to occupy the "place of honor"

within the jurisdiction of the United States and at no time yield
its position to the new United Nations flag.

Periodically through the years the organization has talked as
if it might withdraw its support of the United Nations, but it has
not done so.   Paradoxically, however, in 1948 the organization's
National Defense Committee went out of its way to praise the
United Nations. Beginning in 1945, the Committee's *National
Defense News* had printed for the information of members annual
resumes of United Nation's actions.   In the November-December,
1948, issue, the *News* included a laudatory quotation from Secretary of State George C. Marshall, who said that the UN was
the "symbol of the aspirations of mankind," and urged patience
while the international organization lived through its early years.
"All new efforts to attain order and organization in the affairs
of men require time to grow roots in the loyalties of men," he
pointed out. "Let us not, in our impatience and our fears, sacrifice
the hard-won gains we now possess in the UN."

To this Marshall statement, the DAR policy-making publication
added a report of "extensive interest in the progress and success
of the international body, as indicated by many requests from
DAR members for material to aid them in observing United
Nations Day," praised "advancement in the growth of the UN,"
reminded members that "more than six years had been spent in
tearing down world civilization in a manner unparalleled in
history," and asked, "How can this humpty-dumpty world be
put together again in the three years since V-J Day?"

Up to then, the Daughters had found no serious fault with the
United Nations except the unbased fear that it might lead to
world government.   By 1950, however, they began worrying about
possible changes in the UN charter, and wanted to safeguard a
section "which gave the United States as a sovereign nation, the
right of secession should a tragic breakdown in international
morality make such action on the part of the United States imperative for survival."   Use of the word "secession" sounded an omin-
ous note which a year later was echoed in five resolutions launch-

ing the society's anti-UN policies. These resolutions opposed the Genocide Treaty and the Universal Declaration of Human Rights. They warned of an "attempt to supplant the pledge of allegiance to the United States flag with a universal pledge of allegiance and the U.S. National Anthem with a UN anthem." The resolutions also repeated the 1950 attack on the UN flag and again urged legislation to protect the U. S. flag from encroachment. Still another resolution recommended further legislation to insure the supremacy of U.S. state and national laws over the treaties, global agreements or conventions made by the United Nations.

To the supporters of United Nations, the Genocide Treaty and the Universal Declaration of Human Rights rank high among the humanitarian proposals of the international organization. The Genocide Treaty was drafted and adopted in 1949 by the UN General Assembly in response to public horror over the kind of mass murder and persecutions committed by the Hitler regime in Germany. Making such actions against groups or individuals of a group, for the purpose of group destruction, a crime under international law, the Genocide Treaty was first proposed by UN delegations from Cuba, India, and Panama and has been gathering dust in Senate Foreign Affairs Committee files since 1949. The Universal Declaration of Human Rights adopted December 10, 1948, by the United Nations General Assembly, states that "no one shall be held in slavery or servitude or subject to torture or to cruel, inhuman or degrading treatment or punishment; all are equal before the law and are entitled without any discrimination to equal protection of the law; everyone has the right to own property alone as well as in association with others."

With regard to the Genocide Treaty, the organization expressed the fear that it would "endanger the rights of U.S. citizens" and added: "we have no laws that approve these inhumane principles and these actions are against the moral and civil laws in this country." Of the Declaration of Human Rights, a 1955 resolution said the "Declaration of Human Rights propaganda is used to confuse and conceal the true purpose of the Covenant of Human Rights—which would, if adopted, destroy free speech, free press, free religion and the right to own private property." Earlier in 1951 this Declaration was called an attempt by a "few to dictate one set of rights for all peoples of the world, regardless of background, traditions, achievements and beliefs."

At the time the organization passed its first resolutions opposing certain aspects of the United Nations, it had not turned its attention to UNESCO—that was soon to come.

Meanwhile, Mrs. James B. Patton, from Columbus, Ohio, widow of a lumber dealer, had succeeded Mrs. O'Byrne as President General in a surprise victory in the 1950 election, in which she defeated Mrs. Edwin Stanton Lammers, a Texas candidate whose election seemed assured.

It was in 1952, during Mrs. Patton's administration, that the organization passed such a rash of resolutions critical of the UN that Mrs. Franklin D. Roosevelt remarked that she "knew many fine people are members of the DAR, but I believe we are living in an era too dangerous for any group to pass resolutions without careful study."

Settling back into its entrenched nationalism only seven short years after the end of the war, the society demanded that the U. S. Congress keep tight purse strings on all special UN agencies; opposed an "international flag" at Atlantic Fleet headquarters; charged that the prerogatives of the U. S. were endangered by the "policy of appeasement by the UN in Korea;" denounced the use of UNESCO booklets in public schools; and criticised what it regarded as efforts to bring about partial world government through the UN.

In 1952 Congress delegates cheered to echo the attack on the UN by Senator William E. Jenner and Representative John T. Wood, to whom the UN Charter was a crime perpetrated against us by a coterie composed of out and out minions of Soviet Russia, pro-British Fabian socialists, Rhodes scholars and just plain traitors to America.

Congressman Wood and Senator Jenner were joined in the Anti-UN-free-for-all by Republican Senator Everett Dirksen of Illinois who told the delegates that Americans are free "except that under the United Nations they are committed directly or indirectly to the defense of 750,000,000 people throughout the world."

"This year's batch of DAR resolutions," *The Nation* observed editorially, "is alarming evidence of the growth of the campaign launched a year or so ago in the know-nothing press to 'get the U. S. out of the UN and the UN out of the U. S.' . . . A portion of its $20,000 appropriation to carry on a campaign against subversive activities might well be used by the DAR to find out who is subverting its own policies and by what means."

DAR apprehension concerning UNESCO seems to stem primarily from a fear that it is advocating in the nation's classrooms and elsewhere, a world viewpoint and a loyalty to an international organization which might take precedence over loyalty to the United States. And the organization has continued adamant no matter what proof or protestations to the contrary have been brought forward. Not even Soviet non-participation in UNESCO until 1954, and the withdrawal of three Soviet satellite nations from the agency in 1953 on the ground that it was serving "American war mongers" brought about a change of heart.

In the United States, sponsorship of UNESCO is vested in a U. S. Commission for UNESCO that includes representatives of sixty national organizations named by the State Department. Among these is the United States Chamber of Commerce, as well as the National Catholic Welfare Conference, the National Conference of Christians and Jews, and the American Federation of Labor-CIO. Chairman of the Commission at this writing is Dr. John R. Richards, Chancellor of Oregon's State Board of Higher Education.

An official statement of purpose issued by the State Department said UNESCO's sponsors hoped the organization would help restore the educational and cultural heritage of war-torn countries, repair whole generations of minds which had been warped with "frightening efficiency," and promote better international understanding. It was difficult to quarrel with those objectives or to criticize such UNESCO work as setting up more than 100 "fundamental education" projects in countries like India, the Philippines, Peru, and Nigeria, to teach the essentials of hygiene, nutrition and agriculture; helping forty nations build new school systems or reorganize outmoded ones; supporting thirty-one elementary schools for Arab refugee children from Palestine; and setting up a UNESCO coupon plan by which soft currency countries could purchase educational materials from others with hard currency, including the United States.

Despite its good works, however, UNESCO made a serious error from the DAR standpoint when it issued a series of pamphlets called "Toward World Understanding." Phrases like "world mindedness" and "citizenship in a world society" were seized upon as evidence that the agency aimed to abolish the teaching of loyalty and love of country to American children, and substitute indoctrination in an international society. Actually, the pamphlets were written as a result of UNESCO seminars by teachers from many member countries, including the U. S., and the controversial publications were the work of educators interested only in improving world understanding and international education.

At the time, Assistant Secretary of State Howland Sargent found it necessary to assure a Senate Appropriation subcommittee that this phraseology would be eliminated from further UNESCO publications and explained that it had been used in the British sense—the British conception of a "world citizen" being a citizen of any country who is willing to cooperate with other countries.

In October, 1951, further trouble over UNESCO resulted from the issuance of a newsletter, by the American Flag Committee of Philadelphia, attacking the UNESCO pamphlets. The original newsletter had a very small circulation, but Republican Representative John T. Wood of Idaho inserted the attack in the *Congressional Record* for October 18, 1951, and by the late Spring of

1952, more than half a million reprints of the item had been circulated.

Another member of Congress, Democratic Representative A. S. J. Carnahan of Missouri defended UNESCO and denied that, as charged by the Flag Committee, the offending pamphlet said the "teacher is to begin by eliminating any and all words, phrases, descriptions, pictures, images, or other classroom material or teaching methods of a sort to cause his pupils to feel or express a particular love for or loyalty to the United States of America". Congressman Carnahan continued: "This statement is a complete fabrication. Nothing of the kind can be found in any of the pamphlet series." The DAR remained unmoved.

In the months that followed UNESCO underwent a number of investigations—first by the Senate Appropriations Committee, then by the United States Chamber of Commerce; next by a special mission sent to Europe by the House Foreign Affairs Committee; and finally, by three distinguished Americans assigned by President Eisenhower to "explore" UNESCO.

None of these investigations produced evidence that the agency was trying to undermine love of country or loyalty among American children. President Eisenhower's representatives specifically reported that "UNESCO does not attempt, directly or indirectly, to undermine loyalties or to encourage the substitution of loyalty to and love for a super-national authority for loyalty to and love for one's own country, as has been alleged in some quarters . . . . UNESCO does not attempt to interfere in the American school system." The DAR turned a deaf ear to these reports and reiterated that its members were definitely against several "ramifications" of the UN which "today has a socialistic trend."

DAR emphasis on the preeminent display of the American flag entered the controversy over the UN when, in 1952, the Daughters took credit for a Defense Department ruling that the UN flag must not be displayed in this country except on special occasions or by authority of the President of the United States, and that on such occasions it must not be larger than the United States flag, and must not be flown at a greater altitude or placed in a position other than a subordinate one to Old Glory.

Another incident in which the DAR was successful concerned the opening of the naval headquarters of the North Atlantic Treaty Organization at Norfolk, Virginia where the NATO flag—described by Congressman Wood as "a strange and alien rag"—was displayed more prominently than the flag of the United States. President-General Patton began "voluminous correspondence and arguments" in regard to the Norfolk flag display. Admiral Lynde D. McCormick, naval headquarters NATO commander, stood out against the DAR assault and insisted that under his command the flag of the United States was properly honored at all times. A year later, however the Congress of the United States passed a resolution requiring that the American flag be given the top spot everywhere in this country except at UN headquarters in New York. Mrs. Patton and her successor as President-General, Miss Gertrude S. Carraway, made a special trip to Norfolk to see for themselves what action had been taken to conform to the terms of the new Act. They found the NATO flag had been moved from a semi-circle of flags of member nations, to the headquarters building. "And thus again a stand of the Daughters of the American Revolution in behalf of 'due glory for Old Glory' has been fully vindicated," Mrs. Patton concluded.

When the 1953 Continental Congress convened, there was no lessening of anti-UN resolutions. Looking toward the revision of the UN Charter which was expected by 1955, the Society reiterated its warning that advocates of world government were zealously working to convert the Charter into an instrument that would further their ends. The Congress pledged DAR support for the UN again only as a "deliberative body of sovereign nations working together for peace." It demanded an investigation and a report showing to what extent command over American armed forces had been limited, divided or shared with UN or any other international agency; and then told the U. S. Congress it should review all programs of the UN and affiliated agencies, instead of giving the State Department authority for program approval.

These resolutions brought the first dramatic debate at an annual DAR meeting on policies involving the UN. In the pro-UN corner was a lady from Illinois, Mrs. Emma Waring Walbridge, who said she believed in the United Nations and felt, like many other members that it is "the world's best hope for peace." Relating some of the achievements of the UN since its founding in 1945, Mrs. Walbridge emphasized that through work of the specialized agencies "whole peoples have learned to read and write; millions of hungry children have been clothed and fed; and the most widespread health program ever undertaken in the history of mankind has reduced disease in some areas by 75 to 85 per cent."

President-General Mrs. Patton interrupted: "I am sorry; the three minutes are up."

Mrs. Walbridge wasn't quite ready to quit. "May I just say that this all cost you, each individual, 62 cents in 1952. Is it not worth a try?" she concluded.

Mrs. Patton inquired if there were further remarks and Mrs. Arthur E. Thevenet of New Jersey rose to challenge the resolution's charge that the UN might supersede the American Constitution.

Mrs. Philip R. Peck of Glens Falls, New York urged the Daughters to "turn the strength massed within this great, influential and highly esteemed organization to a constructive force for the UN. . . . The National Society . . . professes to support the UN", Mrs. Peck went on, "but none of the resolutions submitted to the DAR Congress, to my knowledge, has ever commended any action of the UN—on the contrary, they have always been critical or lukewarm in praise or support."

Continuing unusually open debate on both sides of the question, Mrs. Frank Leetch of Washington, D. C. said tartly that if the United States withdrew its financial support from UN, the international organization would "fall on its face." Mrs. Ernest W. Howard, also of Washington, added that the United States does not have to care whether foreign countries like it or not. "As long as we hold the purse strings they'll love us to death."

Further discussion was cut short when the Congress was told that a recital of UN accomplishments was not germane to the resolution supporting the UN as a "deliberative body of sovereign nations working together for peace." The disputed resolution was passed over six Nays, and the other anti-UN resolutions were approved quickly. One opposed the Human Rights Covenant: another attacked the bogey of world government; and a third opposed any re-drafting of the UN Charter which might interfere with United States sovereignty over its own affairs.

By 1954 there were straws in the wind indicating a considerable cooling of the White House attitude toward the Society and its activities. Following half a dozen conflicting bulletins from President-General Carraway concerning President Eisenhower's scheduled appearance at the 1954 Congress, the President appeared belatedly to give the briefest talk any chief executive had ever given to the Society.

A year later, President Eisenhower broke a date for a reappearance with Mrs. Eisenhower at the 1955 Congress. The President was at the White House, barely two blocks from Constitution Hall; Mrs. Eisenhower, who had become a member since her husband had been elected President, was at the family farm in Gettysburg, Pennsylvania. Up to 1957 Mrs. Eisenhower had not made a personal appearance at the organization's meetings and had personally received delegates at the White House only once. Tours of the White House after regular public visiting hours were substituted for afternoon receptions. These receptions with music by the Marine Band and White House aides presenting DAR officials and delegates to the current First Lady and to wives of Cabinet members had been a high point of the DAR program in 1952 and many preceding years.

Possibly President Eisenhower had been annoyed with the 1955 resolutions opposing some of his special projects, chief among these being his dramatic "atoms for peace" plan, which he personally had presented to the United Nations in a speech that made world headlines.

The DAR position was that the proposed atom plan "would result in the accumulation of unlimited physical energy by an international oligarchy which through its monopoly, would be enabled to hold all nations of the world in terror and achieve such a tyranny as never before has been witnessed in human history" and in consequence it would create "immeasurable potentials for the destruction of the United States by its openly avowed enemies."

A resolution embodying these views was adopted almost without discussion. But when the delegates were about to urge that the U.S. Congress "declare the sovereignty of the United States" and demand that the United Nations " cease all interference in domestic affairs of the United States," one lone voice rose in dissent. There followed a brief debate which inspired the *New York Times* to write an editorial criticizing the society for acting on the basis of "antediluvian prejudices."

Mrs. Roswell Tripp of Washington, Connecticut offered a brief but effective defense of the UN. She compared the international organization with the U.S. Congress, "which is able to thresh out all problems of the forty-eight states," and continued, "many of us loyal DARs—and, I may say, our President of the United States—feel that the UN is needed for this same purpose."

"Let us observe before we condemn," Mrs. Tripp concluded soberly. "Let us send accredited observers to prove or disprove rumors about UN activities." To this suggestion, however, Mrs. Ernest W. Howard of Washington, D.C. attending as a delegate of a Clarence, Missouri, Chapter, sprang from a front row seat to reply heatedly that the delegates should not "undignify this great organization" by sending observers to the UN. "Let us do our own personal observing and do as our forefathers did when they went out with their clubs or what have you."

After the resolution warning the UN not to interfere in U. S. affairs was adopted, President-General Carraway scolded the editor of the *New York Times* for use of the phrase "antediluvian prejudices," reminding him that "in almost every case our stands for our Republic have been fully vindicated by time."

In 1956 the UNESCO issue again came before the DAR.

An American Legion committee headed by a former commander of the Legion, Ray Murphy, had made an investigation of
UNESCO and released a report that in general had cleared this
UN affiliate of the charges against it. Declaring the source of the
principal charges against UNESCO was the Philadelphia Flag
Committee whose news letter of 1951 had been inserted in the
Congressional Record by Representative John T. Wood, Mr. Murphy called the Flag Committee "a one-man organization, virtual
successor to the Nationalist Action League which was designated
by the president of the United States as 'fascist'." But the former
Legion commander's defense came too late. After a stormy
session, the 1955 Legion convention had refused to accept the
report of his committee, and had voted a demand for the elimina-
tion of all UNESCO material from American public schools.

The 1956 DAR Congress commended the Legion for its stand
and echoed the demand for the removal of UNESCO material
from American public schools.

Meanwhile, Mrs. T. B. Throckmorton of Des Moines, Iowa, who
had been Resolutions Committee Chairman for six years, held
a press conference. Reporters accepted with alacrity as well as
surprise, and met Mrs. Throckmorton in a second-floor office of
the Society's administration building. The grey-haired, well-
dressed lady from Iowa had never talked to the press about the
dozens of controversial resolutions which had come to her commit-
tee· in six years. She admitted that before taking the unusual step
of calling a press conference, she had consulted a prominent Des
Moines, Iowa newspaper man, Pulitzer Prize winner Lawrence
Toth.

Still flustered, the Resolutions chairman confided that she had
been a "little unhappy" because "some of our own membership
and church women" disapproved of the United Nations resolution
passed in 1955. "They thought we were against the United
Nations," she said. "We have always been for the United
Nations as a parliament working for peace. We have decided

we will have a clarifying resolution, to make our position clear."
Explaining further, she reminded the reporters that 1955 was
the year in which the UN Charter was to come up for possible review and revision and admitted naively: "So the internationalists
of the country were pretty much out to disagree with the DAR on
their nationalistic thinking. It was the wrong year to get a good
press on our action."

Mrs. Throckmorton confided further that the Society had been
misunderstood on its 1955 "atoms for peace" resolution. "We
aren't against pooling our atomic know-how with other nations, if
other nations would do likewise," she said. But she indicated
there would be no clarifying resolutions on atoms for peace, and
in fact there were not.

As good as her word, however, Mrs. Throckmorton brought
in separate UN resolutions which summarized the time-worn position without introducing any new elements. In one the organization
pledged itself to continue support of the UN "in its original
purpose" as a group of sovereign nations working together for
world peace and understanding. The resolution also pledged
continued opposition to UN's threatened conversion into a world
government.

In another resolution the Society repeated its opposition to
the "many agencies which purport to be a part of the UN, formu-
lating policies such as the Genocide Convention and the Covenant
of Human Rights which would deprive us of the individual
liberties and free enterprise on which our nation was founded . . .
and which have made it so strong and so great." A third repeated
strenuous objection to "propaganda disseminated by UNESCO,
which tends to indoctrinate and train for world citizenship" and
highly commended the American Legion for its critical appraisal
of UNESCO.

So the DAR yielded a little, but did not surrender. The ground
yielded in 1956 was recaptured the following year. In January,
1957, the DAR magazine printed an editorial-type article headed
"Shall We Withdraw?" This article was reproduced for distri-

bution by the National Defense Committee with other literature at the 1957 Congress. It outlined what "would happen to our future as a free people if we remain in the UN, and what would be the results if we should withdraw."

The article charged that Stalin himself originated the idea for such a post-World War II organization within three weeks after Hitler's surprise attack on Russia, and that Stalin made "formation of a world organization" one of his requirements for agreeing to an Anglo-Russian Mutual Assistance Pact signed by Eden and Molotov in 1941.

"In view of the United Nations record," the article continued, "let us ask ourselves what might be the result of our leaving the United Nations. The only casualty would be the death of a few naive and unrealistic ideals held by starry-eyed people in the face of unassailable facts. . . . The first benefit would be the saving of our self respect, our prestige as a world power and enormous sums of money. . . . The property and buildings of the United Nations in New York should be returned to the donors if we left the organization. The United Nations could meet in Paris or it could use the League of Nations buildings in Geneva. . . The United Nations could still function without us as it does now. . . .

"In time we should be able to establish a framework for economical and political collaboration between free peoples, in which each nation could better its own position by its own efforts, rather than submit to the domination of one of the great powers. Leadership of free peoples is our logical role, rather than our present appeasement and open collaboration with Russia, her satellites and the rising group of neutrals. So long as we are a member of the United Nations. we will of necessity assist Russia to her expansion of power. The first step towards resisting her expansion and helping others to save themselves, is to leave the United Nations to Russia, who conceived and created it for her own evil purposes."

Another anti-United Nations leaflet sold at the 1957 Congress harked back to the Daughters' long-established fear of world government as a by-product of UN. It quoted Clarke M. Eichelberger, Director of the American Association for the United Nations, as declaring that "world government has evolved and will evolve thru the United Nations, as the people are willing to evolve. The process has already begun. . . . "

Still another leaflet renewed the Daughters' long standing charge against UNESCO—i.e., that its primary objective in the field of education is to make "every person international minded, in order to destroy any particular national loyalty"; that UNESCO urges American teachers to dwell particularly on attractive aspects of foreign cultures and less on American traditions and culture, to suppress American history and American geography; and to give less emphasis than has been the custom in this country to "things American."

On this groundwork, the Daughters built a resolution demanding U.S. withdrawal from the United Nations, if it admits Red China; and another calling for a Congressional investigation of UNESCO and demanding that no more U.S. money go to UNESCO. Also for the first time since the United Nations was established in 1945, the Daughters omitted a resolution supporting UN as an organization of sovereign nations to preserve peace on earth. Asked the reason for this omission, Mrs. Throckmorten replied that "nobody had submitted a UN resolution" to the committee and that past resolutions remained in force unless repealed. But her statement about continuing validity of past resolutions conflicted with another action by the Committee. It presented a blanket resolution reaffirming previous DAR support of Congressional committees investigating matters pertaining to internal security; endorsing the principles of a Bricker-type ammendment to the Constitution; and opposing "socialized medicine"; the United Nations' Genocide Convention; and the Human Rights Covenant.

Twenty brave souls rose to oppose withdrawal from UN if Red China is admitted to membership. One said, "That is going too far." But there were no friends of UNESCO in the DAR auditorium. The anti-UNESCO resolution—sharper than any previously adopted by the Daughters— was passed unanimously and with considerable applause.

If there is considerable support for the UN and its specialized agencies among the rank and file members of the DAR, as some observers believe, that support has certainly been effectively buried under the avalanche of hostile resolutions and other actions which have come out of the Society's headquarters in recent years.

CHAPTER IX

NATIONAL DEFENSE

To understand the DAR's national defense crusade of the late 1920's, it is necessary to recall the atmosphere in our country during that period. After World War I came a great upsurge of feeling that there must be no more war, that the world would not survive another such conflict; and there was honest disagreement as to how best to achieve that objective and to safeguard the United States. Although a "little group of willful men" had prevented the United States from going whole-heartedly into the League of Nations, we were parties to the 1921-1922 conference designed to stop the naval race and to the Kellogg-Briand Pact of 1928, outlawing war as an instrument of national policy. Pacifism became almost a religion and peace groups sprang up on all sides. But as at the present time, other conscientious American citizens did not believe that peace could be achieved by education and by creating a peace psychology; they pinned their hopes on a strong national defense. Unfortunately, this disagreement set one group against another and created suspicion and misunderstandings.

Perhaps chief among the leaders of peace groups was Frederick J. Libby of Washington, D. C., executive director of the National Council for the Prevention of War, and as such a target of the DAR. A mellow 83 in 1957, Mr. Libby insisted that he has "never had any hard feelings against the Daughters. They're just like the rest of us. They allowed themselves to be used."

If Mr. Libby had gone further and identified individuals who "used" the DAR in the name of national defense, he might have given prominent mention to one William B. Shearer, who was investigated by a Senate committee in 1929. As far as the record shows, the DAR has never mentioned Mr. Shearer's name or admitted that it had any connection with him. Nevertheless, testimony given the Senate committee shows that he was equipped with letters of endorsement from the society and other patriotic groups when he went to a naval disarmament conference in Geneva, Switzerland, in 1927, as a paid representative of shipbuilding interests. In the society's long and varied history, this association with shipbuilders' agent Shearer is one of the less happy events.

William B. Shearer was a handsome, mustached gentleman whose connection with the shipbuilders became embarrassingly clear in 1929, when he sued Bethlehem Shipbuilding Company, the New York Shipbuilding Company, and the Newport News Shipbuilding and Dry Dock Company for $257,000. He claimed that that amount was due him under a verbal agreement with the three corporations to pay him $25,000 a year for ten years, plus $7000 owing on the $58,885 he said he had spent as their agent. The shipbuilders employed him, he said, to represent them at the 1927 Geneva disarmament conference between the United States, Great Britain and Japan—a conference which collapsed when the three nations failed to agree on terms of navy cruiser limitation. Naturally, the shipbuilders and their agent were interested in ship construction as opposed to disarmament.

The Daughters became involved with Mr. Shearer as a result of the national defense crusade they launched in 1926. This crusade included support of a Big Navy. Thus they were plunged into the middle of the national controversy between militarists and pacifists. Ironically enough, Mr. Shearer traced his personal interest in this controversial subject to the Harding armament conference held in Memorial Continental Hall in 1922.

The Shearer testimony, which began on September 30, 1929, and which continued for many days, gave clear proof in his own words that he had hoodwinked the patriotic organizations whose endorsement he had secured. He insisted that these organizations "supported me, more or less, in my own ideals of what I was trying to do in bringing out the important points of National Defense." One of the committee members, Republican Samuel

M. Shortridge of California asked him a blunt question; hadn't he said "in so many words" while in Geneva as agent for the shipbuilders that he was there as the representative of certain patriotic societies in the United States?   Mr. Shearer hedged but had to admit it.   "I will not say 'representative.' I said 'endorsed.' If you wish to interpret that as representative I will acknowledge it," he replied.   Senator Shortbridge followed up; "Did you mention the DAR?" he asked.   "Yes sir," Mr. Shearer replied.

But if the DAR had been "used" by Mr. Shearer, so had many other people more experienced than the society's leaders of the 1920's.   There is no evidence whatever that the Daughters knew of his connection with the shipbuilders or were themselves other than completely sincere in their crusade for a bigger army and navy in the name of an "adequate national defense."

It is hardly likely that the earnest ladies, far from Geneva, knew what their "representative" was doing or how he was spending the shipbuilders' money.   The Big Navy agent, according to *New York Times* correspondent Wythe Williams, rented a sumptuous apartment in Geneva's most exclusive section, entertained lavishly, was acquainted with every member of each delegation to the conference, and was friendly with most Americans in official attendance.

Strangely enough, Mr. Williams reported, Mr. Shearer had been given a secret U.S. Navy Department report showing naval armaments of the three nations attending the conference, and was able to get out of closed sessions information not available to the correspondents covering the conference.   Mr. Shearer himself issued to the press a daily "progress" analysis, which consistently contained correct data.   When the three nations failed to reach agreement and the negotiations collapsed, one of Geneva's leading newspapers printed a story about Mr. Shearer, calling him "The Man Who Wrecked the Conference."

The Sunday after Mr. Shearer had begun his spectacular testimony, the Reverend William L. Stedger of the Coply Methodist   Church, Boston, told his congregation the Senate should investigate the DAR and other organizations "which have allowed themselves to be made tools of the Big Navy agent." In blunt nonclerical language, Mr. Stidger called the Daughters a "lot of old ladies who sit at home basking in the unearned increment of dead ancestors, satisfying their feeling of self-importance by sending forth the stupid propaganda of war and allowing Mr. Shearer to use their organization as a cat's paw to rake his hot coals out of the fire. . . ." The Boston clergyman continued: "Mr. Shearer is the same man who used the DAR to flood the land with propaganda of enmity against President Hoover, with a statement branding the President's delay in building cruisers as unwarranted, unsafe and unconstitutional, and condemning any limitation of 10,000-ton cruisers."

The national magazine *World Tomorrow* followed Mr. Stidger's attack by reporting in a caustic editorial that the Society's attorney, H. Ralph Burton of Washington, had announced a forthcoming suit against the Boston clergyman "for critical remarks," and that other suits "allegedly" were to follow. "It is hinted darkly that all those who have given the DAR a bad name (except its own leaders) are either to be put into the stocks or driven into exile," the magazine chuckled. No suits actually materialized.

After Mr. Shearer's suit to recover fees was filed, Senator William E. Borah introduced a resolution demanding that the Senate Naval Affairs Committee or one of its subcommittees investigate Shearer's connection with the three companies. The expose which followed came about midway in the period of greatest Daughter activity for national defense, but it did not dampen their ardor. On the contrary, at the 1930 Congress— the first to be held after Mr. Shearer's sensational testimony— they passed so many resolutions on military subjects that a number of members resigned in protest.

The organization, though founded to glorify the heroes and heroines of the Revolution, was not always so militaristic. Following World War I it seemed to be groping towards an internationalism of the Wilsonian type; in 1918 the International Relations Committee urged every chapter in the country to conduct a systematic study of international problems such as the causes of war and the rights of small nations, with particular emphasis on the objectives for a peace settlement with Germany. The committee chairman of the forty states which had set up state committees on international relations had suggested that "if the United States is to help establish national policy at the end of the war, it is time the people of the United States were informing themselves as to what this policy might be and on what basis it might be obtained. . . community of purpose must be developed if we are to preserve and maintain America as a great democracy."

In 1919, when Woodrow Wilson was fighting for the League of nations and a just peace, Mrs. George Thatcher Guernsey, President-General, told the Continental Congress that America had entered a new world of democracy, had taken its place among world powers and had realized that no nation "liveth to itself, no man liveth to himself, and we, as Americans, must come to understand that in any righteous league that shall bind the nations together, we must give as well as take." Under Mrs. Guernsey's mid-west leadership the organization endorsed the League of Nations.

Succeeding Mrs. Guernsey as President-General was handsome, deep-voiced Mrs. George Maynard Minor of Connecticut, whose emphasis was spiritual. In 1921 she pointed to the "awful example of Germany, whose ambitions "have been materialistic, grasping for world dominion, without faith or honor or the light of spiritual things," and for whom, she said, there was no hope "so long as deceit, faithlessness to solemn promises and lack of spiritual vision are the characteristics of her people." In 1922 Mrs. Minor triumphantly quoted Lord Balfour, British Prime Minister, as saying that as the result of the arms limitation conference "mutual fear has given way to a spirit of a very different character, confidence has taken the place of mistrust."

In 1923 the organization deviated slightly from its international position when it endorsed the plan for military preparedness proposed by Secretary of War John W. Weeks. The next year, however, it turned international again, and supported President Calvin Coolidge's movement for America's entry into the Permanent Court of International Justice under the League of Nations.

Between 1924 and 1926, the transformation from the society's easy-going past to its future of nationalism and militancy took place. The primary causes appeared to be the growing strength of the pacifist movement and the rise of the Communist menace.

In 1924 *Reds in America*, by R. M. Whitney appeared—first of a flood of volumes on the threat of Communism within the United States. Mrs. Anthony Wayne Cook, who was elected President General in 1923, was so impressed by *Reds in America* that she distributed a copy to every state regent and national officer—nearly 100 ladies.

The theme of the Whitney book was the menace of an underground movement in the United States, the "Real Communist Party," which was charged with plotting to overthrow the United States Government. This accusation was to be echoed in many of the Daughter's later suspicions about "subversive plotting to overthrow our government." Mr. Whitney's book served to inaugurate the fight against the Communist menace which was to continue for some years under the direction of the National Defense Committee.

In describing in detail the secrecy and the elaborate precautions of the Communist Party to avoid detection,Mr. Whitney devoted hundreds of pages to various angles of the "real" Communist menace, with one chapter on women's clubs. The DAR was soon to suspect that other women's groups like the Women's International League for Peace and Freedom, headed by famed social worker Jane Addams of Chicago, and the National Conference on the Cause and Cure for War, whose president was equally famed suffragist Mrs. Carrie Chapman Catt, were tinged with Communism. Carefully refraining from specific charges, Mr. Whitney quoted a magazine, *Woman Patriot* of May 1, 1922, as saying a 1922 Pan-American Conference of Women at Baltimore, called by

Mrs. Catt, was in reality the Women's Third International; and that in 1919 and 1921 "Women's Internationals" were held in Europe under the name "Women's International League for Peace and Freedom." The author declared, "It behooves all loyal American women and men as well to watch their step in these times surcharged with danger."

But post World War I pacifism, with its emphasis on education for peace, also played its part in driving the DAR to support the militarist extreme. Chief among the peace groups were the Women's International League for Peace and Freedom and the National Council for the Prevention of War. The WIL was organized in 1915 at the Hague, Holland, with the avowed purpose of bringing home to world consciousness "the stupidity, brutality and horror of bloodshed." The National Council for the Prevention of War, founded in 1921, was a clearing house of organizations in the United States which believed in "the substitution of law for war as a method of settling international differences."

Also prominent was the Women's Peace Society, whose president was 80-year-old Mrs. Henry Villard, daughter of Civil War abolitionist William Lloyd Garrison, This Society staged a "No More War Day" on July 26, 1924, and almost simultaneously, the National Council for the Prevention of War announced that ministers all over the country would preach about world cooperation on July 27, 1924. In 1925 the Women's Peace Society urged a constitutional amendment forbidding war. At its 1925 meeting the National Conference on the Cause and Cure for War, featured a speech by a young New York attorney who was destined to become a world figure, John Foster Dulles, who declared unequivocally: "Economic conditions, the desire to retain established wealth and the fear that other powers may extend political control over treasured natural resources, are the most fruitful causes of war." Hardly had his words died away when a gathering of patriotic society representatives charged that the Cause and Cure for War program at which the future Secretary of State had spoken, was "blatant propaganda for the League of Nations."

Nobel Prize winner Jane Addams stated that the membership of her organization was composed of persons who believed they were "not obliged to choose between violence and passive resistance or unjust conditions for ourselves or others. We believe that courage, determination and moral power can achieve these ends without violence. We believe that experience condemns force as a self-defeating weapon." These words made the Daughters see Red.

Unique among organizations of its kind because it originated while World War I was still being fought, the Women's International League for Peace and Freedom held its first meeting in this country, in May, 1924, when fifty delegates from twenty-one countries, speaking fifteen languages, arrived in New York City on their way to Washington. Even before the WIL conference, there was a melee at another women's meeting in Washington hotel, when defenders of the international group were hissed by women who demanded a Congressional investigation of WIL and protested its Washington meeting. Republican Congressman Clarence McLeod of Michigan urged the Justice Department to look into allegations that the peace group was allied with Soviet Russia or partly maintained by funds from Russia.

No investigations were made, but following the 1924 WIL meeting, women's patriotic societies not as yet including official DAR representation called a conference whose purpose was to counteract the so-called "peace propaganda." Mrs. Helen Tufts Bailie, protesting in behalf of the DAR, charged that the WIL was viewed with suspicion by persons on the lookout for anti-American propaganda, largely because the organization was international. She said Army men in mufti were at the 1924 meeting as observers, and "realizing the great and growing influence of the peace organizations, prominent among which was the WIL," enlisted women's patriotic societies in opposition because they did not want to do this job themselves.

The chairman of the women's patriotic conference was a lady destined for long association with the militant patriotic movement—Mrs. Noble Newbold Potts, president of the Washington branch of the Daughters of the War of 1812. The program of the meeting, reported Mrs. Bailie, featured speeches praising military training, ridiculing the idea of a warless world, denouncing international cooperation and scoffing at activities of peace organizations.

Almost immediately after the WIL Washington conference the DAR Executive Committee (made up of the President-General and elected national DAR officers), voted unanimously that "our society would not be true to its lofty ideals of patriotic service if it did not take more active measures than it has yet taken in opposing the disloyal individuals and organizations that are striving to pervert our national ideals." A year later, in 1925, Mrs. Anthony Wayne Cook, President-General, insisted that "nothing could be farther from the aims of our society than a militaristic program," but she urged, " it is the duty of every citizen to safeguard the United States against aggression and to support and maintain land, sea, and air forces for our reasonable protection. To this policy the DAR is solemnly committed." Mrs. Cook deplored the "spirit of pacifism and the undermining of our ideals of national service by foreign agencies and by our native born, emotional theorists, who have been swept from stable moorings by skillful propaganda."

Thus by the time when Mrs. Alfred J. Brosseau was elected President-General in 1926, succeeding Mrs. Cook, the way had been thoroughly paved for the organization to launch its National Defense Crusade. A woman of direct action, Mrs. Brosseau lost no time in acting upon a resolution passed by the Congress that elected her, authorizing a National Defense Committee. Within the same year she led the society into the Women's Patriotic Conference on National Defense, an outgrowth of the 1924 meeting of women's patriotic societies. For the half dozen years to come, the Patriotic Conference was to be the spearhead of super defense activities and the DAR was to be one of its most important member organizations. In 1927 President-General Brosseau told

the DAR Congress that the conference call had been issued jointly
by the American Legion Auxiliary and the DAR, that the response
of "other societies was enthusiastic," and that the DAR contributed
the "gratuitous use of Memorial Continental Hall" as its share
of the conference expense, while other heavy incidental expenses
had been borne by the American Legion Auxiliary.

At this 1927 Congress, Mrs. William Sherman Walker made
her first report as National Defense Committee chairman. She
was warmly praised by Mrs. Brosseau for having made a significant contribution during her first year in that post. Mrs. Walker
stated her committee's two objectives—to support adequate national
defense and oppose subversive influences. She said the committee was cooperating with all other agencies which supported
principles of adequate national defense, was collecting information
about subversive forces in the United States and was planning to
display and disseminate this information. "Cooperate. Collect.
Evaluate. Disseminate. That is our task," the Defense Chairman
concluded.

A year later Mrs. Walker's success in collecting "subversive"
material was attested by the *Boston Herald,* which reported that she
had gathered together the country's outstanding display of such
material.

Flushed with the excitement of this new project, Mrs. Brosseau
warned the 1927 Congress that already their organization was
being called "militaristic" in some quarters. Denying the charge
without identifying its source, Mrs. Brosseau added a statement
that could have been echoed by any peace-loving DAR opponent.
She said her complete ignorance of a militaristic "state of mind"
made the task of refuting the allegation exceedingly difficult.
"Being an American," she continued, "I have never gone abroad
for the express purpose of making a study of the military tactics
of aggressive warring nations. But from my knowledge of history
and my personal experience with two wars, I know my country
has never been prepared for wars into which it has reluctantly been

forced. Our Society believes in national defense—the kind that defends only and does not propose war, indulge in imperialism or impose its will upon others."

If the opposing post-World War I philosophies could have been supported without creating suspicions and animosities, without setting one group against another, the country would have been saved an unpleasant interlude and the Daughters could have gone their way in support of national defense without reaping a bitter harvest of adverse criticism. In the late 1920's, however, crusading groups fought bitterly and gave no quarter; suspicions and animosities set sincere and earnest men and women against each other.

An outstanding example of this struggle is the history of the National Council for the Prevention of War, the most active and influential of the peace groups, which in two years after its founding in 1921 had grown to include thirty-five national organizations, with a combined membership of approximately 10,000,000 persons.

In 1921-1922 its budget was $40,000, and in 1922-23, $73,150. Its objectives were progressive world organization, reduction of armaments by international agreement, and worldwide education for peace.

Originator Frederick J. Libby, who was executive secretary of the Council from 1921 until his retirement in 1954, was a New England Congregational minister and instructor at Phillips Exeter Academy, before World War I. On leave of absence from the Academy, he worked with World War 1 Quaker relief in Europe and later joined the Society of Friends.

To date DAR fire has not withered the Women's International League for Peace and Freedom. In 1958 it still survived with a U. S. branch maintaining offices in Philadelphia. In a 1954-55 leaflet, the League reported that three of its founders' 1915 proposals—the abolition of secret treaties, the right of a population to determine its own government, and a permanent court of justice—

reappeared in President Woodrow Wilson's famous fourteen point program for lasting peace.

In its most active and influential years, the National Council for the Prevention of War included in its membership organizations which should have set it above suspicion—among them, the American Association of University Women, American Farm Bureau Federation, the Foreign Policy Association, the National Board of the Y.W.C.A., the National Council of Jewish Women, the National Education Association, the National League of Women Voters, the Women's Trade Union League, the Peace Association of Friends in America, and the Women's Christian Temperance Union.

The Council spread its message throughout the country by means of literature and speakers, and it was one of the latter—Mrs. Lucia Ames Mead—on whom the DAR National Defense Committee trained its guns in 1926. The Committee sought to prevent Mrs. Mead from addressing the students of southern colleges largely on the ground that the Council was an "organization sympathizing with and promoting socialist and radical ideas."

In Mr. Libby's file are copies of letters written by Mrs. Julius Y. Talmadge, the prominent Georgia member, to the presidents of two Florida colleges at which Mrs. Mead was to speak. One letter, addressed to Dr. Hamilton Holt, president of Rollins College, Winter Park, Florida, on August 20, 1926, charged that a "serious menace is facing Florida, in that the National Council for the Prevention of War is sending Mrs. Lucia Ames Mead on an extended lecture tour through the southern states in November and December.

"Some authentic data as to who Mrs. Mead is has been gathered by the Daughters of the American Revolution through the assistance of the Military Order of the World War and other patriotic organizations who are helping to stem the tide of radicalism which threatens the best institutions of our country," Mrs. Talmadge continued. "Mrs. Mead is the wife of Dr. Edwin D. Mead of Boston, well known with his wife as a pacifist worker who is a vice chairman of the National Council for Prevention of War, an organization sympathizing with and promoting socialist and radical ideas. Mrs. Mead's long career as a leader in such un-American movements is evidence of what she stands for."

Dr. Holt of Rollins, a noted educator, replied with a forthright rejection of Mrs. Talmadge's plea to cancel Mrs. Mead's lecture. Dr. Holt stoutly defended Mrs. Mead, saying he had been her friend and in close touch with her for twenty years, "as a speaker from the same platform in conferences and conventions in behalf of the cause which is now to bring her to the South." He said he understood that both Mrs. Mead and the National Council for the Prevention of War advocated U.S. disarmament only as a joint project with other nations, and added: "Mrs. Mead is not a Communist, although you doubtless remember that the early Christians were. She does not approve the Soviet government in Russia, being a firm believer in the democratic and representative system. I think she does believe in the recognition of the existing Russian government as a temporary political necessity. . . . I am therefore in position to inform you, and it is a pleasant duty, that there is no woman on the American platform who is rendering abler, wiser or more devoted service for the great cause of peace and good will among men, which every patriotic man and woman ought to promote. This is peculiarly the duty of our 'Patriotic Societies,' especially the Sons and Daughters of the American Revolution, who surely can never forget that the great founders of the Republic were the preeminent peace statesmen of their time."

Although Dr. Holt thus refused to ban Mrs. Mead as a speaker, a similar letter from Mrs. Talmadge succeeded in intimidating a smaller college in Decatur, Georgia, which cancelled her address.

Mr. Libby himself spoke in at least 500 schools, on behalf of the objectives of the council—though not without difficulty and often fighting against the Communist label. He collected two filing cabinet drawers filled with clippings and other material about "efforts to keep me from speaking and attacks from other quarters." In Indianapolis, Indiana, the Mayor ordered Mr. Libby's

arrest as a Communist but cancelled the order on discovering that
150 local dignitaries were waiting to hear him speak.

In this period, the DAR was attacked on many sides by liberal
publications. An example of this adverse publicity may be found
in a 1929 issue of the *Christian Century,* which printed an article
giving its answer to the question, "Are DAR Women Exploited?"
The author of the article, Mrs. Elaine Eastman, was a member
of the DAR protest committee headed by Mrs. Helen Tufts Bailie.
Mrs. Eastman asked, "How can the average well meaning DAR
save herself from being exploited by socially ambitious leaders
who are themselves conceivably made use of by more powerful
personages for motives of their own?"

Mrs. Eastman described the activities in support of national
legislation of a combination of women's groups called the Women's
Joint Congressional Committee, from which she said, "women's
patriotic societies have stood grandly aloof, and united upon
occasion for aggressive action under the banner of the DAR."
Reporting that of 1000 DAR's living in ten cities and towns, in
five scattered states, 268 belonged to the General Federation of
Women's Clubs, 78 to the National League of Women Voters,
Parent-Teacher Association or American Association of University
Women, the critical Daughter charged that "individual DAR's
who are members of other women's organizations cancel themselves
out," because the DAR has been so manipulated by its national
officers as to "bitterly oppose almost every legislative item advocated by sister organizations." The society's labeling of some
of the sister groups as "communistic" or "interlocking" with
radical organizations had also embarrassed its relations with
those groups, Mrs. Eastman pointed out.

Further, while most other women's groups supported the child
labor amendment to the Constitution, according to Mrs. Eastman, the DAR, under Mrs. Brosseau's leadership, had lined up
with manufacturers' organizations and other interested groups
in opposition. She pointed out that the DAR was "conspicuous
by its absence "from a list of women's organizations supporting

a federal Department of Education with a Secretary of Cabinet status, charged that the organization "aggressively pushed" measures providing for increased armaments, "each and every project fathered by the professional warmakers," and that when an international agreement to refrain from the use of poison gas and bacteria in warfare was humanely urged, the "ever militant ladies warmly upheld" these barbaric weapons, "although they were not long since damned as a German atrocity."

Mrs. Eastman attributed part of the difficulty to the society's organizational framework, declaring that this makes the DAR "chapters creatures of the national society to which each member individually adheres," and "is contrary to the organizational plan of most other women's groups, in which local chapters or branches are independently organized under a state charter and can withdraw from the federation at will." For the individual member she urged "more personal initiative, more independent thinking, more serious study of the complicated issues of government," saying that while this would no doubt "lessen the artificial prestige of ambitious women at the top, it would greatly enhance the essential worth and influence of our regimented womanhood."

However, the organization's old guard was not without some defenders—among them a Washington magazine, the *National Republic,* whose editor, Walter S. Steele, was given an award of commendation at the 1956 Congress. As a result of the militant resolutions adopted in April, 1930—on the heels of which many membership resignations followed—the *National Republic* printed a lengthy laudatory article, including a defense of DAR policies. The magazine called it "significant that because this organization stands firmly against socialist internationalism and pacifism, it is the constant target of attack by individuals and organizations standing for the policy of rendering the nation helpless against invasion or insurrection, and which would subordinate American to European interests and make the security and prosperity of this country dependent upon the people of the rest of the world. . . . It is fortunate that America has this great national organization of patriotic women who have not yielded to the tremendous force of European propaganda which has misled so many American women to spurn nationalism in favor of internationalism."

Another supporting voice came from a gentleman in Chicago named N. E. Hewitt, who wrote an answering letter to the *Christian Century*, after it published Mrs. Eastman's article about the Daughters. Mr. Hewitt called Mrs. Eastman, who had resigned from the Society, a "frustrated rebel who is now an ex-member of the DAR," and added, "The old quotation, 'Hell hath no fury like a woman scorned,' is applicable to her. . . . . Mrs. Eastman is suffering from a serious case of sour grapes." He reminded readers that in "every great organization there are renegades who naturally oppose everything supported by the majority, irrespective of merit. These borers from within are generally the dupes and tools of minds far superior to their own, minds that are distorted and dedicated to a program of destruction. I feel quite sure that personally Mrs. Eastman is a lovely woman, but it is quite apparent that her mind has been perverted by those who have fruitlessly endeavored to disrupt the DAR . . . . Mrs. Eastman has condemned the DAR for its refusal to endorse any program of legislation calculated to socialize government by centralizing power. She has represented the many women's groups who are working tooth and nail for socialistic legislation. As the dupe and tool of the agencies sponsoring such legislation, of course, Mrs. Eastman could not agree with loyal Americans. I thank God that we have loyal, staunch American women in the United States, who have the courage to openly back their convictions and to unswervingly support the Constitution of the United States against the attacks made upon it."

Thus within three years after leaving their quiet patriotic paths, the DAR's new militancy had led them to suspicion, dissension, and strife.

CHAPTER X

THE COMMUNIST MENACE

The Daughters' battle for national defense has been inextricably tied in with their fight against the Communist threat. Both struggles are still looked upon with pride and approval by many members; others view them as nightmares which might have gone on indefinitely, had it not been for the Black List expose. Before this point was reached, the DAR had become thoroughly and, at least in some quarters, embarrassingly identified with irresponsible anti-radicalism.

Undoubtedly the organization believed, as did other Americans after World War I, that the war had made the world safe for democracy. In 1919, Mrs. George Thatcher Guernsey, President-General, told the Society in ringing phases: "Yesterday we said, 'Autocracy must die.' Today we say, 'Autocracy is dead'!" In 1921 her successor, Mrs. George Maynard Minor, declared that the organization would have nothing to do with either Hun or Bolshevik. The Germans, she said were a nation without hope, "so long as deceit, faithlessness to solemn promises and lack of spiritual vision are their characteristics." Russia, Mrs. Minor said, presented "the awful example of a nation too childlike and undeveloped to have much character at all, too simple minded to withstand the hideous lure of Communism. For Russia there is great hope when her soul awakens."

In 1924 the Daughters passed resolutions against Sovietism, Socialism, Communism and Bolshevism. They congratulated Secretary of State Charles Evans Hughes for his "splendid and courageous stand against these radical, subversive and destructive principles," and for opposition to any recognition of the Soviet regime. In 1925 they sounded their first alarm about the threat of a Red-inspired revolution in the United States. A year later, they established a National Defense Committee, but the operative resolution said more about Red internationalists and revolution than it did about national defense. The document declared that the "plan for destructive revolution in the United States by Red internationalism is not a myth but a proven fact; that its emissaries are working unceasingly to spread their propaganda by insidious, effective and well financed methods; that this plan to overthrow the government of the Republic and set up a Communist Soviet rule in its place is well organized and far-reaching, including the recognition of the USSR, peace propaganda, total disarmament, the destruction of courts, the organization of Communist units within our army and navy personnel, and the organization of workers' leagues to create and develop world consciousness and hatred." Therefore, the resolution called upon the state chapters to unite in a nation-wide campaign to strengthen the country against communism; and the faithful members lost no time in complying. Their President-General, the wealthy, experienced and eager Mrs. Alfred J. Brosseau, appointed a National Defense Committee, with Mrs. William Sherman Walker, former Washington state regent, its chairman.

With the full backing of her organization, Mrs. Brosseau made national defense and war against the Communist menace her administration's chief objectives. Mrs. Brosseau led the society into the Women's Patriotic Conference on National Defense, thus lending its prestige to the founding of this strange coalition of organizations. She also provided the Patriotic Conference with a free meeting place in Memorial Continental Hall. A charge by Mrs. Helen Tufts Bailie of Boston that Mrs. Brosseau proceeded without the society's consent or knowledge in helping to organize the Patriotic Conference has apparently never been refuted. That she did so seems substantiated by the fact that no authorization for such action had been given her by any resolution of the previous Congress. However, her efforts were never repudiated. In 1933 the Daughters voted themselves out of the Conference.

In the name of national defense, the DAR had joined with

other patriotic organizations in endorsing William B. Shearer and had distributed his intriguingly titled pamphlet, *The Cloak of Benedict Arnold.* For its crusade against Communism, it distributed another pamphlet, *The Common Enemy,* by Fred R. Marvin who also provided ammunition for the society's critics. This pamphlet lumped communism, bolshevism, socialism, liberalism and ultra-pacifism as "tending to the same end"—the abolition of government, patriotism, property rights, inheritance, religion and family relations—and charged that the "world revolutionary movement" was operating through Communist organizations as well as prominent liberal and pacifist organizations.

Although not as exciting an international operator as William B. Shearer, Mr. Marvin made a business of exposing the Communist menace. Beginning as a columnist for a small short-lived New York newspaper, he became a lecturer and pamphleteer. He wrote anti-Communist articles for business publications and compiled a so-called "Daily Data Sheet" which specialized in Communist news. Finally, he was to become involved in the controversy over the DAR's Black List.

In 1927 the Daughters, pushing with great vigor their two-fold battle against Communism and on behalf of national defense, became embroiled with Mrs. Carrie Chapman Catt, the famous woman suffrage leader, over the charge that Jane Addams was a Communist. Miss Addams, President of the Women's International League for Peace and Freedom, had become a target for patriotic groups obsessed with the belief that peace advocates were serving the cause of the Soviets, wittingly or unwittingly. Under Mrs. Brosseau, the Daughters became the most articulate of these groups.

In an open letter to the DAR in the National Woman Suffrage Association's magazine *Woman Citizen,* Mrs. Catt stated flatly, "Jane Addams is not a Communist." Mrs. Catt pointedly charged that the society had been "active distributors of literature that slanders other women as well educated, honest and loyally American as are you. . . . Literature subtly designed to throw suspicion upon and impair the reputations of other women's groups and organizations quite as high minded as your own." Warning that DAR leaders "were assisting in a campaign directed and financed by parties unknown, which professes to aim at the destruction of an alleged Bolshevik plot to overturn this government," the suffrage leader said these would be worthy purposes, provided the campaign had brought forward one single proof that such a plot actually existed. Continued Mrs. Catt, "it has not," unearthed a single Bolshevik nor discovered any evidence of a plot that the newspapers had not previously revealed to the public. Instead it has made slanderous, mendacious and brutal attacks upon thousands of Americans who never saw a Bolshevik in their lives. It has charged them with direct or indirect connection with Moscow, with plots and plans to overturn the government, until a veritable hysteria is sweeping the country."

Mrs. Catt's warnings and protests were not the only ones that failed to make any impression on the now adamant orgnization. Mrs. Bailie, who was to touch off the Black List controversy, also protested to Mrs. Brosseau against the policies of national and local officers, but to no avail. This protest was registered on February 2, 1928, nearly two months before the Black List expose, and was ignored by the DAR President-General, who at first paid no attention to Mrs. Bailie's letters; and who, when the protests were repeated, replied with aloof dignity and complete unresponsiveness. "The petition you addressed to me personally I shall take great pleasure in presenting to the National Board of Management, for I assure you that it does not share your point of view," the President-General bluntly stated.

Having disregarded these warnings, the organization found itself in 1928 battered by waves of persistently and increasingly unfavorable publicity. On April 1 the climax was reached, when Mrs. Bailie dropped a bombshell in what might otherwise have been an uneventful meeting of the Boston Ethical Society. Addressing the Society, she described a list of prominent people which had been sent out from DAR headquarters to state regents with a warning that these persons were "not acceptable" to the organization and should not be used as speakers at chapter meetings. The proscribed citizens were so prominent that the reported Black List instantly became a national sensation and Mrs. Bailie herself —hitherto a relatively unknown pacifist and inactive Boston member—a national figure. On the list were Methodist Episcopal Bishop William F. Anderson of Boston; Judge George W. Anderson of the U.S. Circuit Court of Appeals, Boston; Prof. Irving Fisher of Yale University, prominent economist and author of numerous books on finance; Dr. David Starr Jordan, president emeritus of Leland Stanford University; Rabbi Harry Levi of Temple Israel, Boston; Methodist Episcopal Bishop Francis J. McConnell, President of the Religious Education Association; President William A. Neilson of Smith College, Northampton, Mass.; Dean Roscoe Pound of the Harvard Law School; Professor Felix Frankfurter of the Harvard Law School, later named to the U.S. Supreme Court; Clarence Darrow, most famous criminal lawyer of his day; Editor William Allen White of Emporia, Kansas; and Republican Senator William E. Borah of Montana. There were, said Mrs. Bailie, a "host of others against whom the charge that they were unsafe to address a group of women like the DAR is preposterous."

The rebellious Mrs. Helen Tufts Bailie a descendant of Anne Tufts, decorated Revolutionary heroine who nursed wounded soldiers under fire at the Battle of Bunker Hill—organized a DAR Committee of Protest, which later in the same year issued a pamphlet telling how the list of banned speakers came to be known. The pamphlet reported that the discovery was almost accidental. A Massachusetts member, trying to obtain speakers for chapter meetings, could find none acceptable to the chapter regent. Learning that the matter must be referred to her state regent, she discovered that the society's officers had a list of blackballed speakers. Mrs. Bailie managed, with some difficulty, to get a copy of the list, and found on it the name of the husband of a fellow member—a highly respected clergyman of Greater Boston. When the bewil-

dered wife of the clergyman tried to find out why her husband
was on the list and where the list came from, she was denied information on both points. Later, according to the pamphlet, a
trivial reason was given for his inclusion, but the source of the
list was still not admitted.

From the beginning, the Black List blew up a storm of proportions such as the DAR have never experienced before or since.
Staunchly denying the existence of the Black List to the end, even
the skillful Mrs. Brosseau was unable to head off the storm, which
raged for years. Liberal magazines printed satirical articles about
the Black List and the Daughters. Probably the most effective
rebuttal came from editor William Allen White, reportedly included on the list, who wrote that the Daughters were all right but were
just victims of foolish leadership. He laid the blame at the
doors of "idle, apoplectic old gentlemen in red flannels, who
escape the boredom of their rich wives by sitting in Washington
club windows bemoaning the decadence of a changing world.
Retired army officers in Washington hypnotize the nice old girls
of the DAR." Mr. White quipped: "If the rebels of 1776 had
been the same kind of people as their timid daughters, the DAR
would be Daughters of the American Tories."

The Kansas editor who virtually laughed the Ku Klux Klan out
of his state, was well known for pouring scorn on anybody guilty
of trying to strangle ideas with any form of coercion—such as
what he considered to be the DAR fetish of patriotic orthodoxy
and ritual. "The DAR", wrote Mr. White, "has yanked the Klan
out of the cow pasture and set it down in the breakfast room of
respectability, removing its hood and putting on a transformation."

Mr. White's criticisms echoed and re-echoed in other journals.
The famous, now extinct, *Literary Digest* featured the list and
ran comments on it from all over the country. The *New York
Times* observed that it was fortunate for the organization that DAR
ancestors were made of sterner stuff. "Fancy Sam Adams of Boston
proscribed because his utterances might be radical," the *Times*

commented, reminding the Daughters that "Americans of that elder day were not afraid to have issues threshed out in public."

The St. Paul *Pioneer Press* thought the Society "might have displayed some sympathy for Russian revolutionists, since they came from revolutionary ancestry." Mercer G. Johnson, Director of Baltimore's Open Forum, was quoted as saying, "What the DAR needs is a good stiff drink of the simon pure brand of the spirit of '76." The *New York Graphic* wondered what George Washington would say if he knew the DAR had eliminated people of liberal tendencies from their speaker lists. The *Philadelphia Bulletin* considered the Black List much too ludicrous to deserve any serious attention.

Outlook Magazine expressed surprise and indignation that the DAR President-General had stood sponsor for an "amazing list of people and organizations to be barred from a hearing by chapters of the historic organization. . . . Many DAR's are wondering why it was compiled and why their President-General thinks they are not mature enough to judge for themselves the type of speakers they would like to hear." The *Outlook* article continued: "The President General appears to have fallen under the spell of the witch hunting gentry who were so alarmed lest America turn Communist after the World War. . . . . But apparently there still are some sections of the United States which cling to the old doctrines of free speech. For instance, when Senator James Wadsworth, a pronounced anti-suffragist, visited Honolulu last winter, he was cordially invited to address the strongly pro-suffragist League of Women Voters. By the same token, we think the DAR could at least afford to listen to that terrible radical, William Allen White, without loss to its essential Americanism."

A *New York Times* Boston correspondent reported that the Reverend E. Talmadge Root, executive secretary of the Massachussetts Federation of Churches, was given an ovation when he told Congregational ministers of Greater Boston about his experience as a black listed speaker. He said he had learned he was included in the notorious list because he was advisor for the Fellowship of Youth, a position he had accepted as an innocent and presumably useful service, though he had rendered assistance to the group only once in several years. "The ladies of the DAR do not realize the seriousness of the Black List they are abetting," Mr. Root told his colleagues. "A good name is rather to be chosen than great riches. It is the chief asset of a clergyman. Is a man who is unfit to address the DAR, fit to represent the churches? The unthinking may assume that a certain military coloring justifies and authorizes such black lists. To my mind the very connection constitutes a danger compared with which the danger from the 'Red Menace' is negligible. If once we admit that our army and navy and those formerly connected therewith are by that fact constituted censors of public opinion, their power will insensibly grow and the liberties of America will be lost."

Although Mrs. Brosseau staunchly denied any connection with the Black List, she could not ignore an incident which had created such a furor of adverse publicity, and circumstances were to provide her with a plausible explanation. The United States Congress then was considering a Big Navy bill, and Mrs. Walker testified on behalf of this legislation in February, 1928, as chairman of the organization's National Defense Committee. Mrs. Bailie and thirteen other Boston members protested Mrs. Walker's appearance as a witness and particularly her statement: "The Chairman of the National Defense Committee, National Society, Daughters of the American Revolution, desires to affirm personally and to record in behalf of her society that the women who claim descent from patriots lend their sanction to the pending naval program." Mrs. Brosseau rushed forward at this point with a denunciation of those responsible for revealing the Black List.

"They are the outcries of minor members of our order who are not entirely in sympathy with our stand on national defense," Mrs. Brosseau claimed. In another statement she said: A "few pacifists within our organization who oppose our support of the Navy bill" are responsible for the Black List publicity, and added that the dissidents "who have undertaken to villify this society are not even what we classify as active working members. One of them has never held an office in her chapter, while the other has not attended a chapter meeting in two years."

Mrs. Brosseau's recognition of the Black List controversy initially appeared to have some hopeful aspects. "The DAR stands for constitutional government and American Institutions," she said. "No man or woman who adheres to these principles need fear repudiation from us." But less than two months later the organization's top officials, headed by their President-General, repudiated Mrs. Helen Tufts Bailie by dropping her from the organization and meanwhile Mrs. Walker joined Mrs. Brosseau in denying existence of the Black List.

The National Defense Committee chairman announced she simply abhorred the term "Black List" in all its implications and insisted, in a masterpiece of understatement, that if the Massachusetts chapter had compiled any list of banned speakers, it must have been solely of an advisory nature and not intended for circulation or public reference. "We are nationalists and proud of it," Mrs. Walker explained confidentially. "We love our country and put our country first; not that we wish to deal unjustly with any other nation —ever— but we just choose to love our country best. How then could we have sympathy with those who would make of our country one grand international conglomeration?"

Ousted Helen Bailie organized her protest committee, distributing a pamphlet on her position to various chapters all over the country, and the storm of criticism continued. William H. P. Faunce, President of Brown University, whose name was on the Black List, said "public laughter would take care of it." The *Nation* gave a dinner for distinguished blacklisted men and women, and put on quite a show, with speeches and stunts by such public figures as Heywood Broun, Arthur Garfield Hays, Groucho Marx, Ruth Hale, James Weldon Johnson and Norman Thomas. Among the 250 people present were Mrs. Bailie and Mrs. Joseph

Whitney, a prominent New Haven member who had resigned from the organization in protest. A message of regret came from Clarence Darrow, who wrote that being a poor boy he never was able to get a college degree, so "this is the first degree I have ever had and I am proud of it." Senator Borah also wired that it was not his disposition to "rejoice over honors and exceptional distinctions" such as appearing on the Black List. William Allen White sent along his contribution: "Some people have all the luck and I am one of them." Members of the Lewis and Clark Chapter, Eugene, Oregon, who had protested the Black List, sent "greetings from all true daughters of Revolutionary ancestors." The Liberal Club of Harvard University was "delighted" to see its name on the DAR roll.

Writing more seriously in a dispatch to the *Baltimore Sun*, White declared he had positive proof that the Black List was a DAR product. He had a copy, he wrote, which had been mailed officially by the society to the regent of the chapter in his home town, Emporia, Kansas. He also named the well known and highly respected listed organizations including the Y.M.C.A. and Y.W.C.A., religious organizations of many denominations, the Foreign Policy Association, and the National Association for Child Development. "What have these societies to do with preparedness and national defense?" Mr. White asked.

On April 21, two months after the Black List expose, the society filed charges against Mrs. Bailie for "conducting herself in a way calculated to disturb the harmony and injure the good of the society."

The organization's Board of Management gave Mrs. Bailie a lengthy hearing (216 transcript pages with both parties represented by counsel) and then formally voted to expel her. The following November Mrs. Bailie appealed to the Continental Congress, the supreme governing body. The case came before the 1929 Congress with Mrs. Brosseau in the chair.

Helen Bailie's day of reckoning was at hand. She had committed the crime of divulging the Black List—she had washed the society's dirty linen in public and her sisters were not going to let her get away with it. Constitution Hall was nearly completed and was to be dedicated during Congress week, the society planning to move into it a year later. Still meeting in a nearby auditorium they had used for each Congress since 1925, the gathering made headlines by the Bailie expulsion. It was election year, with Mrs. Brosseau going out of office, but until Mrs. Bailie's fate was decided no one thought about electioneering. This happened earlier than anybody had expected.

Under parliamentary rules, Mrs. Bailie's case normally would have been brought up under new business at the very end of the week-long Congress; but that was not Mrs. Brosseau's strategy. Abruptly, in mid-morning on the second day of the Congress, with no advance notice to Mrs. Bailie, who was not present at the meeting, a delegation rose, no doubt by pre-arrangement, to move consideration of her appeal. The motion carried with Mrs. Brosseau's approval; she said it would not be fair to wait until the end of Congress, because by that time many of the delegates would have gone home—which probably was not true, so long as the Bailie case was still pending. She ordered the meeting into executive session, with reporters and guests excluded. Ever in command of the situation, the President-General explained: " I will have to ask you to leave for a moment—maybe for a few hours," and her audience laughed.

Some members of the press managed to eavesdrop, and the proceedings were fully reported in the newspapers. Mrs. Brosseau wasted no time; she told the delegates (which they must have known without being told) that nineteen members had filed charges against Mrs. Bailie, and that the National Board of Management had acted on the charges. Making it clear that the delegates must understand they were not trying Mrs. Bailie, she explained they were only to consider her appeal.

The proceedings got swiftly under way with a motion by an Iowa Daughter to sustain the expulsion, and this was promptly seconded. With only a brave few of the two-thirds vote necess-

ary to grant the request, Mrs. Bailie's attorney's plea to be heard
on the appeal was promptly denied. Mrs. Bailie's expulsion was
sustained by 1,000 shouted "Ayes" and only one "No". The
delegates had certainly not studied the 216-page transcript of
the hearing. They had heard no facts brought forward on the
appeal, but they thoroughly endorsed their President-General's
stand; their vote and their prolonged applause demonstrated that.

In a triumphant announcement to reporters, according to the
Washington Daily News, Mrs. Brosseau said, "The 38th Congress
has spoken. You can figure from this what the DAR thinks of
Mrs. Helen Tufts Bailie." Mrs. Bailie said she was "through",
and added: "I'm glad it's over. I had to keep on fighting—I
couldn't stop without an appeal. But I don't want to belong to
such an organization."

So the rebel descendant of Revolutionary heroine Anne Tufts
was no longer a Daughter of the American Revolution. The *New
York Times* reported that, although the delegates were strongly
in favor of Mrs. Bailie's expulsion, because she had caused the
society so much trouble, many felt it was unfair not to give her
attorney a hearing. The Continental Congress might have answered Mrs. Bailie, but the organization had not heard the last of
the Black List, which, said *The Nation*, "like Banquo's ghost, just
will not down." It lost some members, too, through protest
resignations, but there was no mass exodus. As a matter of fact,
there were more resignations in 1930, over the militaristic and
anti-disarmament policies of Mrs. Lowell Fletcher Hobart.

Of the reams of criticism written about the Black List and the
society's joint crusades, generally speaking, none were more dev-
astating than the appraisals contained in long, carefully written
articles published by two influential newspapers, the *Louisville
Courier-Journal* and the *Springfield* (Massachusetts) *Republican*,
and later printed in pamphlet form. The *Courier-Journal* accused
the DAR of attempting to "interfere with freedom of speech," not
only through the Black List but through incidents like Mrs. Julius
Y. Talmadge's partly successful effort to prevent Mrs. Luela Ames

Mead, National Council for the Prevention of War lecturer, from speaking in southern colleges. The paper cited Frederick J. Libby's experience in Indianapolis, when he was threatened with arrest as a Communist; this, it said, was a "sample of hundreds of similar instances" in which attempts had been made to interfere with freedom of speech. As an even more extreme instance of the organization's Communist fears, the *Courier-Journal* told of a speech made by Mrs. Walker at a Columbus, Ohio, conference on national defense, in which she "discovered possibilities of Communist boring from within" at clinics conducted under the U. S. Children's Bureau. Vividly picturing the plight of the defenseless American woman, Mrs. Walker was quoted as having asked: "Can you imagaine any situation in which the centralized control of maternity and health centers by any bureau of the federal government does not offer a most dangerous technical mechanism for propaganda among women, whatever benevolent or revolutionary cult of propagandists strive to make use of it?"

Ironically, the Children's Bureau clinics indirectly added evidence of the DAR-sponsored Black List. They were established under the Sheppard-Towner Act, which was supported by almost all women's organizations, including the DAR, but which was allowed to expire in 1927. At that time the organization refused to cooperate with other groups in a campaign for the extension of the clinics. Mrs. Walker evidently suspected that the clinics were Communist infested. In 1929 it was reported in the *Christian Century* that Julia Lathrop, first director of the Children's Bureau, and Grace Abbott, her successor, were on the DAR Black List.

The *Springfield Republican* devoted considerable space to a "spider web chart" purporting to show that the "interlocking directorates" of national women's societies were involved in a conspiracy to undermine the American Government and that their leaders were linked with Bolshevism and revolution.

The Springfield paper announced that this chart emanated from the office of General Amos A. Fries, head of the Army's Chemical Warfare Service from World War I until 1928. Fries'

wife was the publicity chairman of the DAR during part
of this same period.   The chart brought such a feminine hue and
cry, the *Republican* reported, that Secretary of War John W.
Weeks ordered the destruction of all the copies remaining in the
possession of the Chemical Warfare Service, and ordered General
Fries to notify people who had received them from his office that
the charts contained errors and must be destroyed.

Reporting that the "spider web chart" was drawn up by Lucia
R. Maxwell, Chemical Warfare Service Librarian, the *Republican*
cited some supplementary verse she had prepared:

> *Miss Bolsheviki has come to town*
> *With a Russian cap and a German gown*
> *In women's clubs she's sure to be found*
> *For she's come to disarm America.*
> *She sits in judgment on Capitol Hill*
> *And watches the appropriation bill*
> *And without her OK it passes—NIL*
> *For she's there to disarm America.*
> *She uses the movie and lyceum too*
> *And alters the books to suit her view*
> *She prates propaganda from pulpit and pew*
> *For she's bound to disarm America.*

The *Republican* also produced evidence of Mrs. Brosseau's connection with Fred R. Marvin.   Subsequently some of his remarks
before a New Jersey chapter elicited a strong protest from Mrs.
Mary P. MacFarland, wife of Dr. Charles S. MacFarland, then
General Secretary of the Federal Council of Churches of Christ in
America; her protest, however, only brought from Mrs. Brosseau
an equally strong endorsement of Mr. Marvin.   According to the
Republican, Mr. Marvin's *Daily Data Sheet* was published under
the auspices of a patriotic organization called "Key Men of Amer-
ica," whose advisory council included Mrs. Brosseau and Lucia
R. Maxwell of "spider web chart" fame.

Mr. Marvin and the other person who had generated a great deal
of unfavorable publicity for the DAR, William B. Shearer, were

destined to disappear from the public eye under widely different circumstances. Mr. Shearer's suit against three shipbuilding companies never came to trial, but on June 11, 1933, was settled out of court. A year later Mr. Shearer was reported as having completely retired from public life, living the life of a gentleman farmer in Connecticut.

Harder luck was in store for Fred Marvin. He was sued by Mme. Rozika Schwimmer, a well known international figure of the time, who charged that he and his newspaper, *The New York Commercial*, had libeled her by reporting she had been a German spy during World War I and a Bolshevik after the war ended. The first woman ambassador appointed by her native Poland, dynamic Mme. Schwimmer later became a noted lecturer in the United States. She organized the Henry Ford peace ship expedition to Europe in 1915, by which the multi-millionaire hoped to get the soldiers "out of the trenches by Christmas." The "Open Forum" of July 13, 1929, reported that Mme. Schwimmer had been awarded $17,000 damages in the Marvin suit, and that the "propaganda of the Key Men of America, Fred R. Marvin's organization of professional patriots, will be discontinued for lack of funds," adding that officers of the American Civil Liberties Union ventured the opinion that the $17,000 verdict might explain Mr. Marvin's financial difficulties.

Far from defunct despite the waves of adverse publicity, the society continued unswervingly on its course. Mrs. Brosseau's three-year administration ended in 1929, and a lady who saw eye-to-eye with her became the new President-General—Mrs. Lowell Fletcher Hobart of Cincinnati, organizer of the American Legion Auxiliary, which, with the DAR, had taken the lead in setting up the Women's Patriotic Conference on National Defense. Continuing as National Defense Chairman, Mrs. Walker was elected a Vice President in 1930. In the same year the organization rubber-stamped resolutions already passed by the Women's Patriotic Conference, which by that time had grown to a membership of forty organizations. The resolutions pledged the society to combat and expose Socialist and Communist activities in schools and colleges; expressed opposition to the recognition of the U.S.S.R. and charged that the Communist International was pursuing its objective to overthrow all non-Communist governments even while seeking recognition and friendly relations; and demanded legislation to rid the country of all seditious and Communist agitators aiming to overturn the government by force, violence or deceit.

By 1930 the depression had begun to be felt even by the DAR who promptly blamed it on the Communists. Mrs. Walker told her fellow members at the 1930 Congress that communists had been caught putting on whispering campaigns to start runs on banks, "thus breaking down the confidence of the American people."

A year later the Daughters bolstered their anti-Communist spirit with two talks by arch foes of the Soviet—Reverend Dr. Edmund A. Walsh of Georgetown University, and Princess Julia Cantacuzene, granddaughter of General Ulysses Grant, wife of a Russian nobleman and a leader of "White" anti-Soviet Russians. Father Walsh said: "The world is the Communists' area and the United States their principal objective," and Princess Cantacuzene added that "insidious propaganda for the Bolshevists in Russia reminds me now of the propaganda we find in the United States today." Keynoting the annual meeting, Mrs. Hobart blamed Communists for some of the depression woes then afflicting the country. Furthermore, she went on, there was a movement under way for expropriation of private property by "distressed people whom the Communist leaders would show how to bring about private property seizure, and then the Communists would be ready to take over power when the violence had been done." She also attributed to Communist leadership "disagreeable events" such as depression parades, riots, street demonstrations, and marches on city halls and on state and national legislatures. The Communists, she charged, had reaped rich rewards in party membership by exploiting unemployment and by directing the minds of sympathizers towards hatred of the U.S. government and opposition to all owners and managers of business enterprises.

In 1931, although the Daughters themselves did not then know it
and no outside observer would have believed it possible, the DAR
was approaching the end of the most controversial era of its history.
Two vastly different leaders were about to lead the organization
into calmer waters—Mrs. Russell William Magna of Holyoke,
Massachusetts, and Mrs. William Louis Dunne of Washington,
D. C.

For years Mrs. Magna had been one of the most popular Daughters. Called their "little gold digger", she had raised hundreds
of thousands of dollars by travelling thousands of miles to visit
chapters and by wheedling money out of pockets at annual meetings to pay off the debt on Constitution Hall. Her wealthy father,
Colonel Walter Scott, a paper manufacturer and Son of the American Revolution, was a loyal supporter of the society and a familiar figure in a box at Constitution Hall when his daughter presided
as President-General or stood at the microphone raising money
like an auctioneer. Tiny Mrs. Magna, with reddish blond hair
and a predilection for wearing blue dresses and hats, was unopposed as a candidate for President-General in 1932.

Publicity chairman for Mrs. Magna was Mrs. William Louis
Dunne, a former newspaperwoman with a good understanding of
public relations. Now a Federal employee living with her husband in a modest Washington apartment, Mrs. Dunne was deeply
concerned about the difficulties the organization had got itself into
since 1926. She was a self-effacing but effective force in Mrs.
Magna's program, bringing an improved slant to DAR public relations. When the "little gold digger" was nominated for President-General without opposition, *The New York Times* reported
"it became known" that Mrs. Magna had not asked Mrs. William
Walker to continue as chairman of the National Defense
Committee, and this "was regarded as confirming rumors that national defense would be less prominent on the program than it
had been in the previous six-years." The *Times* also reported a
"growing feeling in the organization that the menace of Com-

munism had been absorbing a disproportionate amount of the society's time and efforts," and added pointedly that "while ready
at all times to join in the defense of the Republic, the society did
not wish to assume the position of sole or even most responsible
defender." But months passed before anything happened to carry
out this prophecy, beyond the fact that Mrs. Walker was not continued as Defense Committee chairman.

Elected unanimously, Mrs. Magna could have harvested newspaper headlines by announcing her plans to lead the organization
into the more moderate paths. But her moderation was complete
and she did nothing of the kind. Instead, she waited until January 19, 1933, the eve of the annual meeting of the Womens'
Patriotic Conference on National Defense, and then announced
that the society had withdrawn from that coalition of patriotic
groups. Making no self-justifying statement or charges against
the conference or former DAR policies, Mrs. Magna merely said
the society would not support the conference "in a body,"and gave
as her reason for withdrawal the inability of members to pay their
way to the Patriotic Conference "at this time of depression."

Every member familiar with what had been going on in the organization was aware of the real significance of Mrs. Magna's
action. For six years the society had not only participated in the
Patriotic Conference but had been its most important member.
The opening salvo of the Daughters' super-patriotic and anti-Communist campaign had been their alignment with the Conference,
which had been initiated by Mrs. Brosseau in 1927. Friends
for years during their period as leaders, the two ladies gave no
indication of dissension over Mrs. Magna's action. Mrs. Brosseau
was on hand as usual at the 1933 Patriotic Conference, from which
the DAR had withdrawn, and she presented the defense program
of affiliated groups. But at the 1933 Congress, when there was a
determined minority movement to defeat Mrs. Magna's "moderate" policy and return to affiliation with the Patriotic Conference,
Mrs. Brosseau voted with the majority which supported the President-General, explaining that she had cast her vote to uphold the

National Board of Management under Mrs. Magna's leadership, and with the understanding that "the President-General is willing for any member to cooperate personally with other societies."

The organization never returned to its ultra-national defense and anti-Communistic campaigns nor did it return to the Women's Patriotic Conference, which survived the withdrawal, but which exercised increasingly waning influence. When Mrs. William A. Becker of Montclair, N. J., succeeded Mrs. Magna as President-General in 1935, there was some intimation that she might abandon her predecessor's moderate course and take the society back into the Patriotic Conference. Instead, Mrs. Becker announced that it was illegal under the DAR constitution to "affiliate" with any other group, thus making the break final.

Mrs. Magna had put the case more bluntly on March 19, 1934, in words which might almost have been those of Mrs. Carrie Chapman Catt or even Mrs. Helen Tufts Bailie. She lamented that "through bitter experience" the Daughters had learned that the power and influence of their organization were fully appreciated by certain individuals seeking to disseminate certain propaganda under the guise of patriotism, particularly 'highly paid agents who for their own ends seek to use patriotic societies for their own selfish purposes . . . and earn their own livelihood thereby." She added that 99.99 per cent of the Society's membership had come to the same realization.

CHAPTER XI

CONTINENTAL CONGRESSES

The first DAR Continental Congress, held in Philadelphia and considering the most urgent problems of Colonial America, could hardly have taken itself—or its problems—more seriously than do the annual meetings of the DAR. The Republic itself hangs in the balance and is only temporarily eclipsed by orchids, ladies' teas and the white-gloved brigade.

The early Congresses bore little resemblance to the elaborately staged productions of today. Those meetings of the 1890's featured a patriotic song or two—"The Star Spangled Banner" or "Hail Columbia"—and the necessary business details incident to any organization. At first held in a small Universalist church in downtown Washington, the Congresses have long since outgrown such modest quarters. So elaborate are the present-day meetings that the end of one is the beginning of preparations for the next. The Congress machinery is handled by 14 committees—house, hospitality, pages, credentials, program, tellers, pages' ball, seating, marshal, flowers, President-General's reception room, banquet, guest and transportation.

Biggest of all is the House Committee, with a chairman, four vice chairmen and 10 subcommittees of 300 members. Its job is to adapt headquarters and Constitution Hall to the needs and convenience of delegates and alternates from every state in the Union, outlying United States possessions and a few foreign countries. The House Committee members arrange for parking cars on nearby streets, issue parking tags to members officially in need of space, assign lobby space and make contracts with concessionaries who set up shop in the basement lounge of Constitution Hall. In addition it provides facilities for the sale of insignia, DAR literature, postcards, heraldic jewelry and flowers.

It also sponsors a lost and found table and an information center.

The House Committee aranges for first aid facilities with a nurse in attendance and contracts with a caterer to operate three eating places for delegates who prefer not to leave the premises between sessions. Daughters who have to budget their expenses, however, troop across to the Department of the Interior cafeteria.

One of the tougher problems facing the platform committee is the literal shepherding of the hundreds of delegates and guests who participate in the program. These persons must be gotten on and off the stage and, when on the stage, must be seated according to their rank. Observing all protocol and keeping everyone happy calls for the maximum of tact and smooth handling.

Closely allied with this platform duty is the work of the seating committee that must allot space for 4,000 delegates and alternates. Not everybody can sit in front rows within arms' length of the ferns banking the edge of the stage; and consequently, to avoid favoritism in seating arrangements and the inevitable hard feelings that result, seats and states are divided into two groups— low numbers for the floor and higher ones for the balcony, state regents in alternate years drawing lots for downstairs and for balcony seats.

Adding a touch of youthful charm to the generally mature annual gathering are the young women pages. At the first Continental Congress in 1891, there were two pages with not much to do. In 1898, 13 pages, representing the original 13 states helped dress up a DAR ceremony in a downtown Washington theater, for the special awarding of Gorham-designed, jewelled, thousand-dollar medals to the organization's four official founders. By 1957 the number of pages had increased to about 300.

Between the ages of 18 and 30, the pages are DAR members appointed by the President-General on the recommendation of their respective state regents. The pages always wear white dresses and pay all their own bills.

The girls run errands, deliver notes and flowers, stand on guard at key spots throughout the auditorium, ready to do the delegates' bidding; stuff kits with mimeographed handouts for reporters covering the Congress; clip DAR stories from newspapers; put notices on bulletin boards; try to satisfy members seeking special publicity for pet DAR projects, and in general provide the meeting's communications system. The girls' rewards are organizational prestige, fun, and particularly dance partners for the annual pages' ball given by the President-General and the National Board of Managers in the Mayflower Hotel Ballroom.

Briefing the pages on their positions and functions in the processions of national officers which are a feature of Congress programs, is one of the duties of the Marshal Committee. Its biggest job, however, is the overall organization and direction of the processions, when the President-General and the various national officers enter the hall for the official openings of program sessions.

Another committee, assisted by pages, receives and distributes all flowers sent to the Hall and to honored participants. A guest committee sends out invitations to the Congress, acknowledges replies, issues guest cards for admission, greets guests as they arrive, presents them to the President-General and escorts them to their seats in auditorium boxes or on the stage. Members of a President-General's Reception Room Committee act as hostesses to members and guests who come to the handsome and formal reception room to be received by the President-General or who have a part in Congress programs. The banquet committee sells 2000 tickets for the dinner climaxing each annual gathering.

The annual Congress is always held in the week of April 19, the anniversary of the battle of Lexington, but the machinery is well oiled before delegates begin pouring in. Every nook and corner of the $7,000,000 headquarters building is made spick and span in order to pass the critical inspection of thousands of housewives. Hedges are clipped. Grass is like velvet. Voter badges are ready. Programs are stacked for distribution by registered delegations. The DAR genealogical library is temporarily closed to the public, so delegates may browse at will.

Though all Daughters take great pride in their impressive headquarters building, many delegates find the block-size structure confusing and wander around looking for the rooms where state delegations meet, the museum, the library and even for the way to Constitution Hall. The headquarters can be confusing because it was built in four sections, beginning with Memorial Continental Hall, which at first stood alone in the middle of an almost marshy waste. To the rear is the DAR administration building, also built in two sections, and beyond that is Constitution Hall. Corridors leading from Constitution Hall dead-end at Memorial Continental Hall and elevators are not always adequate to carry the rush of delegates to second and third stories. To make things easier for the annual visitors from all over the country, the management has published maps showing the exact location of all major points of interest in the building. In short, very little is overlooked.

Constitution Hall, which requires little preparation for the annual meeting, was designed by architect John Russell Pope, who also designed the Jefferson Memorial in Washington. Large enough to accommodate the organization's expanding delegate body, the Hall also serves as a cultural center for the nation's capital, with its concert and lecture rentals totalling approximately $82,000 in a season and an estimated half million ticket buyers.

The Daughters love their auditorium and their annual Congress. Demand for seats at the Congress has become so great—particularly on opening Monday night and National Defense night—on Tuesday—that in 1955 Miss Gertrude S. Carraway, President-General, said 1,200 were turned away on opening night. In 1956 Miss Carraway took care of this overflow by using the air-conditioned Interior Department Auditorium just across the street. The society had the latter auditorium equipped with loud speakers to relay the Constitution Hall program on Monday and Tuesday nights, and invited delegates to come "and bring their husbands."

These are the "big nights" of the annual event. On Monday night the President-General makes the keynote address and announces the special theme of the Congress sessions—"Our Goodly Heritage" was the 1957 theme. Tuesday night formerly was a gala break in the week's proceedings, when the President General and other national officers received delegates at a formal reception. This frivolity has been abandoned, and Tuesday night is now the occasion for weighty speeches on the organization's defense policies.

The week's program begins Sunday afternoon, with a memorial service for members who have died during the previous year. The organization is far from a youthful one and the mortality rate is high—3019 in 1954, 3058 in 1955 and 3276 in 1956. The service is as impressive as practice and planning can make it. Presiding, the Chaplain-General slowly intones the number of deceased members in each state, and after each number is read, a page inserts a white carnation in a huge memorial wreath. Before the service is over, the wreath is studded with white flowers.

Also beginning on Sunday there are hotel luncheons, breakfasts, dinners, buffet suppers and teas (thirty-seven of these in 1957) given by various state chapters for their own delegates, who buy tickets and attend or save their money and stay away, just as they choose. At numerous "openhouse" state meetings, there are no refreshments or admission fees. Monday is devoted to state get-together meetings and committe meetings. On Monday evening the program opens with a grand processional—music by a section of the Marine Band, the President-General leading other national officers in a slow walk down the left aisle of Constitution Hall, preceded by pages carrying flags. The climax of this performance comes when the President-General approaches the stage and a great American flag is unfurled from the middle of the auditorium's vaulted ceiling to wave over the crowd—a never failing breath-taker.

The Daughters are really friendly souls and many of them come to Congress after Congress ("This is my 38th" said a lady from the West Coast before the opening day in 1957). They meet old friends and make new ones, chat in the lobby, and shop in booths in the basement lounge.

In most cases the rank and file delegates get their only glimpses of their national leaders as they sit on the stage in Constitution Hall, make speeches and reports, march to and from the stage in processions, or appear at formal parties.

Perched halfway in and halfway out of the lobby is a sort of vestibule where representatives of Washington's daily papers take orders for complete sets of "Congress Week" issues. Four thousand ladies buy a lot of "Congress Week" issues, which may explain the press coverage given the annual meeting. *The Star* and *Post and Times-Herald,* which publish on Sundays, lead off with large pre-Congress spreads, and these Sunday sections are sold all week long. A third Washington newspaper, *The Daily News,* with no Sunday edition, gives the organization less space and fewer complimentary articles. In 1956 the *News* got some black looks for printing an unflattering realistic picture of the elderly Daughters. In 1955, the *Post and Times-Herald* waited until the delegates had gone home and then wrote a biting editorial about their "perennial antediluvianism." Naturally this drew fire. President-General Carraway wrote a letter to the editor, regretting that a "number of members had felt it imperative to cancel their subscriptions" after reading the editorial. Another lady, Mrs. W. L. Walton of Kenosha, Wisconsin, criticized the paper for waiting until the Congress was over before printing the editorial. She warned that vengeance would be hers "If God spares me and I am able to attend Congress next year."

Another important focal point of great interest, with doors wide open to delegates, is the museum, where a program is held on Monday morning before the opening Congress session each year. For this program the Curator brings experts to talk about subjects pertinent to the background of the well arranged Revolutionary relics. In 1951 John Kent Tilton, director of the Scallamandre Museum of textiles, described in fascinating detail an exhibit of beautiful fabrics used in the restoration of famous American homes throughout the nation. The founder of the Scallamandre Museum, a New York expert who specializes in made-to-order hand-woven fabrics, has furnished some of the expensive uphol-stery and window hangings in the DAR headquarters and donated a $400 silk damask backdrop for the museum's Martha Washing-ton portrait.

At the 1953 museum program staid teetotalling members were shocked to hear their ancestors probably were consistent topers. Philip H. Hammerslough of Hartford, Connecticut, dis-playing early American silver tankards from his own collection, told them: "History books don't say so but it is a well known fact that early American settlers were heavy drinkers and never lost a chance to down a tankard of cider or ale." In his display of tankards Mr. Hammerslough also showed some made for women; particularly a very large one which he said a father gave his daughter in 1762 as a wedding gift for her own use.

At the same Congress genealogically-minded delegates heard of the sad plight of old family Bibles in a day of small ramblers and smaller apartments. Miss Maud Kelly of Alabama's state Arch-ives Department, said there's no place in such homes for these "big old ragged family Bibles," and reported that her department has provided space for them in its archives library.

Another feature which maintains its popularity all through Congress week is a second floor exhibit of publicity scrapbooks kept by state societies competing for the annual prizes awarded for scrapbooks with the most inches of newspaper clippings. The principal subject in all 1955 scrapbooks was the celebration for the first time of "Constitution Week," September 17-23, for which President Carraway took personal credit. In a newspaper inter-view, Miss Carraway said she was making a radio talk in Norfolk Virginia, when she was suddenly struck with the thought that among all special "weeks" celebrated by Americans, none com-memorated the preservation of the country's constitutional gov-ernment. Returning to Washington, she queried the United States

Chamber of Commerce and promptly launched a drive to establish a "Constitution Week."

Her first step was to persuade Senator William F. Knowland, the California Republican, to introduce a joint Senate and House resolution authorizing the celebration. After Congress had passed the resolution and President Eisenhower proclaimed the celebration, the governors of forty-seven states and top officials of Hawaii, Alaska, the District of Columbia, the Canal Zone, and of thousands of cities, counties and towns, issued similar proclamations. Reports from 2173 DAR chapters showed that the organization reached millions of school children through Constitution week programs. More than five hundred newspaper editorials praised the project, which also won one of five top 1955 awards from Freedom Foundation, Valley Forge, Pennsylvania.

In a basement room of Constitution Hall, typewriters and telephones are installed for reporters covering the Congress. Next door is a room where the public relations director and press pages hold forth. There the usual advance copies of speeches are handed out, reporters' questions are answered and press errands are run by hard working pages. The Daughters furnish free sandwiches and coffee for reporters at lunch time, but thriftily limit this to days when the Congress actually is in session.

Passing on the qualifications of delegates is the important work of the credentials comittee. This process begins four months in advance of Congress week, when credential blanks and registration cards are sent to each chapter with instructions to elect delegates and alternates on or before March 1. A typewritten list of delegates and alternates from each chapter, with the date of their election, must be mailed to the Credentials Committee at National Headquarters and to state regents in time for receipt before March 10. No member is eligible to be a delegate unless her membership dues are paid by February 1, and all delegates and alternates (two alternates for each delegate and regent) must have been members for at least one continuous year immediately preceding the Congress for which they are elected. Exceptions to this rule are the Regent or Vice Regent of a newly organized chapter, or a 21-year-old Daughter transferred to the DAR after at least a year of membership in the Children of the American Revolution.

Chapters with 12 to 25 members are allowed no delegates in addition to their regent. Chapters with 50 to 199 members elect one delegate each, and another delegate is added for each 100 members exceeding 199. A chapter regent is authorized to fill vacancies on her list of delegates from duly elected alternates, the regent herself serving without election.

At Congress time, delegates arrive in Washington and stand in line to register and receive red and white "voter" badges, which they wear as prominently as their insignia. Registration begins on Friday before the Congress and continues each successive day except Sunday, until half an hour following adjournment on Wednesday afternoon. Credentials Committee members check delegates' papers against lists and hand out voter badges. A voter badge is not transferrable by the delegate to whom it was issued except to an alternate if the delegate cannot stay until voting day.

Located close by the main entrance is an efficient ground floor registration and voting room with wall panels which open outward to form twenty-one voting booths. Delegates mark their ballots by hand, though as early as 1919 they tried voting machines. Mrs. Rex Hays Rhoades of Washington, D. C., who was Credentials Committee chairman for eighteen years up to 1947, when she was elected Treasurer-General, declared it took so much time to show the voters how to use the machines that it was faster to "X" the ballots. Also, there is apparently some distrust of the machines; in the closely contested 1944 election—as the story goes—supporters of the defeated candidate for President-General charged ballots were extracted from the machines by the winner's henchwomen.

Precautions against the abuse of the voting privilege are now numerous and thorough. A fifty-five-member tellers' committee handled a three-candidate President-General election in 1956. A teller stood guard outside each voting booth; tellers were ordered not to speak to each other or to anyone else while voting was in progress. They silently handed out ballots, waved voters to voting booths, and watched each voter deposit her ballot in the box. In silence they went to lunch and dinner in a nearby room. In silence they counted ballots after the polls closed at 2:30 p.m. Thursday and again on Friday, when a second run-off ballot had to be taken. They went silently to the powder room in pairs— no teller was allowed to be alone outside the voting room. When a reporter asked to talk to Miss Louise Bullock of Parkersburg, West Virginia, teller committee chairman, Miss Bullock came out of the voting room with a page at her elbow. Even the teller chairman could not be trusted to talk to anyone without a witness!

Voting is obviously a solemn business with the Daughters. Only twenty-one ladies have been elected President-General, and competition for this high honor has been continuous and keen. Examples of dramatic election battles prove the necessity and wisdom of precautions for policing voter credentials and guarding against voting irregularities.

In 1947 Mrs. Roscoe C. O'Byrne of Brookville, Indiana, a judge's wife, became a candidate for President-General just one month before election day, because of the sudden death of the head of her ticket—Mrs. John Logan Marshall of Clemson, South Carolina. Her hesitancy in taking up the race at such a late date was only overcome by her husband's insistence that it was her "duty." So that delegates would quickly get to know her, Mrs. O'Byrne wore the same sailor hat and pink dress during the four days before the voting. There were stories that O'Byrne supporters beat the bushes as far afield from Washington as Philadelphia, to bring in delegates and add O'Byrne votes. Finally to boost their ticket and put their slate over the top, O'Byrne candidates gave a massive reception for all delegates and officers at the Mayflower Hotel—with a bill of $4000. This was the most costly non-alcoholic reception ever held in Mayflower Hotel history.

That was before the voting room was built during the O'Byrne administration. They call it the O'Byrne room, and a portrait of white-haired Mrs. O'Byrne hangs there, though there now is a standing rule that no more portraits of Presidents-General will be accepted by headquarters. A miniature of each top lady is presented to the society when she goes out of office, and is displayed in the President-General's reception room. In 1956 President General Carraway said North Carolina Daughters would have been delighted to present a portrait instead of a miniature of her, except for the no-more-portraits rule.

Before the voting room was added, voting moved slowly and was dangerous to life and limb. With booths set up in Memorial Continental Hall, voters had to climb precariously up and down steep stage steps to cast their ballots. Voting was so slow that in 1947 it was 3:15 Friday morning before Mrs. O'Byrne was declared winner over Mrs. Stanley T. Manlove of Newburgh, New York. Delegates had waited more than four hours for the result—a close 1186 to 1131 contest.

Another spectacular contest winner was Mrs. Julius Talmadge of Athens, Georgia, who was elected in 1944 when the organization held a wartime meeting at the Commodore Hotel in New York City. Though long known as an aspirant for President-General and enjoying much support, particularly among southerners, the beautiful and charming Mrs. Talmadge seemed destined never to be a winner. She had been defeated badly by Mrs. Lowell Fletcher Hobart in 1930, and reportedly agreed not to run in a later election on the understanding that her turn would come thereafter. Apparently the promise was broken.

Finally, in 1944, Mrs. Talmadge and two other candidates ran for President-General and none of the three polled a majority vote on the first ballot. After this vote the Daughters had to evacuate their convention rooms in the Commodore Hotel because of the hotel's prior reservations; on the second ballot they voted in a hotel corridor. It was in that election that the defeated candidates suspected tampering with voting machines. Winner by only one vote in excess of the 814 she needed for a majority, Mrs. Talmadge broke the stranglehold of New England and other Eastern Daughters who had dominated elections for years. Several candidates on her ticket were defeated, however, leaving the opposition heavily represented in her "Cabinet" and giving her trouble with the ill-assorted "team." In fact, according to older members, the principal officers "fought like mad" at Board of Management meetings throughout Mrs. Talmadge's administration.

Under a rigid "no politicking" rule, candidates are disqualified if they let it be known officially, before the close of an annual Congress, that they will run the following year. The same rule prohibits campaigning within DAR buildings at an election-year Congress. When the last gavel had banged in 1955, a distinguished, grey-haired lady from Chicago, Mrs. J. DeForest Richards, announced a full slate of candidates with herself at the top and the others well selected in terms of geography and prestige. This was a strong ticket; Mrs. Richards, the widow of a banker, had been elected Treasurer General in 1953, and had only recently returned from a trip around the world. She seemed a sure winner for 1956, though there were some whispers that because of deafness she might be handicapped as a presiding officer. At that time there was no opposition; but Mrs. Richard's death two months after her announcement threw the field wide open.

Mrs. Frederic Alquin Groves of Cape Girardeau, Missouri, held second spot on the Richards ticket as candidate for First Vice President-General. Mrs. Groves and her fellow candidates met, decided to go through with the campaign as they believed Mrs. Richards would have wished, and Mrs. Groves moved up to top spot. She was opposed by Mrs. Thomas Henry Lee of Philadelphia, past Pennsylvania State Regent and Recording Secretary-General under Miss Carraway, and Mrs. Charles Carroll Haig of Silver Spring, Maryland, who had been Buildings and Grounds Committee chairman under Miss Carraway and a past President of the Children of the American Revolution.

All three ladies campaigned long and hard. Mrs. Haig lost twenty pounds. Mrs. Groves put her whole time in on the campaign for ten full months. Mrs. Lee made an eighteen-state speaking tour between February and April, 1956, and Mrs. Haig was not far behind; she talked to Daughters at sixteen state conferences. Mrs. Groves made her final speaking trip to Florida the week before the Congress opened on April 16, 1956.

The three ladies and their respective slates opened headquarters in suites at the Mayflower Hotel, official DAR hotel headquarters. All held continuous openhouse until the votes were finally counted a week later. With their associate candidates, Mrs. Lee and Mrs. Haig not only held open house but provided a lavish table of refreshments for visiting voters. Candidates brought such dainties from their home states as apple candy from the far northwest apple country, wheat sweets from Kansas, and Maryland beaten biscuits with home-baked ham and turkey.

By contrast, Mrs. Groves opened her headquarters with a prayer and a salute to the flag. Only piping hot coffee was served to her callers.

According to the supporters of Mrs. Groves, all three candidates had agreed not to give a huge party like the one given for Mrs. O'Byrne's ticket in 1947 (the last of that size up to 1956). But Mrs. Haig and her associates tossed a bombshell the weekend before Congress opening day, by sending out invitations for a reception at 10:30 Monday night, immediately after the end of the first Congress session. Like Mrs. O'Byrne's, this party was held in the Mayflower Hotel ballroom, with refreshments but no liquor, and all delegates were invited. Reporters estimated the crowd at 3,200 and experienced members figured the party must have cost more than the $4000 tab picked up by Mrs. O'Byrne's supporters in 1947. Leading off on Saturday afternoon, Mrs. Haig also held a press conference at which cocktails were served after her fellow candidates were presented.

Mrs. Groves countered with a mid-morning press conference on Monday. Mrs. Lee was featured at a reception in one of Washington's finest mansions, given for one of her associates, Mrs. Robert Duncan of Alexandria, Virginia, by Mrs. Duncan's chapter. Apologizing to a District of Columbia chapter because she was the only candidate who failed to attend its party, Mrs. Lee gave what must be the perfect all-time DAR explanation: The Mayflower moved from her room a chest of drawers containing her white gloves and failed to return the chest and gloves until it was too late for her to go to the party!

In a sample poll, a reporter discovered that delegates had come uninstructed and some were doubtful about how they should vote. They had heard the three candidates speak at 1956 state conferences, but felt best acquainted with Mrs. Haig, who had made earlier swings around the country as Children of the American Revolution President. One asked her State Regent how she should vote and was told to make up her own mind. Another remarked: "They say Mrs. Groves has more money than Mrs. Lee or Mrs. Haig. She could do more for the organization."

According to reports, Mrs. Haig lost votes because she went to a beauty parlor for a shampoo and delegates didn't like the shade of her hair rinse; also some ladies swung away when Mrs. James B. Patton, 1950-53 President-General and 1953-56 National Defense Committee chairman, stepped into line beside Mrs. Haig at the big Monday night party, thereby indicating that Mrs. Patton was a Haig supporter. There was some feeling that the organization had had enough of Mrs. Patton, inasmuch as she had served as a national officer and committee chairman for nine years. Reportedly, too, some delegates disapproved of Mrs. Haig's big Monday night party—it was attended by some 3,200 persons—because it was held so soon after the unfortunate death of her husband.

Thrusting at her chief opponent, Mrs. Lee said she thought the President-General's job should go to an unmarried woman or a widow who could give it full time. A far cry from the early days of the organization when a husband in Washington official circles was a prime requisite! Both Mrs. Lee and Mrs. Haig were widowed, while Mrs. Groves had a husband who was so anxious about her electoral prospects that after the final ballot she rushed out to telephone him long distance before talking to reporters. The lady from Missouri, whose husband was a successful businessman, had taken up Mrs. Lee's challenge. "I think a husband as good as mine would be a help to any President-General," she proudly chirped.

A new contender like Mrs. O'Byrne in 1947, Mrs. Groves, however, did not wear a sailor hat and the same dress all through pre-voting preliminaries. Instead she gave her eleven associate candidates enameled necklace watches, so that delegates would recognize them as members of her slate. Mrs. Haig and Mrs. Lee also devised identifying but less lavish insignia. Mrs. Haig and her associates were decorated with small lapel corsages made of forget-me-nots in the form of an "T." The Lee group wore ribbon rosettes with "Lee" in prominent lettering on the blue and white streamers.

Mrs. Groves' diamonds—earrings, necklace and brooch—were eye-catching, especially when she wore them with a formal evening gown. Reportedly, the diamonds worried her fellow candidates, not only because they outshone the latters' rhinestones in a receiving line, but because there was some feeling that voters would eye them with envy. There was a similar report about Mrs. Alfred J. Brosseau in the 1926 campaign on account of her beautiful rubies. Mrs. Groves refused to doff her diamonds, reportedly insisting that "I've always worn them and I'm going to wear them now".

However solemnly the Daughters take their elections, equally vital business on Congress programs are the yearly resolutions, many of which have aroused public criticism and estranged members. From the very first meeting in 1891 there have been resolutions. In the Library of Congress is a slim volume listing "statutes" passed by the Daughters at annual meetings from 1891 to 1902. These early "statutes" were simple and practical, providing the framework on which the expanding organization built.

For example, it was voted that "literary papers" should be banned from annual programs, which should be devoted strictly to business; that the Treasurer-General should be bonded at the society's expense, and that the society should furnish the First Vice President-General with stationary and stamps for official use in connection with her duties.

Showing a consideration for headquarters workers in advance of their times the Daughters in 1896 voted them thirty days' annual leave and an eight-hour working day. In 1897 authorization was given for employment of a bookkeeper at a monthly salary of $100—excellent pay for that period. They adopted a standard form for letters of condolence sent out by the organization; and they decided that the national board of management could accept no communication, written or oral, derogatory to the character of any member, unless it was supported by proof and unless the member were given an opportunity to defend herself. Gossips were plainly put at a disadvantage.

During the years of great expansion, few resolutions worthy of mention were passed. A notable exception, however, was one passed in 1913 setting up a committee on the welfare of women and children, but this manifestation of developing social consciousness was voted down without protest five years later. In 1913 a motion to sell Christmas seals as a money raising plan to pay off the debt on Memorial Continental Hall was tabled in order to avoid competition with Red Cross and Tuberculosis Association seals. In 1914, just before World War I, the Daughters were absorbed in decisions regarding their magazine on which they had lost $7,000 the previous year. In 1915, with the world deep in the war, they passed resolutions showing a blissful unconcern which now seems incredible. They urged the U. S. Congress officially to adopt the "Star Spangled Banner" as the national anthem, and to establish a "Great Seal Day," in honor of the Great Seal of the United States.

Except for often being equally out of touch with the country's real concerns, the simpler "statutes" of the earlier years have little in common with the work of the present-day fifty-odd member Resolutions Committee, whose resolutions are approved almost unanimously by obedient delegates. Under the rules rigidly limiting debate, there is little chance for successful opposition. Not much can be said in the three minutes allotted a speaker, and the record shows that the few rebels who have raised their heads in recent years have achieved nothing but publicity. Resolutions that provoke vigorous outside criticism whiz through the Congress, which has been primed by key speeches of public figures supporting the resolutions and after delegates have been fed large doses of policy literature.

Meeting behind closed doors, the Resolutions Committee accepts resolutions up to Tuesday of Congress week and gives delegates proposing them an opportunity to be heard. How many delegates take advantage of this opportunity is unknown because of secrecy of the Committee's operation and the fact that proposals may be buried by a two-thirds vote. That this happens was evidenced when Mrs. T. B. Throckmorton, Resolutions Committee chairman, admitted in a 1956 press conference that the committee had refused to report several suggested resolutions on the controversial issue of public school desegregation.

Resolutions and other action by the annual Congress set the policy to be carried out the following year by elected officers. Such importance thus attaches to the resolutions that there have been recurring protests because chapters and members are given no advance information about them and delegates come to each Congress with no idea what they will be asked to approve. This is contrary to the democratic practice in some other large women's organizations such as the National League of Women Voters, which requires its state and local branches to discuss and vote in advance on proposals to come before its annual convention.

Protests seemed to have borne fruit when Mrs. James B. Patton, 1950-53 President-General, announced a new policy. She sent to the chapters in January summaries of resolutions expected to come up at the April Congress; but even this failed to make everybody happy. There were complaints that the summaries gave little idea of the resolutions as finally drafted. At any rate, Gertrude S. Carraway, successor to Mrs. Patton, also disliked the new system. "It's a long time between January and April," said Miss Carraway, announcing that the Patton experiment had been abandoned. "A lot of things can happen to make resolutions proposed in January out of date in April."

However, the Carraway administration initiated another minor reform. Beginning in 1954, and still effective, delegates were given at least twenty-four hours to study resolutions before voting on them; they were read one day, mimeographed copies were distributed to delegates, and voting began the next day. Meanwhile, reporters were forbidden to mention the resolutions except as "proposals."

The organization did not always operate under a three-minute rule. Up to 1920 there was no limit on debate, which went on and on—as did Congress sessions. The candidates for President-General found this open debate served them well. For example, in 1915 Mrs. George Thatcher Guernsey's supporters talked at great length about an embarrassing DAR magazine situation and an even more embarrassing financial mix-up in the administration of Mrs. William Cumming Story, whom Mrs. Guernsey was opposing for re-election. Retaliating, Mrs. Story herself took advantage of loose Congress rules by insisting on the deletion of a section of the report of one of her fellow officers (a Guernsey supporter), which she claimed put her unjustifiably in a bad light.

Having won the election in 1917, Mrs. Guernsey succeeded in making a start on limiting debate. The first limitation was a five-minute rule; delegates were allowed to speak only five minutes at a time and twice on the same subject during a Congress session. A similar rule was adopted in 1923 "to avoid filibustering," and in 1925 the *Washington Post* reported that such limitation of discussion had been "the ambition" of many Presidents-General before Mrs. Guernsey.

Even as recently as 1956, with the three-minute gag rule in

effect, delegates have found their voices and talked freely about a matter close to their hearts—a proposal to change the name of their Flag Committee. Daughter after Daughter made suggestions, and the name of the committee was completely revised. At the same Congress, a newspaper reporter watched President-General Carraway handle the revolt of Mrs. Franklin Peabody against the restrictive immigration resolution, and commented that the machinery made it as difficult as possible for delegates to stage such a revolt. Miss Carraway had asked for a rising vote, after Mrs. Peabody had been shouted down by thunderous "Ayes" supporting the resolution. "See how it works?" asked the reporter. "There wasn't any reason for taking a rising vote. But that forced opponents to stand up and show themselves."

A review of Congress programs also indicates that they are planned to feature speeches preparing delegates for policy resolutions. The speeches build up to a specific result and have a single-minded clarity. The organization has not felt it necessary to present more than one side of even the most controversial issues. It must often be the envy of the better informed and infinitely more puzzled members of the United States Congress! In 1952 three nationally known speakers hacked away at the United Nations, before the DAR first openly attacked it. National defense speakers have been and still are high up on their list, and probably no other organization has heard so many anti-Communist talks.

Meeting out of Washington during World War II, the Daughters were warmly welcomed by four cities—Chicago, Cincinnati, New York and Atlantic City. In Cincinnati in 1943 they included on their program a typical DAR ceremony—the gift to the city of two historic elm trees.

But the DAR Congress really belongs to the nation's capital. It is a yearly phenomenon like the cherry blossoms, the sweltering summers and the Senator's opening game. To press and public alike, it has become an established part of the Washington scene.

CHAPTER XII

PERSONALITIES AND DISSIDENTS

High on the list of DAR personalities and dissidents is Mrs. Franklin D. Roosevelt. Although the former First Lady resigned from the DAR in 1939, protesting the society's refusal to allow Marian Anderson to sing in Constitution Hall, there are members who hold that technically she is still a Daughter. To support their contention, they cite by-laws which contain no provision for the resignation of "life members", of which Mrs. Roosevelt was one. As such, Mrs. Roosevelt did not apply for membership, but at the age of 50 allowed herself to be enrolled. Up to that time she had shown no interest in the society, even though six Revolutionary ancestors made her eminently qualified for membership.

Two years after she became a life member, however, Mrs. Roosevelt's sympathy for peace and "radical" groups embroiled her with the society and in a President-General election. Mrs. Roosevelt had been named as a "radical" in *The Red Network*, a sensational book whose jacket bore the name—as though in endorsement, though this was later denied—of Mrs. William A. Becker, then running for President-General.

Keeping discreetly silent on the election battle, Mrs. Roosevelt could hardly have failed to consider it at least a mild slap in the face when Mrs. Becker was overwhelmingly elected. She took no active part in the organization, except to give a reception for delegates to the annual Congress at the White House each year, and she paid no dues or initiation fee. Approached by Mrs. Russell William Magna, Mrs. Becker's predecessor as President-General, Mrs. Roosevelt allowed her genealogy to be traced and her name recorded as a life member at large—that is, affiliated with no DAR chapter. There are indications that the organization never was enthusiastic about the former First Lady even before she resigned in 1939. More specifically, there still are whispers that Mrs. Roosevelt never was eligible for membership. It is alleged that her many Revolutionary ancestors made her only a collateral, not a direct, descendant of patriots, and that when the genealogists turned up this information the leadership chose to ignore it and admitted her as a member.

Whatever the truth may be, Mrs. Roosevelt became a life member without paying the $100 fee, which was paid by the society to gain the prestige of having another First Lady on its rolls. She was assessed no dues, in accordance with life membership prerogatives; and when the Daughters were received by the President and Mrs. Roosevelt at the White House on April 21, 1933, she was presented with an embossed certificate bearing the names of her six Revolutionary ancestors.

After Mrs. Roosevelt resigned in 1939, a Gallup poll showed that 67 per cent of Americans approved her break with the organization. The Daughters themselves, from Mrs. Henry M. Robert Jr., President-General, downward, kept mum. Officially they said nothing; they closed ranks as they have done time and again in tense moments, and rode out the storm. If it was indeed true that Mrs. Roosevelt was ineligible for membership, or that she could not resign life membership, the Society at least made no capital of either of those details. Nearly twenty years later, in 1956, Mrs. Robert—a parliamentarian herself as well as the daughter-in-law of the Robert of "Rules of Order" fame—could see no reason why any member, life or otherwise, should not resign at will, regardless of the wording of the by-laws.

After Mrs. Roosevelt resigned, Mrs. Robert as President-General saved the controversial First Lady from open repudiation by angry Daughters. That year the annual White House reception was held as usual, but Mrs. Roosevelt wasn't on hand. She had gone to Seattle to keep a year-old promise to help celebrate the birthday of a grandson. Substituting for her, Cabinet wives— Mrs. Cordell Hull, Mrs. Henry Wallace and others—received the ladies of the DAR. "So Mrs. Roosevelt is going to Seattle for the

DAR Congress," quipped the society columnist of the *Washington Times-Herald*.

Later in the DAR Congress, when "courtesy" resolutions were read to the delegates for routine vote, there was an angry flurry over a "thank you" for Mrs. Roosevelt's reception. After Mrs. Robert had called only for "Yes" votes on this resolution, a delegate rose to ask why Madame President-General had not called for "Noes" as well. Mrs. Robert calmly explained that "No" votes never are asked for on courtesy resolutions, since they always are passed unanimously. Still the delegates were not satisfied. Another rose to ask if Mrs. Roosevelt had arranged the reception, and Mrs. Robert replied that many letters on arrangements had been exchanged with Mrs. Roosevelt. The flurry ended; the parliamentarian had saved the day for the First Lady. Of a considerable number of dissident Daughters who have protested the Society's policies by resigning their membership Mrs. Roosevelt is by all odds the most outstanding.

If the top dissident title may be awarded to Mrs. Roosevelt, the opposite title of top creator of DAR dissension can probably be shared by Mrs. Alfred J. (Grace Lincoln Hall) Brosseau and Mrs. William Sherman Walker, who led the National Defense and Communist Menace crusades in the 1920's and 1930's. Bearing the brunt of persistent adverse publicity, the two ladies became nationally-known public figures. Largely because of their leadership, the organization was severely critized by many of the nation's leading newspapers and magazines.

Because they stood their ground in silence under this barrage and made no concessions to their critics, the two ladies became almost legendary figures. Little was publicly known about them personally except that Mrs. Brosseau was the wife of wealthy industrialist Alfred J. Brosseau, President of Mack Trucks, Inc., and that Mrs. Walker was a lady from Seattle, Washington, of little prominence until she skyrocketed to fame as first chairman of the Daughters' National Defense Committee.

Nearly thirty years later, however, in 1956 Mrs. Walker broke her silence and talked freely about Mrs. Brosseau and herself. Neither aggressive nor defensive, she told how and when the Daughters first became alarmed by the Communist menace, how their National Defense crusade began, and what she thought it had accomplished. About DAR controversies, she exercised the same discretion she had shown in the 1920's and early 1930's and had nothing to say. Without defending Mrs. Brosseau, she said the society's most controversial President-General did not initiate the national defense crusade and its accompanying battle against the Communist menace. She gave that credit to Mrs. Anthony Wayne Cook, who had gone down in DAR history as a rather innocuous President-General and, ironically, the last of the old school which had managed to keep the organization out of public controversies.

The picture Mrs. Walker painted of Mrs. Brosseau as a person differs sharply from the ruthless dictatorial personality presented to the world when, for example, she led the organization in expelling Mrs. Helen Tufts Bailie without a hearing by the Congress. To Mrs. Walker, Mrs. Brosseau was a steadfast friend and a cheerful, gay companion. Friends since before the days of their joint crusade, for 20 years they had vacationed together at Swampscott, Massachusetts, until, in 1956, Mrs. Brosseau—probably in her 80's—had a bone injury and was kept at home. In the same year Mrs. Walker was still good looking, well preserved and for years had worked actively with the American Coalition, a group of patriotic societies whose chief objective, she said, was to oppose unrestricted immigration. "American Coalition" was lettered on the door of her office in a remodelled apartment building at 1025 Connecticut Avenue in the downtown section of Washington—a pleasant place, just cluttered enough to give a feeling of action.

Mrs. Walker has kept a worn leather-bound volume, privately printed, in which Mrs. Brosseau had collected for her friends a number of speeches and messages she had written as a DAR official. Perhaps the best of them was one written before she became President-General, when, as chairman of the Ellis Island

Committee, she was intensely interested in the work with immigrants on the Island.

In that message she described the restriction imposed by the United States Immigration Service along with the "privilege" of helping women in the Ellis Island detention room. "We were to keep our sympathies in leash and not become interested in 'cases.' Our job was to provide the women with work for their hands and thereby relieve the mental strain under which they suffered." She told of the "window of hope" through which workers issued free materials to long lines of patiently waiting women—cloth for bungalow aprons, blouses and undergarments; remnants for children's clothes; yarn with which to knit socks and sweaters for their men; and crochet cotton and embroidery materials for those needing diversion. "This work ended quarrelling in the women's room," Mrs. Brosseau wrote. "No woman will quarrel with another when she is being shown how to make something pretty for her baby."

A strictly feminine message and one that would have rocked her patriot ancestors, written for the organization when she was President-General, describes Mrs. Brosseau's school girl thrill when she reached the height of her social ambition and was presented to Their British Majesties at Buckingham Palace in 1928. This happy interlude occurred just after Mrs. Helen Tufts Bailie had exposed the DAR Black List. In Europe to visit chapters there, Mrs. Brosseau was one of 33 American women presented to King George and Queen Mary that season. Her presentation added a fillip to the unfriendly publicity the Society then was reaping; one magazine writer reported with amusement that Mrs. Brosseau had "bowed her 100 per cent American knees" to royalty. Of all the 33 American women so honored in 1928, Mrs. Brosseau was the one chiefly mentioned in the American press at the time of the court presentation and when she came back to New York.

Describing the experience for fellow members, Mrs. Brosseau said it was a "wonderful adventure" which she wanted to share.

With an enthusiasm almost comical in an entrenched DAR, she told them the "setting for the royal ceremony holds all the grandeur, the beauty and the dignity of historic pagentry, but the presentation itself is marked by such quiet, orderly regulation that it appears to border upon simplicity." Although some Daughters no doubt would have been more interested in their President-General's court dress than the grandeur of the ceremony, Mrs. Brosseau refrained from giving them any details although she revealed indirectly that the court train held terrors for her strictly American imagination. Referring to the skill of court attaches in handling the ceremony, she reported that the "train of the dress, which could be provocative of so much grief," was laid on the carpet by attendants and removed from the carpet and thrown over the arm by other attendants, with perfect timing at the "right moments" of entrance and departure. Mrs. Brosseau described how "one walks past the throne and pauses to make a slight curtsey before the King and Queen, one receives in return a gracious bow from Their Majesties. The custom of backing out of the room no longer prevails, but the presentee faces the Queen until Her Majesty faces the next comer and then passes quickly out, to mingle with the throng, to partake of Supper or to return as an observer to the Throne Room."

Concluding with a Patriotic Postscript Mrs. Brosseau in self defense said: "Let it be here recorded that one is not compelled to make concessions with one's 'democratic spirit' in the 'unique and delightful experience.' The question is merely one of orientation and for a brief time becoming a part of and enjoying the highest social honor that one nation can bestow upon a guest from another country."

The *New York Times,* which covered Mrs. Bosseau's court experience rather thoroughly, stated that the day before her presentation on May 9, 1928, she practiced the "low, sweeping curtsey which she would perform before King George"—a gesture which would certainly have raised her patriot forebears from their graves if they could have seen it.

In addition to preserving statements and acounts concerning Mrs. Brosseau, Mrs. Walker kept some of the personal Christmas cards sent out by that lady over a period of years. Messages on the cards are quite self-revealing. One expressed the hope that the writer's "own dear world would impose upon the acts of my life, a verdict ever tempered by the belief that I had kept as the white plume of human endeavor the steadfastness of my own convictions." Another, undated but apparently written at some time during the Daughters' almost hysterical preoccupation with the "menace" of world government, professed to read a lesson from the birds feeding outside her Greenwich home: "Our little feathered friends would not tolerate a world government in birdland, for they know their own methods of self-government are the wisest and best." Still another, possibly written during the Korean War and reflecting the strain over the United Nations flag issue, asked: "Are we right in allowing the youths of our own country to again sacrifice their lives on foreign shores? Are we right in ignoring the fact that they are dying, not under the protecting folds of the Stars and Stripes, but under the same banner that is claimed by the enemy?"

Warm in praise of her friend, Mrs. Walker was modest about her own spectacular leadership. She said the national defense work "was necessary, has served a great cause and has served the country," but added "it just happened" that she became national defense head in 1926, because she had moved to Washington from Seattle and could give the organization a great deal of time, while other officers commuted great distances back and forth to Washington. "I had so many different jobs, some of the Daughters called me 'Pooh-Bah,'" Mrs. Walker gaily explained.

Friendship between Mrs. Brosseau and Mrs. Walker began in 1923, when both ladies were elected to the Cabinet of Mrs. Anthony Wayne Cook—Mrs. Brosseau as Treasurer-General, and Mrs. Walker as Organizing Secretary-General. Between the lines of Mrs. Walker's reminiscence can be seen a developing pattern of cooperation between the two women who were destined to share

criticism as well as friendship. Both were capable, vigorous and
devoted to the organization. As Secretary-General of the DAR
Mrs. Walker travelled around the country with Mrs. Cook to state
DAR conferences. Both Mrs. Brosseau and Mrs. Walker were
on the list of officers who received from Mrs. Cook a copy of *"Reds
in America,"* the book which was their first source material on the
Communist menace; and both were increasingly absorbed in what
they believed was a national defense and subversive crisis. "We
were working along those lines from 1923 to 1926," confides
Mrs. Walker.

The record leaves no doubt of Mrs. Walker's efficiency as Defense Committee chairman. Appointed in 1926, she sold the DAR
on the double-barreled national defense and anti-Communist crusade. When Mrs. Brosseau went out of office in 1929, Mrs. Walker was elected Vice President-General and led the ticket among
candidates for that office. After Mrs. Brosseau had retired, Mrs.
Walker stayed on as National Defense Committee chairman under
Mrs. Lowell Fletcher Hobart. But unlike Mrs. Brosseau, the former National Defense Chairman did not keep up her active participation after the policy shift represented by Mrs. Russell William Magna's election. She continued to live in Washington, and
from 1950 to 1957 was vice chairman of the Resolutions Committee but the organization saw little of her. Mrs. Brosseau ended
thirty years of married life by divorcing her husband in October
1930, charging "intolerable cruelty" and winning a reported
million-dollar settlement. Her ex-husband then married a neighbor in Greenwich, and some members attribute the estrangement
to the fact that Mr. Brosseau had become a DAR widower.

In their happier days, Mr. Brosseau had given DAR headquarters one of its handsomest memorials—a solid silver, wall-height
bas-relief of the Declaration of Independence, topped by a silver
reproduction of the famous Trumbull painting of the Declaration's
signing, which adorns Memorial Continental Hall's entrance lobby
and was presented by Mr Brosseau in honor of his wife. Another
beautiful gift is a stained glass window donated by Mrs. Brosseau.

To her public, Mrs. Brosseau presented, after her divorce, an
unchanged courageous front, as she had after the organization
abandoned its ultra-national defense and anti-Red policies by withdrawing from the Women's Patriotic Conference for National
Defense. A woman of a different type, less devoted to the DAR,
might have sulked in a corner and withdrawn from active participation. But not Mrs. Brosseau. On the stage at every Congress
sit the *grande dames* of the Society—its past Presidents-General,
who are designated Honorary Presidents-General as soon as their
three-year terms of office have ended; and Mrs. Brosseau never
missed one until 1956 when she became physically unable to be
present. Her voice was raised as usual on DAR issues. She even
saved the society a magazine editor's salary by donating her services from 1947 to 1950.

Perhaps because they represented the extreme in devotion to
the society and certainly a degree of fanaticism in their crusades,
Mrs. Brosseau and Mrs. Walker created much dissension in its
ranks.

Among those who bitterly opposed their policies, the most
aggressive was Mrs. Helen Tufts Bailie of Cambridge, Massachu-
setts, who was expelled from the society for her expose of the
Black List. Less well known was Mrs. Mary P. MacFarland of
Mountain Lakes, New Jersey, wife of the distinguished General
Secretary of the Churches of Christ in America, Dr. Charles S.
MacFarland; she also was expelled from the society on November
12, 1928, in the controversy which was climaxed by Mrs. Bailie's
expulsion. A graduate of Smith College, Mrs. MacFarland was
President of New Jersey's American Association of University
Women and an officer of the National League of Women Voters.
Her protest against DAR policies began when she publicly doubt-
ed statements made by Fred R. Marvin, source of much of the
material on alleged Communist activities collected by the organiza-
zation under Mrs. Brosseau and Mrs. Walker. Both Mrs. Mac-
Farland's chapter regent and the President-General refused to
listen to her protest.

Then in her 50's—about the same age as Mrs. Brosseau—Mrs. MacFarland wore brown hair in coronet braids and, also like Mrs. Brosseau, was attractive although no beauty. A damaging pamphlet which Mrs. MacFarland distributed both within and without the organization included affidavits from two members who swore they had received copies of the Black List from their state's National Defense Committee chairman, and that the state chairman verified that the list was authentic and authorized by the national society. The pamphlet charged that "men of prominence and unquestioned patriotism" had been black-listed by the society for alleged participation in a movement to establish a world Soviet. Such allegations, according to Mrs. MacFarland, were false fabrications.

As could have been expected, Mrs. MacFarland was ordered to appear before the National Board of Management and stand trial for "creating disunity in the society." She refused to appear but did submit sworn evidence in support of her charges. After her expulsion, she issued a statement in which she said: "They clearly intimated that they would like to be rid of me, and tried to intimidate me. . . ."

A dissenting Daughter from Witchita, Kansas, was the first to demand that the chapters be given a part in deciding the society's national policies. Mrs. Omer St. Roy had the courage to introduce resolutions on the floor of the 1929 DAR Congress making this proposal. She had come to the Congress prepared to introduce the resolutions, and with the support and knowledge of her Witchita chapter. But delegates found it hard then, as now, to oppose the society's top leaders. Mrs. St. Roy resigned her membership in the society, but the regent and secretary of her chapter wrote a letter to Mrs. Brosseau apologizing for her resolutions. After the Black List expose in 1928, eleven women resigned in a body from two New Haven, Connecticut chapters and a twelfth followed soon after. This protesting group included wives of Yale Professors Irving Fisher, internationally known economist, and William Lyon Phelps, almost equally well known writer (both gentlemen were included in the Black List). Also in the group were Mrs. Edward B. Whitney, widow of a former U. S. Attorney in New York City; Mrs. Hannah Townshend, first New Haven woman to sit in Connecticut's state legislature; and Miss Elizabeth W. Farnam, president of the New Haven League of Women Voters—all prominent in local and civic affairs. Mrs. Phelps and Mrs. Whitney signed a joint statement saying they resigned because they felt the organization had "adopted a policy which strikes at the root of American freedom."

Although the Black List received more public attention than the organization's militant defense policies, the latter cost the society more resignations. In 1930, under Mrs. Lowell Fletcher Hobart, resolutions were adopted so strongly denouncing disarmament and the World Court that a number of resignations followed. Their opposition was dramatized because President Herbert Hoover made a major policy speech at the DAR Congress advocating disarmament and predicting that the United States would enter the World Court.

The 1930 Congress was still in session when the wealthy and generous Mrs. William Thayer Brown of West Orange, New Jersey, resigned her membership. She sent her resignation to Mrs. Hobart, saying she had long been in disagreement with official policies, particularly regarding the Black List, disarmament and the World Court. At about the same time came the withdrawal of Mrs. Carroll Miller of Pittsburgh, a prominent Democrat, who had seconded the nomination of Al Smith for President at the 1928 Democratic convention in Houston, Texas. Mrs. Hobart said of these two resignations: "Just another attempt to use the DAR for peace propaganda."

The following week two more prominent women quit: Mrs. Lois Kimball Mathews Rosenberry of Madison, Wisconsin, wife of the chief justice of Wisconsin's Supreme Court; and Miss Margaretta Fort, West Orange, New Jersey, sister of Democratic Representative Franklin Fort and daughter of a New Jersey governor. Next, on May 16, 1930, nearly half of the members of the Stanford University Chapter in California resigned in protest against the "political activities and reactionary policies of the National Board of Management in regard to peace, disarmament and the World Court." This group, which included wives of two former Presidents of Leland Stanford University, Dr. David Starr Jordan and Dr. John Cooper Brannen, also protested against the "high handed methods of the DAR administration, by which chapters have no effective voice in the determination of the national policies of the organization."

Many of the society's most prominent members, beginning in 1890 with that self-appointed first organizer, Mrs. Flora Adams Darling, have been centers of controversy and fair game for the press. Mrs. Darling's career was a brief one and the next major figure on the scene was Mrs. Caroline Scott Harrison. A relatively inactive President-General, Mrs. Harrison lent tremendous prestige as the First Lady and seems, to this day, to inspire a kind of worship that the Daughters have accorded no other leader.

Long after the death of their first President-General, grateful Daughters built a dormitory in her memory at Miami University, Oxford, Ohio. Mrs. Harrison's Oxford associations were many. She had grown up there, the daughter of Dr. John Scott, President of Oxford Female Institute; and President Harrison was a graduate of Miami University, class of 1852.

In the earlier days when Presidents-General were uniformly the wives of prominent Washington officials, another favorite personality was Mrs. Adlai E. Stevenson. Her husband, Vice President of the United States, had earned President Cleveland's gratitude during the first Cleveland administration by taking on the unpleasant job, as First Assistant Postmaster General, of dismissing some 40,000 Republican postmasters and replacing them with members of the President's own party. And Mrs. Stevenson is the only woman in the history of the society to be elected President-General four times.

Mrs. Stevenson's immediate successors were wives of Cabinet members, and unopposed in their candidacy for President-General.

It was not until 1905 that the organization put on the first of its electoral battles.

In that year, the winner was Mrs. Donald McLean, a lawyer's wife who had been New York City regent for ten years. Partly a geographic choice, Mrs. McLean easily triumphed over her opponents—Mrs. Charles Lippitt, Rhode Island state regent, and Mrs. George M. Sternberg, who was opposed partly because she had lived in Indiana and three previous Presidents-General had been residents of that state. Opponents of Mrs. McLean whispered that if elected she would kill the Memorial Hall building project, and that she was unpopular with her own chapter. Countering, Mrs. McLean charged that her "great, cosmopolitan chapter" had been ignored for seven years, and added "I came to the Memorial Continental Hall ground-breaking ceremony with a spade which had been offered by the New York City chapter for this ceremony and had been unanimously accepted by the Congress of the previous year. But the spade wasn't used."

At the end of four years Mrs. McLean chose her successor— Mrs. Matthew T. Scott of Bloomington, Illinois, sister of Mrs. Adlai E. Stevenson and a woman of consequence on her own account. For many years Mrs. Scott had been active head of her business interests, including 20,000 acres of Illinois farm land. In 1908 she had distinguished heself by inaugurating an experiment in education for scientific farming. She sent forty farmers of her area, at her own expense, to take a short course in scientific agriculture at the University of Illinois.

Mrs. Scott was neither beautiful nor young. Over-plump, snub-nosed, she often wore a bonnet like Queen Victoria's. Mrs. Scott was opposed by Mrs. William Cumming Story, New York State regent, a pretty lady who knew how to make dramatic appearances at the right moment, and who attracted devoted followers. When the 1909 Congress had barely opened, according to the *Washington Post*, Mrs. Story already had worn one trunkful of gowns but had many more in reserve. On the defensive because she was backing Mrs. Scott, retiring President-General

McLean bolstered her spirits by wearing the most gorgeous outfit ever seen at a Congress event—trailing white crepe de chine with a train, black hat with blue ostrich plumes, and an emerald dog collar with matching bracelet. At one point during the Congress sessions, Mrs. Story, in yellow satin and a large black plumed hat, her arms full of flowers, walked slowly up the main aisle of the auditorium, only to be brusquely dismissed by Mrs. McLean because she had failed to answer when Mrs. McLean called for her regent's report. Nevertheless, Mrs. Story's dramatic appearance set off a frenzied demonstration by her supporters.

Loser by only eight votes, Mrs. Story tried again in 1911 and lost once more to Mrs. Scott, this time by 154 votes. On a third try in 1913 she was elected. The organization's most indefatigable office seeker, pretty Mrs. Story ran in four heated elections at two-year intervals, beginning in 1909 and ending in 1915, when she defeated a Daughter of an entire different type, Mrs. George Thatcher Guernsey,wife of a prominent banker in Independence, Kansas. Calling herself a "plain woman from Kansas," Mrs. Guernsey wore her straight hair parted in the middle and drawn back in a knot on the back of her head—she seemed almost like a Grant Wood painting come to life. Her evening dresses had cap sleeves, her floor length tailored suits were topped by small, severe hats. She ran on a reform program; its chief plank was three-year terms for Presidents-General and no re-election.

Although she lost to Mrs. Story in 1915, Mrs. Guernsey won in 1917 and quickly made a name for herself not only as a reformer (the three-year term was adopted), but also as a World War I President-General. Her 1917 election was a victory over three opponents.

In a 1919 speech, Mrs. Guernsey made statements that have been excellent ammunition for the society's critics, just as was Mrs. Scott's reference to "pink teas" in 1913. Both ladies meant well. Mrs. Scott was advocating a more realistic socially conscious program for the society, and Mrs. Guernsey was preaching the dangers of a population with foreign born, un-Americanized citizens. The "plain woman from Kansas" began by ridiculing British-aping Americans. "What," she asked, "can we hope for from the Americanism of a man who insists on employing a London tailor? Ten to one he will say 'bawth' for 'bath', 'bean' for 'been', and 'ither' and 'nither,' in violation of the best usage in England and America." Then she went on to deplore the tendencies of many foreign-born Americans to cling to the language, customs and even the food of their mother lands, and asked another question: "What kind of an American consciousness can grow in an atmosphere of sauerkraut and limburger cheese? What can you expect of the Americanization of a man whose breath always reeks of garlic? If I had my way, I would transfer thousands of Minnesota Scandinavians into the South, Wisconsin Germans into New England and New York Jews to the far West."

In their own fashion the Daughters did something about the Americanism of the foreign born. Meanwhile, their "plain woman from Kansas" served three years under the terms of the reform she herself had originated, and was succeeded by a lady of very different personality and background—Mrs. George Maynard Minor of New Haven, Connecticut, first unopposed President-General Candidate since 1901. Although Mrs. Minor was considered a wealthy woman it was during her administration that the Daughters authorized a $3,000 annual expense account for Presidents-General. This was reportedly done because Mrs. Minor could not—or would not—pay her own expenses as her predecessors had done. The yearly allowance since has been increased to $6,000.

Mrs. Minor's election in 1920 signaled the rise of Connecticut Daughters as "Queenmakers" in the society. Perhaps one reason she had no opposition was that 150 Connecticut delegates came en masse to Washington, moved into the Willard Hotel, set up Minor headquarters and passed out campaign buttons in pairs, one decorated with a picture of the Connecticut State flag, and the other lettered "Minor". The campaign was successful and Mrs. Minor for years was the grande dame of the DAR, most spiritual of all the Presidents-General. Recalling this New London personality in 1956, Mrs. William Sherman Walker described her as sharing her ocean front home with a friend, painting in her third floor studio and skippering her own little sail boat.

The chief claims to fame of Mrs. Anthony Wayne Cook of Cooksburg, Pennsylvania, are that her son was called a draft dodger when she ran for President-General in 1923, and that her husband gave two $5,000 contributions to Constitution Hall at the 1925 Congress. In her honor, the society planted a memorial "Cooks Forest" on family owned property. Within the organization she is known primarily for an unsuccessful attempt to win the society's support for the already doomed prohibition amendment to the Constitution.

Mrs. Lowell Fletcher Hobart of Cincinnati, Ohio, who succeeded Mrs. Brosseau, was made to order for the job in that period of frenzied militancy. Organizer of the American Legion Auxiliary, Mrs. Hobart joined Mrs. Brosseau in issuing the call for the first Women's Patriotic Conference on National Defense, into which Mrs. Brosseau led the unprotesting Daughters in 1927.

The immense popularity of little Mrs. Russell William Magna with her fellow members not only enabled her successfully to usher in a period of moderation but also to ride out the depression with its reduced membership.

Mrs. William A. Becker of Glen Ridge, New Jersey, balanced an aggressive campaign for teacher oaths with her own youth movement—helping poor "Becker Boys" and "Becker Girls". This movement, inspired by Mrs. Becker, flourished during her administration; in 1937, she was delighted to report that Massachusetts Daughters alone were helping more than one hundred "Becker Boys and Girls." Asked recently what happened to her youth program, Mrs. Becker replied: "Oh, I went out of office and I guess it was just dropped."

A former tennis star became President-General when Mrs.

William H. Pouch, World War II leader, was elected in 1941.
In addition to a multitude of war projects, Mrs. Pouch also
sponsored a youth movement in memory of her own daughter, a
lovely girl who died at the age of 16; Mrs. Pouch is "Aunt
Helen" to DAR Juniors. Several years ago, to get "Aunt Helen"
away from the rigors of the most recent and very hot election, her
wealthy husband took her on a world cruise with a group of
Daughter-friends, and from shipboard Mrs. Pouch merrily radioed
the 1956 Congress that she had been elected "regent" of the DAR
cruise party.

Chief problem confronting Mrs. Julius Y. Talmadge, successor
to Mrs. Pouch, was Clare Boothe Luce's "white artists" campaign.
Boosted for election as a business woman of ability who had managed her husband's cotton plantation and pecan groves after his
death, Mrs. Talmadge succeeded in riding out the segregation
storm. Since her term as President-General, she has served as
a member of Georgia's State Board of Education.

Chiefly noted for tackling the organization's last big building
job—remodeling and rebuilding its administrative offices at a
cost of $1,250,000, when building was so expensive that people
thought the society was crazy to think of such a project—is Mrs.
Roscoe O'Byrne of Brookville, Indiana, President-General from
1947 to 1950. She also led the Daughters in their successful
fight in state legislatures against world government tendencies.
Her successor, sweetly pretty Mrs. James B. Patton of Columbus,
Ohio, widow of a lumber dealer, promised the Daughters a vaca-
tion from moneyraising by launching no new projects during her
administration. She kept her promise and also put the official
magazine on a money-making basis by recruiting local members
to solicit advertising for issues assigned to states. This idea came
from Miss Gertrude S. Carraway of New Bern, North Carolina,
magazine editor under Mrs. Patton, and it helped win the
President-General's job for Miss Carraway in an uncontested 1953
election.

First and only spinster to be elected as head of the DAR, a

predominantly "housewife" organization, Miss Carraway's slogan was "economy, efficiency and expansion." In her final 1956 report she stated modestly that she had lived up to this slogan. She had renovated the twenty-five-year-old Constitution Hall out of magazine profits; kept expenses to a minimum; originated a plan to recruit new members and extract prompt dues payments from old ones; accumulated investments totalling $618,000, more than twice the $298,000 reported in 1953; and expanded the work of all the DAR committees.

There were some members who called the efficient Miss Carraway—another redhead who slightly resembles Mrs. Magna—a "dictator." This charge was especially hurled at the 1956 Congress when she ruled that there could be no applause from the floor for President-General candidates after their nomination, and thereby prevented the ladies from gauging the strength of their respective candidates by the applause method. Miss Carraway's own successful campaign for leadership was reported to have been backed by a wealthy North Carolina member, who according to the story, said she "would spend a million dollars to make Gertrude Carraway President-General."

An aftermath of Miss Carraway's administration is one of the minor amusing incidents in recent DAR history. Among Miss Carraway's innovations was appointment of the organization's first full time public relations employee. With the aid of her services Miss Carraway was able to put out and revise a number of booklets. Just before her administration ended, 10,000 copies of a very attractive library booklet were printed at a cost of several thousand dollars. Generously illustrated and printed in color, the striking booklet included a handsome view of the library with Miss Carraway herself in the foreground; also, although the Carraway administration was so soon to be over, names of Miss Carraway and other members of her administration appeared on cover pages, as well as a statement from the retiring President-General on the role of genealogy in history, family life, national pride and patriotism.

It was a good quote and the booklet was attractive and well-written; but apparently the new President-General, Mrs. Frederic Alquin Grove, did not care for the prominence it gave the retiring administration. She ordered new cover pages printed, and had them pasted over the originals. The new pages substituted the names of her fellow officers and a different quotation on genealogy from the new President-General, together with a foot-note explaining that "these booklets are being distributed for use temporarily until revision is available."

CHAPTER XIII

CHILDREN OF THE REVOLUTION

At the annual Congress in April 1936 complacency seemed to be the order of the day. The worst of the depression was over, the organization's controversial teacher oath campaign had not yet been launched, Mrs. William A. Becker's youth movement was doing nicely, the debt on Constitution Hall was almost paid, all appeared to be peaceful and happy in the DAR. But Mrs. George Thatcher Guernsey, the "plain woman from Kansas," who was getting to be an old lady, startled the Daughters, indeed frightened them, by the picture she painted of a very new problem confronting the society.

Mrs. Guernsey had a booming voice well known to her fellow members, an indomitable spirit and a DAR record second to none. Probably the most practical of all Presidents-General who had led the society through its history, she made a pronouncement at the 1936 Congress which was the essence of sensibility. Looking the Daughters over, she told them that they were getting old and needed young women to swell the ranks. She also warned them they would have to "change their ways" if they wanted to attract new blood.

"We cannot expect to recruit members from the many thousands of eligible young women unless we can offer to youthful energy, enthusiasm and intellect proper forums and opportunity for the use of their intelligent activity," said Mrs. Guernsey. "There are too many Junior Leaguers, university women and sorority girls who have not 'followed mother' into our society, for the simple reason that somewhere along the line we have become too 'sot in our ways'."

The Daughters never had ignored Mrs. Guernsey, nor did they ignore her now, though her warning posed a problem; how would they attract young women? DAR membership qualifications from the very beginning had made 18-year-olds eligible for admission; programs, as Mrs. Guernsey said, were "sot"; for half a century members had been following the same course. Could they change? And what could they offer that the other women's organizations did not?

More important, the Daughters never conducted membership drives or made open bids for new members. In its great past, the society had trouble keeping up with genealogical research on membership applications and its growth had been considerable in the early 1900's. It was not the Daughters' fault that they had lost some of the fine enthusiasm for Revolutionary history and heroes which had fired their predecessors; Mrs. Lockwood had warned that some time they would complete their self-appointed mission—the really great task of finding and marking Revolutionary graves, marking historic spots and restoring historic homes and buildings—and have nothing left to do. Patriotism had come to mean something different to members who were then growing old in the organization. They had lived through their period of most severe criticism, and had developed an almost professional stance of keeping their banners flying. But the Daughters had no recruiting experience.

Mrs. Guernsey had tossed them the gauntlet, however, and with characteristic determination they began the job of recruiting "Juniors".

In the DAR vocabulary, a "Junior" is a member from eighteen to thirty-five. She must establish eligibility like any other Daughter, and she must join a regular chapter; there are no "Junior" chapters. Once in, however, a Junior is not bound by the same restrictions as are her elders. Although she must pay her dues, she is not expected to support as many projects as are her "seniors". Because she is likely to be employed, in college or a young mother, she is "encouraged" but not required to attend the usual daytime chapter meetings. Also encouraged to have its own meetings, with tables of bridge, if they like, the Junior organization is more like a typical neighborhood club than a DAR chapter except that it is geared to the society's projects.

Juniors in chapters have no separate organizations of their own and no annual meetings except a Sunday night dinner preceding the April Congress. Always present and ready to declaim at the April dinner is the President-General; her remarks usually follow the line she will take when she makes later orations from the stage of Constitution Hall. Also during Congress week there is a Junior discussion meeting and the Juniors are allotted space in Constitution Hall for a bazaar at which they sell the usual bazaar articles to raise money for their only national project—a scholarship fund established in 1937. The girls aren't everlastingly pressed for donations, as are older members; they raise such moderate amounts as the $6,437.45 they collected in 1955-56 for their scholarship fund. This money sent eight children to the Daughter's school at Tamassee, South Carolina, and fourteen older students to Lincoln Memorial University, Harrogate, Tenessee, one of eleven schools approved and aided by the organization.

As with other DAR projects, the recruitment program is being carried out by a committee. A National Junior Membership Committee was created, and its chairman encouraged state societies to appoint state Junior membership committees. By 1942 there were committees in all of the forty-eight states, and the National Junior Membership chairman proudly presented Juniors to the Congress which met that year in Chicago. The Juniors entertained with an original skit, "Salute to the Women of 1776."

Accepting Mrs. Guernsey's challenge in 1936, President-General Becker had appointed a recognized leader as first director of Junior Membership—the wealthy and charming Mrs. William H. Pouch of New York City, who was well known as being on her way to the President-Generalship. She pushed the Junior Membership program vigorously, and made it a major project when she was elected President-General.

Evidence of the importance attached to Junior Membership is found in the society's handbook, detailing its organization and operations. The handbook urges every chapter regent to appoint a Junior-age member as chairman of Junior Membership and to organize and guide Junior activity within the chapter. It also recommends appointment of young women to serve on other chapter committees . . . . "to give them better opportunity to serve the society and learn DAR work by sharing in it. Juniors are capable and have good ideas—the number of young women serving as chapter and national officers is evidence of this."

The handbook says "the society has provided activities which are particularly appealing to young women, including 'paging' at state conferences or national DAR Congresses . . . . Pages usually return home with a new concept of the society and with a desire to enter into its work more actively." Other "activities particularly appealing to young women" are not defined, and a search of Junior Membership committee reports indicates only that the girl concentrate on scholarships and donations to schools, including payment of students' medical bills. In the handbook's reference to "paging" there is no mention of the pages' most glamorous reward for service—the traditional Pages' Ball. A standard Congress feature long before Junior membership became a major project, this is what the girls call a "lovely ball"— not a wallflower party, with too many girls and too few men. The Daughters see to that.

No better place than Washington could be found for a glamorous party given by generous and socially minded members. The nation's capital takes its social life—official and residential— seriously, with a social register, social secretaries and ladies who earn their livelihood by "arranging" successful debuts, with an adequate number of eligible young men, for the daughters of socially ambitious mothers. A pair of professionals who "take care of lists" for debut parties have been engaged by the Daughters for the pages' ball. "Taking care of lists" means seeing to it that the "nicest types of young men" are present. White House aides usually are there; nearby military posts, of which there are many, furnish young officers; foreign Embassies are staffed with many young secretaries and other attaches, who are delighted to attend; and, finally, hand-picked civilians complete the group which totalled 600 young men in 1953. The girls also are permitted to invite their own escorts if they wish to do so. "They're lovely girls and they have a perfectly wonderful time," said a young married page.

However, despite Junior Membership committee drives and encouragement from top organization officials the Juniors grew slowly. In the early 1940's the National Junior Membership chairman made no report of the numbers of girls enrolled but in 1942 her report showed that Juniors in thirty-one states were sufficiently strong to hold state assemblies—Junior meetings. In 1947 Maryland had only 40 Juniors, all closely associated with their senior chapters; Colorado 51; California 150; Illinois 245; Georgia 700; Connecticut 390; Maine 64; Massachusetts 120; Michigan 300; Mississippi 150; Missouri 99—and so through the state roster. Pennsylvania led with 750, but in general more Juniors were recruited in southern states than in the north.

In 1956, when the overall membership was at an all-time peak of 185,000, Miss Louise J. Gruber of Drexel Hill, Pennsylvania, national Junior Membership chairman, proudly reported that for the first time the Junior total had reached five figures, with 10,061 members. This may have been due, at least in part, to the Honor Roll set up by President-General Carraway, giving chapters yearly gold stars if they met all requirements on a twelve-point Honor Roll list—one point being the addition of at least one Junior member to each chapter. Only a year earlier, in the latest revision of the Handbook, "lack of junior membership" was called the "chief DAR weakness," and the Daughters were told "nothing is more important to the growth of our National Society than increase in Juniors." But even with the Junior membership reported in 1956, the 1955-56 Junior increase was only 1776, while net general membership that year went up 11,542. In 1957 no new figures were reported.

In small chapters, with few members, the Handbook urges

encouragement of Junior activities. "In small chapters it is not always feasible for Juniors to meet separately on a regular schedule, but they can hold occasional meetings of their own," members are told. "Small groups should not be discouraged—some of the most interested and active Junior committees we have today began with only three or four girls."

In 1956 there was a practical demonstration of Junior interest when eight Juniors gave the Congress something new in election campaigning. The eight—attractive young women from all over the country—campaigned for their mothers, who were candidates for top offices on the winning ticket headed by Mrs. Frederic Alquin Groves. They put out their own campaign literature, headed "Juniors for Groves." Plugging for Mrs. Groves' platform as "giving social recognition to patriotic and historic programs for the young people of our time," the girls promised to "accept the torch from our mother's hands, hold it high and meet the challenge to carry on the work of the DAR, not only now but in the immediate generation of the future." They also told delegates that some of the eight Junior campaigners are third generation DAR members, "now have children who are members of the Children of the American Revolution, and thus are integral representatives of four generations with the National Societies, CAR and DAR."

Children of the American Revolution are a DAR youth group which started much before the Juniors, but has grown very slowly and never has had an impressive membership. Actually in early DAR years, the proportion of Children as compared with Daughters was much higher than it was in 1957, when there were about 17,000. In 1910, the CAR had 10,000 members; in 1924, it had grown to a record 24,000, but ten years later had dropped to 12,000 and 21 years years later, in 1955, it had increased by only 2,000 to 14,000.

One weakness of the CAR, according to some Daughters, is the wide spread in the ages of its members. Children with a bona-fide Revolutionary ancestry—subject to the same requirements as for the DAR—may belong from the minute of their birth until their twenty-second birthday.

As an extreme example of early enrollment, the CAR magazine for June, 1956 featured a picture of a "prize winning baby" who became an applicant for CAR membership ten hours after her birth. The baby is Deborah Lucille Rouse of Dallas, Texas, whose mother and grandmother are Daughters and whose CAR papers were filled out and taken to the hospital when the mother became an obstetric patient. As soon as the infant was born, the papers were completed with name and date, rushed to the Dallas airport, and put on the first plane for Washington, where they arrived ten hours after Deborah's birth. They were approved at the CAR Board meeting on December 6, when Deborah was three weeks old, and at the CAR national convention in April, 1956, Deborah won another distinction; she was given a silver spoon in absentia, in honor of her birthday on a patriotic holiday, Armistice Day, 1955.

Children of the American Revolution were established by the Continental Congress on February 22, 1895.

Still under the DAR's maternal wing, CAR business offices and museum gallery are on the second floor of Constitution Hall, and its board room on the third floor of Memorial Continental Hall. It has senior and junior officers, its societies usually are sponsored by DAR chapters, and its senior officers must be members in good standing of the DAR, Sons of the American Revolution or Sons of the Revolution. Junior officers are CAR members and are elected each year, but ranking Daughters usually head the CAR as National President, national officers and national vice presidents. Among past CAR National Presidents were the wives of a former Governor of Iowa, a Congressman from Montana, and a prominent judge of the highest court in the District of Columbia.

The creator of the CAR was a New England Daughter, Margaret Sidney, the popular author of *Five Little Peppers and How They*

Grew, and many other children's books. Miss Sidney, whose real name was Harriet Mulford Stone, showed writing talent at an early age; her father was one of the earliest professional architects in New Haven, Connecticut. None of her books was as successful as the *Five Little Peppers,* but her output was chiefly responsible for the success of the publishing firm headed by her husband, Daniel Lothrop, whom she married in 1881. The Lothrops bought and lived in "Wayside", Nathaniel Hawthorne's home at Concord, Massachusetts.

The Lockwood-Regan history of the society tells the story of the CAR's founding with many words of admiration for the founder and for the youth group. "It was small wonder," wrote the two early historians, "that from Mrs. Lothrop's loving heart and sympathetic nature should have emanated the beautiful thought of organizing the National Society of the Children of the American Revolution. The conviction that such a move was a necessity and not a sentiment had taken deep root in her alert brain. None but a woman full of tender solicitude for the youth of our country and concern for their future development along patriotic lines would have given the subject the serious consideration which demanded unremitting effort and great sacrifice of time and strength."

Continuing their paean of praise for Mrs. Lothrop, "whose fortunate environment and habit of life early led to serious reflection upon the necessity of implanting in childhood settled principles and fixed trends of thought," the two ladies reported, "She was reared in an atmosphere instinctive with child love and her ardor in child development was not lessened by her marriage to Mr. Daniel Lothrop, who was called the children's friend. . . . At home and abroad Mrs. Lothrop finds herself the object of admiration and affection, not only of the children of myriads of households, but of thousands of mothers who bless her for her true and natural interpretation of child life."

The revered Mrs. Lothrop made a dramatic appeal to the Congress on February 22, 1895, when she urged the authorization of the youth group. "Surely," she told the Congress, "the women of America are, by their Godgiven offices of mother and sister, set apart to do this very work; and the DAR are again set apart from all other mothers and sisters because of their membership in the sacred cause for which the Society works." Her appeal was so well received that Mrs. Lothrop immediately drew up a constitution for the children's organization and submitted it to the Board of Management in April, 1895; it was approved, and Mrs. Lothrop was made Honorary President for life. She also served as National President of the CAR for six years, organized its first society—the CAR calls its groups societies, not chapters—in Concord on May 11, 1895, and sponsored the first CAR public meeting on July 4, 1895, at the South Meeting House in Boston. At the end of that year the new organization had 58 societies and 318 members who, if divided evenly among the 58 groups, would have made an average in each small group of a half a dozen members.

The Handbook lists the objectives of the CAR as identical with those of the DAR, but adapted to the needs and understanding of youngsters. It is, in fact, a co-educational DAR in miniature. The CAR's began by imitating their elders; a month after their first meeting, a tablet was placed on an historic elm tree in Stonington, Connecticut, by CAR societies at Stonington and Westerly, Rhode Island. Later the Westerly society, named for Lieutenant Colonel Samuel Ward, grandfather of Mrs. Julia Ward Howe, also dedicated a tablet in honor of Colonel Ward, one of the more interesting heroes of the Revolution. A well-to-do young man, son of a Governor of Rhode Island, Colonel Ward was among the first Revolutionary War volunteers. He fought through the entire seven years of the war, survived with Washington the terrible winter at Valley Forge, and later became a successful New York businessman who enjoyed the exciting experience of being the first American to visit the Far East, which he did in 1788. His illustrious grandaughter, Mrs. Howe, delivered the address when the tablet was presented in 1904.

Like the Daughters, early "Children" did their bit in the Spanish-American War. The Little Men and Women of the '76 Society, Brooklyn, contributed to the Woman's National Relief Fund during that brief struggle, and the Blue Hen's Chicken Society, Wilmington, Delaware, erected a memorial drinking fountain at a cost of $3,000 in honor of Lieutenant Clark Churchman, a Delaware officer who was a Spanish-American War casualty.

Less than a year after its establishment in 1895, the CAR movement had leapfrogged across the Continent to the Pacific Coast, when on February 1, 1896, twenty-eight charter members were admitted to the first CAR Society in San Francisco, named for a forgotten Revolutionary boy hero, Valentine Holt. At the age of thirteen, Valentine had "with bravery and fearlessness delivered messages as a courier, his pathway beset by marauding bands of Indians and still more dangerous English troops." Eluding both Indians and English, he survived the Revolution and lived to the ripe old age of 80. When 77 years old, Valentine Holt applied for a Revolutionary War pension and lived only three years to enjoy it. The Society named after him flourished until the great 1906 earthquake, when its members were so scattered that although efforts were made to reunite them, the Society never was reorganized.

Less expensive than the DAR, the Children's group charges only $3.00 initiation fee and $1.00 annual membership dues. In a concession to Juniors, the Daughters permit twenty-two-year-old CAR girls to transfer to the DAR with no initiation fee, and still another youth bargain is a charge of 15c for two CAR application blanks, original and duplicate, which go through the genealogical mill of the parent organization.

In 1951, when the "Children" had about 12,500 members, Mrs. Donald Bennett Adams of New York, National President, reported it was just about holding its own at that level from year to year. Calling the Daughters to task, she pointed out that there was an "appalling loss" of CAR members who were dropped for non-payment of the $1.00 yearly membership dues—a trend which she "could not blame on the young people." Not the children but their elders pay their dues, the National President complained. "And," she said, talking to the elder Daughters like a Dutch aunt, "you should have more pride than to allow this to happen." As for grandmothers, Mrs. Adams had a special message for them: "After all, if you are a grandmother we know you are over 21." The forthright National President also wanted to know, speaking from her knowledge of CAR booking, why the entire 1951 crop of 22-year-old girls hadn't been transferred to the Daughters. . . ."Why is it that only 132 of the 419 transfer cards issued to 22-year-olds were used?" she asked. "Give us members and keep them members. Your own future membership is at stake," Mrs. Adams warned.

In 1954 the Daughters took steps to insure more concern about the CAR. The annual Congress authorized a National Children of the American Revolution Committee—which, strangely enough, after all the years since the CAR was founded, had been missing from the long list of national committees. Working to establish a closer relationship between the Children and DAR leaders and members, and encouraging CAR committees in DAR chapters, the new national committee no doubt can be given credit for recent Children's membership growth. But in 1955 the picture still was discouraging. In that year the youth society admitted 2341 young people—more than the number of new Juniors in 1956—but registered a net membership gain of only 489, having lost 610 members by resignations and dropped 464 for the non-payment of dues.

Reporting a new membership drive in 1956, a headquarters staff member said this would emphasize the recruiting of boys to offset the preponderance of girls brought in by the Daughters, who as a much stronger organization than the "Sons" recruit more children. Also, this headquarters staff member added, the Children's organization had suffered because the sponsoring Daughters had been inclined to treat it like an only child, with a smothering domination. The boys and girls were now being given and were enjoying more responsibility.

Actually, so far as official recognition of the Children is concerned, the Daughters do little except bring two small CAR's to the opening session of each annual Congress. Dressed in Colonial costumes, wigs, powder and all, the pair solemnly present the President-General with a bouquet, and this by-play usually gets the little Colonial-costumed boy and girl into newspaper pictures. Children selected for this honor ordinarily are very special members—sometimes grandchildren of current top officers.

Despite its miniature organization and small headquarters offices, CAR has its own museum next door to its offices on the second floor of Constitution Hall. Opened in 1951, the museum features relics chiefly of interest to children; a Colonial doll house, with tiny Colonial garden; a dust-proof, moth-proof, lighted case filled with a collection of dolls in costumes of many countries; a tiny glass punchbowl and six cups used by a little Louisiana girl of long ago; a silver spoon given by a Revolutionary soldier to his little daughter; and heirloom doll dishes of famous Spode and Staffordshire china.

The convention of the Children is held immediately after the DAR Congress each year. Although the Children's projects closely resemble those of their elders, their conventions feature sightseeing and fun, with little or no politics and practically no long-drawn out reports and speeches. Nearly 500 youngsters, mostly between the ages of 14 and 21, attended the 1954 convention. In 1956 delegates trooped through the White House like other tourists, went to the Washington, D. C. Chapter House—a fine old residence at 1732 Massachusetts Avenue, N.W.—for a "get acquainted" reception; had a Dutch treat dinner at one of Washington's best hotels, with waiters and waitresses wearing Colonial garb in their honor; put on an "annual stunt night", with patriotic flag skits; sandwiched business into one morning session, including a message from President Eisenhower praising the youth organization's "patriotic achievements," made a sightseeing tour of the capital, and then went "formal" for a dinner-dance in the ballroom of another large hotel. Decorations carried out the theme of the "Golden West," in honor of Miss Diane Weller, University of Southern California student who was Junior National President in 1955-56. On Miss Weller's table was the CAR museum's perfect miniature of a covered wagon—an exact imitation of the Conestoga wagons which crossed the continent in California's gold rush; and on the driver's seat were Miss Weller and her father in miniature, perfect doll replicas.

Guest speaker at the dinner was Representative Craig Hosmer, California Congressman representing Miss Weller's district. He presented the young lady with an American flag which had flown that day in her honor atop the dome of the United States Capitol. (Members of Congress often thrill their constituents by giving them flags which have flown from the Capitol dome. Employees of Congress run up the presentation flags for a brief period, then haul them down again and turn them over to the solons.) After dinner there was a dance and, according to the CAR magazine, the ballroom was filled to capacity with "beautiful belles and their handsome escorts," who won "countless lucky number prizes." After all this there was a strictly CAR coke party, with seniors excluded, given by Miss Weller and other retiring junior officers for their newly elected successors. "The party was a fitting climax to a wonderful day," the magazine reported.

The CAR convention ended on a distinctly religious and patriotic note. The boys and girls went to the Washington National Cathedral for a memorial service; to Arlington Cemetery and Mt. Vernon to lay wreaths on the Tomb of the Unknown Soldier and the tombs of George and Martha Washington; to a CAR tree on a Mt. Vernon hillside, where they installed newly elected officers "while mocking birds furnished music for the impressive ceremony;" and to the Mt. Vernon picnic grounds for a box luncheon. After lunch they stopped at the Old Presbyterian Meeting House churchyard in nearby Alexandria, Virginia, to visit the Tomb of the Unkown Soldier of the Revolution, erected by earlier CAR's in 1929 and a continuing shrine of the youth group. Here a wreath was laid by a Virginia CAR, Miss Frances Ivy Jordan,

Junior State President, and after this ceremony the boys and girls planted a tree in the churchyard, with Junior Presidents of all northern Virginia societies participating.

In Alexandria, George Washington's home town, fine old houses line the streets in a downtown Colonial section, bordering the Potomac, while sprawling suburbs have added miles of apartments, houses and shopping centers in the outskirts. Prominent in the Colonial section is Gadsby's Tavern, popular meeting place of Revolutionary days, where George Washington presided over a public meeting to celebrate the signing of the Constitution, and where Lafayette slept when he came back to America in 1824 as a national hero of the new republic for which he had fought. Gadsby's Tavern was restored by Daughters and Children, the Children having full responsibility for several of the rooms as their part of the restoration job. The old tavern, surrounded by cars and parking meters of the present, is a constant reminder of the past.

In 1957 about a thousand youngsters attended the organization's 62nd annual convention with a similar program. By way of honoring Bob Barr of Houston, Texas, junior national president for that year, a special plane from his home town brought Texas-shaped sandwiches with an olive marking the spot where Houston is located. A New Orleans lass named Nancy Ann Kern won an award because she was the 800,000th member taken into the national society.

Junior DAR's and Children of the American Revolution imitate their elders by raising money through small contributions for organization projects but of course in more modest sums. In 1955-56, for example, the Pennsylvania Juniors collected almost $1,400 for building and equipping a playground for the Tamassee School; District of Columbia Juniors planted an acre and a half of fruit trees at Tamassee, and Nebraska Juniors "adopted" a student at a school for Indian girls. In 1954-55 the Children adopted mountain schools as their national project. They collected $500 for an electric meat saw at Tamassee, raised another

$500 for an underground silo at the DAR Alabama school, and $1,100 for an electric organ at a third school on the Daughters' approved list. For their 1956-57 national project, the Junior Board recommended the restoration of a little chapel near Jackson, Mississippi.

In World War II, both youth groups concentrated on war projects. Juniors operated their own motor corps and in several states mechanics' certificates were earned by determined girls. They transported patients to clinics, served as volunteers in hospitals and homes, joined the WAVES, SPARS and WACS, bought "locators" for the armed forces—those metal detectors used to locate bits of shrapnel or other metal in the bodies of wounded servicemen. In one year alone they put in more than 534,570 hours of Red Cross service; made and filled 16,000 buddy bags (gifts for service men); gave money for a blood plasma project; sent home-cooked food to Army and Navy posts; entertained servicemen; made cookies by the thousand for USO service men's centers; worked on salvage drives; sold bonds and stamps, met troop trains, and knitted socks for the Coast Guard.

In the same year Children of the American Revolution raised $2,000 for a Red Cross ambulance, oversubscribed the $2,000 by $450 and immediately started to raise another $2,000 for a clubmobile to be used by the Red Cross overseas. Junior President William S. Berner of New Jersey brought greetings from 12,000 CAR members to the 1943 DAR Congress and told the Daughters: "As boys and girls of 1776 took an active part in the War for Independence, so boys and girls of today have a definite work to do for their country. The boys and girls of 1942-43 are taking an active part in the war for the preservation of freedom." Mrs. Pouch, President-General, wrote in a 1942 issue of the DAR magazine that "Letters from CAR members who are in service far from home, sound a note of confidence and acceptance of conditions. . . ."

Naturally, in the Daughters' tradition, both youth groups have their own insignia. Juniors, who of course are entitled to wear the regular DAR insignia, have a simple Junior membership bar pin, while CAR insignia is a complete and separate line, from membership pin and ancestral bars, to official pins and bars for Senior and Junior officers and a grandmothers' pin, not to speak of CAR teaspoons, baby spoons and forks, charm bracelets for girls and tie holders for boys. The American flag and American eagle are featured in the design of the CAR membership pin or emblem, together with the words "Children of the American Revolution." No ribbon, however, is worn by the Children; their insignia is a pin to which can be attached a bar lettered with the official title of the wearer—Promoter, Chairman, National or State Officer, etc. Prices begin with $16 for the membership pin, but this and other pins may also be had in silver gilt at lower rates.

Grandparents are prize commodities in the children's organization. There is no grandfather's pin—grandfathers of Revolutionary ancestry are supposed to be Sons of the American Revolution, and the CAR is a DAR-sponsored group. But the CAR has grandmothers' and grandfathers' committees, which award honorable mention to CAR Societies with grandfathers and grandmothers with the largest number of grandchildren enrolled in the organization.

Once children are enrolled in the youth group, they apparently find themselves exposed to education in the DAR tradition, with emphasis on American history and the flag of the United States. True to this tradition, the CAR magazine for June, 1956, reported an original skit on the history of the flag, written and presented by members of the Sarah Randolph Boone Society at a Vicksburg, Mississippi, DAR meeting. With an immense American flag in the background, nine children in Colonial costume dramatized the history. One child displayed a duplicate of the first liberty flag flown on the village green at Taunton, Massachusetts, on October 21, 1774, in defiance of the British; another produced a copy of the flag carried by Revolutionaries at the Battle of Bunker Hill, featuring New England's green pine tree symbol, while a third

and fourth followed with the Revolutionary Minute Men's flag—
a coiled rattlesnake on a solid yellow background—and the flag
of George Washington's regular army, resembling the United
States flag but still carrying the British King's colors. Finally,
a little girl dressed as Betsey Ross climaxed the show with the
original Stars and Stripes Betsey made on commission from Washington after the Declaration of Independence was signed in 1776.

Another juvenile historical contribution is a refreshingly brief
history of George Washington, written by Tommy Carter, a nine-
year-old from Whittier, California. Concentrating on the high
spots of the great man's career, Tommy reported that Washington's father gave him a horse and when he went to school "he was
one of the strongest boys." Then George's father died when he
was eleven, they were poor and George could not go to school,
Tommy continued. "When he was teen-age he went to see his half
brothers. They were very rich. His half brothers had been soldiers and he wanted to be a soldier. When he was twenty he became a soldier. The government sent him with a message to the
Red Coats. He met some Indians on the way and they showed him
the way. He got back safely. . . . They had a war. The Americans won the war and Washington went home. . . . After a while
they wanted a president and wanted George Washington to be president. He was president for eight years. He died in 1799. He
was 67 years old."

Thus the DAR provides, in effect, patriotism from the cradle to
the grave.

CHAPTER XIV

WASHINGTON HEADQUARTERS

Gradually, over a period of half a century, the Daughters have built and financed their Washington headquarters, which they proudly call the finest "ever built by women for women." A monument to their courage in four times planning and carrying out a building program, their block-size headquarters structure is flanked on the right by the Pan American Union Building, which Andrew Carnegie financed as a contribution to friendly relations among the American republics. To the left is the American National Red Cross Building. The White House is only three blocks distant and the Lincoln Memorial just a litle farther. For blocks in all directions there is no privately owned commercial real estate.

The last of the society's great builders is Mrs. Rex Hays Rhoades of Washington, who directed a $1,250,000 construction project in the years between 1948 and 1950. In 1947 Mrs. Rhoades was elected Treasurer-General and thus assumed much responsibility for remodeling and expanding the organization's administrative offices. Her job was complicated by high building costs which increased the total bill for this final building project from an estimated $900,000 to $1,250,000. Aided by a sense of humor, Mrs. Rhoades gaily and efficiently buckled down to do this big job, but when it was over she was ordered to bed because of high blood pressure.

The DAR Washington headquarters overshadows that of any other national women's organization in the Capital even though the American Association of University Women, the General Federation of Women's Clubs, the Order of the Eastern Star and the National Women's Party also have some fairly impressive real estate in the city. The AAUW is the owner and occupant of a four-story town house which was the Russian Embassy in pre-Soviet days and boasts something the Daughters lack— a Russian ghost or at least the legend of a ghost who at one time was believed to haunt it. The General Federation of Women's Clubs is ensconced in the former home of General Nelson A. Miles, noted Civil War cavalryman and Indian fighter. His stables have been converted into a smart, small restaurant, with the horses' stalls preserved and polished to add atmosphere. The Order of the Eastern Star is housed more grandly in a vast limestone mansion built as the home of a former Washington multi-millionaire, Perry Belmont. The National Woman's Party owns fine property on Capitol Hill—a handsome brick residence with walled garden, which was donated to the feminist group by one of its chief supporters, Mrs. Oliver H. P. Belmont, a New York and international social leader. However none of these structures can begin to compare with the Daughters' marble and limestone grandeur.

To obtain funds Mrs. Rhoades "sold" every last bit of the buildings from the foundation to the ladies' rooms—to chapters, state organizations, wealthy members and others not so wealthy. She even sold sections of outer walls to state societies, but with one reservation:—"I said I wouldn't have any bronze markers on exterior limestone," she laughs. Thus money was extracted more or less painlessly for the last building project, through the organization's pet formula for raising funds.

The headquarters buildings are literally dotted with big and little commemorative bronze markers and plaques. There are markers in honor of state regents and in memory of deceased relatives, markers testifying that the state societies have paid for large blocks of the various buildings, and even markers on the seats in the auditorium of Constitution Hall. Plaques or markers affirm that a marble basement entrance was "bought" by Oklahoma Daughters; that a wall was dedicated by Michigan members to 88-year-old Mrs. Henry B. Joy of Detroit who held many posts but never was elected President-General; that a south corridor was paid for by West Virginia DAR's; that a first floor drinking fountain was installed in honor of Mrs. Julius Y. Talmadge by her Georgia chapter; that the business office was "bought" by Georgia members. And so on throughout the block size structure.

To help pay for Constitution Hall, members bought auditorium seats at $150 each, and according to a DAR story, some thought they really owned the seats and could claim them at Congress sessions. Actually the buyers were only entitled to have the seats marked in memory or in honor of some friend, relative or DAR dignitary. When Constitution Hall was renovated in 1955-56, Mrs. Haig of Silver Spring, Maryland, Buildings and Grounds Committee chairman, reported that some of the seat markers had disappeared and that workmen had removed and replaced more than 16,000 screws when they took off all markers as part of the renovating job. Mrs. Rhoades "sold" so many bits and pieces of the 1948-50 project that she ran out of markers, and Mrs. Haig had similar trouble when she "sold" new chairs for state boxes to state DAR's as part of the 1955-56 renovation. The engraver couldn't keep up with her orders.

The formula of selling markers to pay off the mortgages on their handsome buildings was devised by the organization more than half a century ago, when the first and most beautiful of their headquarters structures, Memorial Continental Hall, was erected. Insisting on the utmost in quality, those DAR pioneers built Memorial Continental Hall of pure white Vermont marble, and in the low priced construction days of the first decade of 1900, it cost only $638,965.94. Even the Daughters could not afford white marble nearly a quarter century later, when they built Constitution Hall of limestone, paying $1,825,000 for it; or when they erected their first administration building at a cost of $385,-000; or when they remodelled and expanded the administration building in 1948-50.

Actually, however, there is no architectural or esthetic conflict between the white marble of Memorial Continental Hall and its limestone neighbors, all joined in the solid block-size headquarters structure. The sections were equally well designed, by outstanding architects. Fronting on Seventeenth Street, Memorial Continental Hall has a fine Colonial pillared main entrance and to the right an open portico with 13 great carved marble columns representing the thirteen original states of the Union. Just as impressive is the opposite side of the block-size structure fronting on Eighteenth Street—the main entrance to Constitution Hall which is also pillared with architectural grace. And framing the administration building are some small lots of green lawn, trimmed hedges, and flower beds in which tulips and irises bloom each spring. An early resolution set aside life membership and charter member initiation fees for a building fund. The fund thus established grew rather slowly at first. When the first Continental Congress was held in February, 1892, the treasury had accumulated only $650; in 1900, with a rapidly growing organization, it had reached $50,366.07, and in 1902, $82,190.57.

In 1902 the DAR's bought the site of Memorial Continental Hall for $50,266, demonstrating a sound approach on real estate values. Although at the time this site was swampy, undeveloped land and they were called "foolhardy women" for buying it, actually it is a site second to none in Washington.

Mrs. Charles W. Fairbanks was the President-General who had the courage to abandon hope for free land from the U.S. Congress, call a meeting of the Memorial Continental Hall building committee and launch the building plan. A committee on architecture was appointed and the committee selected an expert adviser— Professor William R. Ware of Columbia University—and next held a national competition to choose an architect. On October 11, 1902, the twelfth anniversary of the organization's founding, ground was broken on the $50,000 site. Mrs. Adlai Stevenson described this ground-breaking ceremony in her early history of the DAR—a momentous but not a cheery occasion, as she pictured it. The day was dark and it rained almost continuously, but that did not deter the Daughters from attending in large numbers.

"The tent which had been erected over the platform was crowded with national officers, state regents from many distant states and distinguished guests. . . . Mrs. Fairbanks broke the ground with a spade made of Montana copper, gift of Montana Daughters; the handle made of wood cut from the pathway followed by Lewis and Clark as they wended their way through the western wilderness, part of which is now Montana. The handle is to be inlaid with wood from other historic spots and adorned with silver and gold from Montana mines and Montana sapphires of blue and white, the colors of the society."

After Mrs. Fairbanks delivered an "inspiring address," wrote Mrs. Adlai Stevenson, a collection of $492 was taken up for the building project, and a slab of granite was donated by a dealer in stone, to mark the spot where ground had been broken. This was still only vacant land with no immediate prospect of construction, because the Daughters had run out of money. Later a block of white marble was sent from the White House to mark the spot, but instead was kept to be placed in the interior of the building. Where it was placed is now not known; but wherever it is, the inscription bears evidence of Mrs. Harrison's administration: "From the home of the First President-General to the Daughters of the American Revolution."

Nearly two years passed before the cornerstone was laid on April 19, 1904, during Congress week. The cornerstone was appropriately in charge of the Masonic Order and was accompanied by Masonic Rites, with lighted candles on the four corners of the cornerstone, an intoned service and a gavel used by George Washington in laying the cornerstone of the Capitol Building on September 18, 1793. A year later, however, the Daughters put on their own dedication program in the presence of a large and enthusiastic audience. The building wasn't finished, but, Mrs. Stevenson wrote, that "mattered not. . . . At last the Daughters, after years of arduous struggle, were literally under their own roof. They had each and every one contributed in dollars and in cents, some in large gifts, others in contributions by states, so that every Daughter felt she had a personal interest in our Home." For the dedication ceremony, evergreens, wreaths, roses, flags and elaborate wall medallions hid the unfinished interior. The gleaming white marble walls were in place, but the roof was temporary and later had to be replaced. Again the Daughters had run out of money.

In April, 1905, Mrs. Fairbanks went out of office after increasing the Memorial Continental Hall building fund to $175,000 and spending all of this except $2,000. Her successor, Mrs. Emily Ritchie McLean, took over the project and had an immediate stroke of good luck. The dedication ceremony had paid dividends. Inspired by the sight of their partly completed white marble temple, enthusiastic members contributed $50,000 to the building fund at the congress that year. Still, though this response was very encouraging, Mrs. Stevenson reported that $50,000 was "wholly inadequate to the demands upon their treasury and the financial situation looked very bad. Then Mrs. Stevenson reported an energetic move by Mrs. McLean, who, she wrote, "was equal to the exigencies of the emergency. With a courage that bordered on daring, Mrs. McLean borrowed $200,000 from the American Security and Trust Company and this enabled the Memorial Continental Hall Committee to meet its obligations and complete the most beautiful and perfect building in the National Capital."

Spending the $200,000, Mrs. McLean evicted sparrows that had made their nests in the temporary roof; finished wings on either side of the Memorial Continental Hall Auditorium; bought and installed auditorium seats; put in plumbing, electricity and a heating system; and left the building a completed structure when she went out of office in 1909. She also left a disputed final account of $28,000 with the builders, but that was settled amicably by her successor, Mrs. Matthew T. Scott.

Finishing touches were added by Mrs. Scott, first President-General to preside over an annual Congress in the Memorial Continental Hall auditorium. Almost beside themselves with joy over their new building, delegates heard their President-General suggest that they were like priestesses " in a temple whose votaries worship at a shrine dedicated to God and country. . . . Custodians of sacred, historic memories and of noble traditions of public service, we stand as it were upon a moral and spiritual eminence, holding aloft the high ideals for which our fathers died proudly and gladly with a smile upon their lips, and which must be preserved pure, unsullied and intact, if our nation is to retain the proud title it gained in Revolutionary days—that of being the political and moral leader of mankind." Mrs. Scott concluded: "My prayer is that we may keep our motives as pure as these white walls and our deliberations and actions as harmonious as the perfect proportions of this symphony in stone."

Mrs. Scott was hostess at the first notable reception in the new auditorium in 1911—"notable not only on account of the elegance of the costumes and uniqueness of the surroundings," wrote Mrs. Stevenson, "but especially so on account of the distinguished guests, representing every phase of official life in Washington and almost every foreign country."

An additional $52,564.87 was contributed to the Memorial Continental Hall fund during Mrs. Scott's four year administration but even with this encouraging increment, the debt was to trouble the organization for years to come. It tried various schemes for money-raising, such as a DAR cruise, a "Penny-a-day" plan with members literally using the penny bank method to get a $3.65 contribution together in a year; and the so-called "Block plan," named for its originator, wealthy Mrs. Willard T. Block of Chicago. This plan provided that members be asked to buy one dollar certificates, each certificate contributing 90 cents to reducing the mortgage. The organization's official jeweler, J. E. Caldwell & Co. of Philadelphia, printed the certificates and received ten cents in payment for each one sold. By 1915, $15,000 had been raised in this way and 70,000 certificates still were on hand. In that same year, however, Mrs. William Cumming Story, popular President-General, ran into trouble over the Block plan, when it was revealed that Caldwell & Co. had not been paid $8,000 due them for their ten-cent share of the selling price of each $1.00 certificate. With no explanation forthcoming as to why the $8,000 had not been paid over, there was popular demand that this deficit should be paid out of the society's treasury. Resourceful Mrs. Story successfully opposed this demand by reporting that Caldwell & Co. had agreed to accept payment gradually over a five-year period, and two years later, in 1917, Caldwell cancelled the obligation on which $7,855.61 was still outstanding, calling it a contribution from the firm to the Memorial Continental Hall fund.

In 1915, the $60,000 balance still due on the building fund mortgage became a campaign issue when Mrs. George Thatcher Guernsey of Kansas ran against Mrs. Story, who was up for a second two-year term. Ever practical, Mrs. Guernsey figured that $60,000 could be painlessly eased out of current receipts over a three-year period, and her campaign literature explained how this could be done. The society then had 100,000 members, each of whom paid $1.00 annual dues to the national treasury, while another $10,000 came in each year from initiation fees. Out of this $110,000 income, Mrs. Guernsey proposed to set aside $20,000 each year to liquidate the debt, and thus wipe it out in three years.

Regardless of this attractive financial proposal, Mrs. Guernsey was defeated, but she ran successfully in 1917 and the balance due on Memorial Continental Hall was paid off that year.

The Daughters' "bits and pieces" purchase plan first began on the Memorial Hall project when state societies bought a series of "state rooms" in the white marble temple. Flanking the Hall's auditorium on three sides, the handsomely designed state rooms belong to the state organizations and are handsomely furnished by them in period decorations. Each year during Congress week, delegates from all over the country go from room to room gazing admiringly at polished mahogany furniture, rich hangings, beautiful rugs, mantels, mirrors, and grandfather clocks—all collected and cherished by the state organizations, and many highly valuable as authentic antiques.

These twenty-seven rooms are in charge of the museum curator, under the general direction of a committee and a professional consultant. Almost every year one state or another replaces hangings, changes the color schemes of walls and woodwork, or adds new antiques. Planned to depict different types of home surroundings in households of the Colonial, Revolutionary and federal periods, and to preserve in them gifts and cherished heirlooms of members, the rooms constitute an authentic series of little museums, each a beautiful example of early Americana.

Most of the states reproduced parlors, drawing rooms or dining rooms. Maryland's parlor centers around an Empire mahogany sofa which was used by Thomas Jefferson when visiting in the home of the original owner. In Iowa's parlor are prized wooden book ends made of old wood from the White House roof replaced in 1927; the donor was Mrs. Herbert Hoover, an Iowa Daughter. Vermont's typical small New England study is furnished with genuine Vermont antiques, and New York's handsome drawing room with elaborate Colonial pieces. In the Texas music room are an 1830 spinet piano, one of the first harps made in America, and early American music books. Alabama's small reception room features a mahogany desk-bookcase, floor to ceiling height, which was owned by William Rufus King, the first Vice President of the United States elected from the South. California's cozy sitting room is similarly furnished with heirlooms.

New Jersey's room is one of the most historic. It reproduces a formal chamber of the Jacobean period, with handsome wall paneling and hand-carved furniture made from wood of the British frigate "Augusta", sunk during the battle of Redbank, on October 23, 1777, and raised through contributions from chapters and individual members in New Jersey. The room takes its inspiration from the dignified period decor in the "City" of London—the British capital's financial district. Portraits of New

Jersey signers of the Declaration of Independence hang on the walls, and stained glass windows picture the state's historic participation in the Revolutionary War.

Massachusetts members faithfully reproduced a sitting room of a well-to-do family in the Revolutionary period and furnished it entirely with original antiques from that state. The room features a rare grandfather clock and a framed portrait in needlework. It also boasts a wooden mantelpiece taken from a revolutionary home in Dorchester, Massachusetts, and set in the brick of the home's original construction.

Virginia adorned the President-General's dining room with a shining mahogany Hepplewhite dining table removed from the home of a prominent Revolutionary Virginian, Judge Henry St. Clair Tucker of Winchester. Kentucky's southern parlor is decorated with wallpaper of an early floral design, an historic mantel, a fine overmantel mirror with gilt frame, a pair of brass andirons and a Sheraton mahogany sofa. Louisiana reproduced a typical courtyard of the early days in that state; there are authentic copies of cast iron furniture, an especially designed hand-wrought iron gate with matching window gratings, and other reminders of yesteryear.

Oklahoma's kitchen might have come from almost any early American home, its huge fireplace built of original brick from a farmhouse on a road over which Washington's troops marched on their way from Valley Forge. A chair and kettle came from the same farmhouse, and an old pine cupboard is an original from the home of a Rhode Island Daughter. Kitchen utensils are heirloom gifts from members in every state of the Union, including pewter platters and plates decorating the mantel above the fireplace. A huge iron poker now in the room was the only means of defense left to the wife of Sergeant James Taylor of Massachusetts when her husband fought in the Revolutionary War. In a children's attic, sponsored by New Hampshire, are children's furniture and belongings from the past—hooded rocker cradles, childsize rocking chairs and straight-back reed chairs, small tables set with porringers and other old fashioned dishes, and cradle linen.

Many other fine furnishings of the building were gifts from member groups. Massachusetts chapters paid for one of three pairs of memorial bronze entrance doors and Connecticut members another; a Washington, D. C. society woman, Mrs. Francois Berger Moran, volunteered to raise money for the third and finally paid off the last $1,400 installment herself. Pennsylvania chapters donated the entrance hall, as evidenced by the state's coat of arms, done in bronze and sunk in the marble floor. A Rutland, Vermont, chapter had the "honor" of placing the inscription "Memorial Continental Hall," across the front of the building, above sixteen massive columns supporting the roof of the front portico. The south staircase, leading from entrance hall to second story, was a gift of Minnesota Daughters, and Minnesota's coat of arms decorates the wall above the first turn of this staircase. A Brooklyn chapter gave the matching north staircase, and Vermont members added mahogany hand rails. Auditorium light fixtures were bought by New York, Kansas and Baltimore chapters. A massive table and chairs for the auditorium stage (specifically designated for use by the President-General) are reproductions of similar pieces in the room where the Declaration of Independence was signed; they are the gifts of District of Columbia chapters. Furniture for stage boxes and dressing rooms was presented by chapters in Kentucky, Massachusetts and Wisconsin.

As further contributions to the building project, state organizations furnished the Memorial Continental Hall offices for national officers and headquarters for clerical employees. The business office was furnished by Missouri, the historian general's office by Ohio, and so on. Ten pairs of sliding doors, right and left of the auditorium, were gifts of New York, District of Columbia, Illinois, Connecticut, Michigan, Colorado, and Minnesota chapters. Display cases for the Daughters' first museum of Revolutionary relics were installed in space which could be shut off from the auditorium by closing the sliding doors; by opening them, and filling the museum space with chairs, auditorium capacity could be increased.

Thirteen monolithic carved columns, forming a portico memorializing the thirteen original states, were presented to the society by chapters or legislatures of those states; and Illinois chapters gave the pediments on this memorial portico—one of the building's finest architectural features. Early members took so much pride in the memorial portico that in 1913 they planted thirteen ivy plants from George Washington's grave near the columns, and each of the thirteen original states sent a representative to the ceremony.

Only a few years after they were free of debt for Memorial Continental Hall, the Daughters began another building project. Their first administration building was completed and occupied in 1923, at a cost of approximately $385,000. Vastly grown, the organization had needed more office space and in 1920 President General Guernsey appealed for it by describing the conditions under which headquarters employees were working. She noted, for example, that sixteen clerks in two small rooms processed several thousand application papers each year; a similar group in the Treasurer-General's office was crowded into three small rooms and handled $1,094,882.61 in DAR funds during Mrs. Guernsey's three-year term of office. Mrs. Guernsey convinced her fellow members that they must have better administration offices, although construction of the administration building did not begin until her term of office was over.

At that time the organization had not acquired the solid block site of their present headquarters structure. For this site they paid $207,419.88, buying it in three parcels but making sure to buy far enough in advance of need so that no other purchaser would get the additional lots. This property is bounded by Seventeenth, Eighteenth, C and D Streets, and the society was able to get a number which gives them many a patriotic thrill—1776 D Street!

Having completed their administration building, the Daughters might well have been expected to rest. But not so. Still in debt for the adminstration building, they took on their largest building project of all—Constitution Hall, for which they began planning in 1925, also at the suggestion of the influential Mrs. Block of Chicago. Despite the successful completion of Memorial Continental Hall, some members demurred when they first talked of Constitution Hall, even though the Congress had overflowed from their own auditorium into a rented commercial auditorium nearby.

As early as 1922, even before the administration building was completed, Mrs. Minor, successor to Mrs. Guernsey, warned the Daughters that "we have outgrown our hall." Adding up figures Mrs. Minor showed there were more voters at annual Congresses than there were Memorial Continental Hall auditorium seats, which could accomodate 1800 and by use of museum space, 1900. First exploring the possibilities of enlarging the auditorium, they were advised against it by the building's architect, who said it could be done but would ruin the architectural beauty of the auditorium and its fine acoustic properties.

Mrs. Guernsey, the building committee chairman for the administration project, announced in 1922 that half of the $385,000 cost had been paid off and was given authorization to borrow the remaining $187,061 needed to finish this project. Also reporting that the organization itself would finance the actual construction cost, Mrs. Guernsey said various states and members "had requested the privilege of furnishing rooms in the new building and paying for special features." Connecticut, she said, would take over the President-General's office and spend $2,000 for its decoration and furnishing; New Hampshire would spend $1,000 on the Corresponding Secretary-General's office; Children of the American Revolution $1,500 for a committee room; Pennsylvania Daughters $2,700 for two committee rooms; and the National Officers' Club (the Daughters' most exclusive inner group, made up of current and past elected national officers) would assume responsibility for a special assembly hall, spending $10,000 on decorations and furnishings.

It was three years after Mrs. Minor's warning that the society had outgrown its hall before Mrs. Block made the first Constitution Hall suggestion; in 1925 she proposed a million-dollar auditorium. Mrs. Block's suggestion was taken up by influential Mrs. Anthony Wayne Cook, then President-General, who appointed a committee with Mrs. Brosseau, Treasurer-General, as chairman, to study the matter. In 1926 Mrs. Brosseau was elected President-General. At the same Congress which elected her, Mrs. Brosseau proposed a $2,000,000 auditorium and suggested a financing plan; she said bonds should be floated for $1,000,000 and the remaining $1,000,000 raised by the membership. The cost of the auditorium was a little less, $1,825,000, but bonds were floated for $1,000,000, as Mrs. Brousseau proposed, and in 1927 had been oversubscribed and a total of $425,499 had been pledged toward the balance.

Mrs. Russell William Magna, the lady named by Mrs. Brosseau as chairman of the Constitution Hall finance Committee travelled 52,000 miles in three years on her money-raising mission. At each Continental Congress in that period, she took the President-General's microphone and fervently roused pledges of more funds. In 1925, when the project was only a suggestion by Mrs. Block, delegates pledged more than $500 a minute in a money raising hour, promising to give an initial $35,000 for the project; when Mrs. Magna sprang into action as the society's "little gold-digger," they exceeded this record. By 1928 Mrs. Brosseau was able to report that the deficit was "rapidly being reduced"; a year later she announced $1,000,000 had been raised by the Daughters' chief financing plan, through the "sale" of auditorium seats to individual members at $150 each, boxes to state societies at $1500 each and platform chairs and library book units to members or chapters, in addition to cash and pledges.

Money continued to come in for this large project—a phenomenon of the organization is the fact that all its money-raising has been done through its own methods and under its own leadership, without spending a nickel for professional money-raising assistance. In 1929 the Constitution Hall fund reached $1,075,000 in cash and pledges, and was given a $25,000 check by Mrs. Brosseau's husband, Mack Truck President A. J. Brosseau, who had promised this contribution as soon as the million-dollar point had been reached. In the same year, Mrs. Magna reported a new device for money-raising sales to Daughters and DAR groups; space in the new building had been "sold" by the cubic foot, she said, to make it possible for small contributors to feel the pride of ownership. Also 5,870 feet of foundation had been "sold" by the foot.

Actually, Constitution Hall was not paid for in full until 1941; but in 1935 Mrs. Magna, then retiring after three years as President-General, reported that the biggest part of the job was done and that during the nine years since she began raising money for the auditorium, cash pledges had been redeemed almost 100 per cent. "We have never had even a 2 per cent shrinkage in pledges," Mrs. Magna proudly announced, and added "As Finance Chairman, I have given nine years of my life to Constitution Hall."

With Constitution Hall completed, the Daughters entered a new field. They began to book concert artists, symphony orchestras and lectures each year, and after a brush with the tax collector, they were put on the tax-paying list of Washington real estate owners. Previously they had enjoyed tax exemption as a non-profit educational and patriotic society and so they were surprised and chagrined when on September 21, 1934, the District of Columbia government dunned them for $20,908 in real estate taxes and notified them that unless they paid, the big auditorium would be sold for taxes. With money coming in from auditorium rentals, the society could no longer be called a nonprofit organization and District of Columbia business men financially interested in a nearby commercial auditorium (ironically, the very one in which the annual Congresses were held while Constitution Hall was under construction) objected to unfair competition from the tax free hall, which also was much more attractive than its commercial neighbor.

After several legal flurries, the organization capitulated and agreed to pay real estate taxes based on their anual rental returns from the hall, but not on the total value of the property. These tax payments since have gone up to about $16,000 a year. Incidentally, the nearby commercial auditorium soon afterwards gave up and was turned over for Federal Government office space.

In 1929, at the dedication of Constitution Hall, Mrs. Brosseau had predicted that a new administration building would follow; but it was nearly 20 years later when the Daughters grumblingly voted to spend $900,000 for remodeling their first administration building, adding a new section to replace a glassed walkway leading to Memorial Continental Hall.

Some of the members thought that on account of high post-war prices, it was no time to build, but others balked at the plans proposed by Mrs. Rex Hays Rhoades, Treasurer-General, for the transformation of their treasured Memorial Continental Hall auditorium into a genealogical library. Since 1925 the old auditorium had been virtually idle, and in 1946 District of Columbia fire inspectors refused to allow its use except for small gatherings because it lacked adequate exits. The District DAR held three meetings there a year, but otherwise it was silent and empty between elections, when voting booths were set up on its small stage.

Mrs. Rhoades argued and cajoled. She told 1948 Congress delegates that the society's financial record was so good "we are now able to borrow $200,000 at $2\frac{1}{2}\%$ interest on our reputation alone." To those who grumbled that "it was no time to build", she replied: "The District of Columbia Red Cross is preparing plans for a $2,000,000 building. So why is it no time for the Daughters to build?" In due course the delegates approved the $900,000 project, and a few hours later Mrs. Rhoades placed orders for structural steel. When she emerged from a Congress session with the favorable vote in her pocket, Constitution Hall's building manager jokingly told her there was a steam shovel out front and asked if she wanted it to go right to work. "That isn't as foolish as it sounds," she replied. "We have plans ready and we're going to work right away."

The building was completed in 1950, before Mrs. Rhoades went out of office. But in that year she had to tell members that the project had cost $300,000 more than had been expected. Later, when the Korean War sent prices still higher, the $1,250-000 investment was a bargain.

This amount was raised by pledges at annual meetings and by the Daughters' own "sales" method. Mrs. Rhoades ran out of doors, rooms, bookstacks and museum cases. She then "sold" tables, desks, chairs, books, and lamps, thereby raising another $4,000. North Carolina members paid for all the ladies' rooms in the remodeled building and Illinois' chapters bought the entrance door and stairway for $22,000. Miss Katharine Matthies gave $8,000 in addition to $25,000 for the O'Byrne voting room. An ancient box elder, dating back to George Washington's time, was sacrificed to make room for the expanded structure, and its wood was cut up into flag stands and book ends, which were sold very quickly. Pledges at the 1949 Congress totalled nearly $125,000. Delegates pledged the price of the hats on their heads, wore corsages made of dollar bills and turned the corsages in for the building fund. In 1950 the debt stood at $550,000; by 1951 it had been reduced to $390,000, and in 1953 an unpaid balance was wiped out by profits from the society's magazine.

Since then, the only headquarters money raising project was a small flurry at the 1956 Congress, when President-General Carraway interrupted the program to ask delegates to "buy" new chairs for Constitution Hall boxes and stage, as part of the first quarter-century renovation and redecoration of the hall.

In a few minutes they had bought nearly 100 chairs at $40 each, leaving only a few as a liability for the National Society. Announcing the auditorium had been lightened with grey damask seat upholstery and grey tile flooring, Mrs. Haig, Buildings and

Grounds chairman, proudly reported that "We expect to save twenty per cent on electricity bills with this lighter color scheme." She neglected to mention the cleaning bills.

The $1,250,000 project provided a beautiful modern library and a small museum; specially welcome is the new voting room which has tremendously simplified the annual balloting.

One very wealthy member, the previously mentioned Miss Matthies of Connecticut, (reportedly worth $7,000,000), offered $20,000 to build and equip the needed voting room. Mrs. Rhoades asked the architect if that would "cover" the cost of the room and he replied, "It would be better if you had $25,000." So Mrs. Rhoades long-distanced Miss Matthies and told her she couldn't have the voting room for $20,000 but she could have it for $25,000. Miss Matthies cheerfully paid the extra amount.

The new library now is a prized possession. The auditorium's sloping floor has been levelled (the seats were sold to a church for $5,000) and uncomfortably steep balconies have been slightly changed, but not enough to spoil the original architectural effect; handsome carved wall paneling was left undisturbed, as were right and left stage boxes; former museum space was transformed into a working area for genealogists. A central figure is the big reading room occupying the former auditorium bordered with flags of the forty-eight states, the District of Columbia and the United States territories. At the farther end, overlooking what once was the auditorium stage, is a Rembrandt Peale portrait of George Washington reportedly worth $20,000. Reading tables with shaded lamps fill the center auditorium space area and bookshelves are crowded with 45,500 bound genealogical volumes.

Another prized possession is the museum—a long, handsome room with open alcoves for exhibits and beyond these an archway framing a dominating and dramatic full-length portrait of Martha Washington in a red gown. The alcoves are like miniature museum galleries, in which some displays are permanent and others changed from time to time. One duplicates a Colonial parlor, with fireplace, bric-a-brac and Colonial furnishings, all of historic value. Among others are a toy alcove, an alcove featuring early American silver; and several for men's accessories of the Revolutionary period — yellowed lace stocks, knee breeches, buckled shoes, high-collared coats; others for china and early glass, for Revolutionary weapons, uniforms and military accoutrements.

At the entrance end of the museum is a "provincial section," in which are the oldest DAR relics—pewter,wooden and tin articles used by the pioneers in the most primitive period of Colonial life. The outstanding pewter item historically is a charger which bears this inscription: "In 1776, during the New Jersey campaign, George Washington was served pork and beans from this platter at the home of Colonel Daniel Maning." And displayed with the pork-and-beans charger is a carving set which belonged to Francis Scott Key, composer of "The Star Spangled Banner."

Alcove museum cases are fitted with silk, velvet and cotton lining chosen by experts to set off the treasures they contain. Mrs. Cecil Norton Broy of Arlington, Virginia, first curator of the new museum, suggested the alcove design and worked with Miss Genevieve Hendricks, a prominent Washington interior decorator, in the exceedingly meticulous task of finding the right shade for each case and for the museum walls and ceiling. Miss Hendricks hand dyed some of the fabrics; for example, silk dyed the same shade of Williamsburg silver green used on walls and ceiling is the background for china with decorations including that elusive shade.

For heirloom baby clothes they chose cotton chintz, copying an authentic Revolutionary design of tiny rosebuds on pale blue. Soft gray-blue velvet shows off two silver teaspoons made by Paul Revere, and a silver teapot given by Dolly Madison to one of her friends as a wedding gift. Miss Hendricks donated 100-year-old material for case linings. The handwoven red silk wall hanging behind Martha Washington's portrait was contributed by New York silk manufacturer Franco Scalamandre.

Since the museum curator also is in charge of furnishings or replacements in the state rooms, Mrs. Broy had responsibility for the choice of many other fine fabrics. Every piece of upholstery material, every yard used in hangings, is carefully selected. Prices run as high as $25, $30, $35 and even $40 a yard for narrow width silks and satins. The most expensive fabric in the entire group of buildings is $40 a yard material in the New Jersey state room.

The society's museum collections include 7000 different items. Mrs. Broy tells of an elderly Daughter who one day came hurrying through the museum, followed by a taxi driver carrying a hooded mahogany cradle, an heirloom which had belonged to her family in New Jersey. "My nephew is coming to see me this afternoon," she explained. "He wants this cradle as a container for firewood. I'm going to see that it isn't used for firewood. Babies in my ancestors' families have been rocked in this cradle. Once George Washington came to see a baby in this cradle."

To be accepted by the museum, heirlooms and other relics must date back at least to 1830. Many of those offered are worthless as museum pieces; for example, in 1953 the *Washington Daily News* reported that 700 pairs of donated salt and pepper shakers were stored in the museum basement. Beginning with the gift of one beaded bag, the museum collection now includes more beaded bags than can be displayed at one time; it also has innumerable snuff boxes, shawls, (notably, a priceless shawl that belonged to Martha Washington); and spectacles, among them pairs that belonged to Benjamin Franklin, John Paul Jones, and a private in the Revolutionary Army. The soldier's spectacles have a broken iron rim of one lens tied together with a piece of string.

In the jewelry display cases are Martha Washington's mourning pin, worn after George Washington's death—black onyx circled by twenty-four pearls and containing a lock of her husband's hair at the time he died; also a locket containing hair of both Thomas Jefferson and his wife; the mourning pin worn by Patrick Henry's second wife after his death; Henry's finger ring inscribed with his memorable fighting words—"If this be treason, make the most of it"; several rings given by Napoleon to Lafayette; Dolly Madison's earrings; and a lyre-shaped brooch made of George Washington's hair.

In the parlor is John Hancock's desk, beautifully preserved, side by side with a Chippendale sofa which belonged to one of the less famous signers of the Declaration of Independence, Thomas McKean of New Jersey. On a Pembroke table next to a wing chair is an open Bible, and on the Bible John Paul Jones' spectacles. Dolly Madison's fan case is a box two feet long. Martha Washington's teapot, from which she served soldiers at Valley Forge, is a permanent exhibit; so also are three of her initialed silver spoons, used by the Washington family when the seat of government was in New York following George Washington's election to the Presidency. In the glass collection are seven or eight wine glasses that belonged to Dolly Madison; Patrick Henry's big punch bowl; and huge flip glasses worth $100 apiece (flip was a hot drink enjoyed by DAR ancestors, who passed the glass from mouth to mouth with blissful disregard for sanitation).

In 1957 the museum added a replica of Mrs. Harrison's "orchid" gown; carefully reproduced and containing a few surviving remnants of the original material, notably some of the black satin which lines the train. The gown is made of soft grey, heavy lustrous imported silk, with touches of lace and a grey beaded stomacher. For the admiration of 1957 delegates, it was worn by a show case type figure, roped off at one end of the museum and flanked by potted orchids. The grey silk, with the small orchid design woven in the fabric, was reproduced by the same Scalamandre firm that manufactures so many magnificent silks and satins for the DAR.

One of the museum's oldest pieces of furniture is Daniel Boone's rush bottom chair. It speaks of the wilderness, just as John Adams' handsome mahogany chair and John Hancock's polished mahogany desk are silent evidence of the early culture and comfort of Eastern colonies. Another eloquent reminder of daily living among our forefathers is a copy of America's earliest primer, with ABC's in small letters and capitals on one page, and The Lord's Prayer on another.

There is, of course, a system which must be followed whenever state rooms are redecorated or gifts offered for the rooms or the musum. These rooms are owned by the District of Columbia and twenty-six states—Ohio, Missouri, Tennessee, Maryland, New York, Texas, California, New Jersey, Maine, Wisconsin, West Virginia, New Hampshire, Louisiana, North Carolina, Illinois, Iowa, Vermont, Alabama, Indiana, Michigan, Massachusetts, Delaware, Virginia, Kentucky, Rhode Island and Oklahoma. Each state has a room committee, which always includes the state regent, and which must confer with the Curator General in order to make certain that the furniture meets specifications. Pieces must have been made in the state, used there for a long time, or imported for use by some early citizen of the state. Authentic window treatments of the Revolutionary period are copied, and varied from room to room for educational purposes.

The same care is exercised in choosing color schemes for state rooms. For example, Mrs. Broy explains, in the Illinois room "We used a shade of Hamburg red, which was the first color our ancestors used—they made it by pounding brick into powder. For this background Miss Hendricks dyed curtains an exquisite shade of green—she dyed half a dozen samples before she got the exact shade."

Museum donations are subject to screening in states and at DAR headquarters, Mrs. Broy explained. A state museum chairman is given a description of the proposed gift, and she transmits this information to the museum. The gift is received on approval and may or may not be accepted. The organization wants articles that are historic or that belonged to patriots, and does not want duplicates of items already in the museum collection. Under any classification, the accepted gifts must date back to years before 1830 .

The Daughters have certainly housed and decorated their beloved society munificently.

CHAPTER XV

ORCHIDS AND INSIGNIA

When the average American thinks of a DAR he probably pictures a plump lady of more or less uncertain age wearing orchids and a broad blue and white ribbon. These are only part of the trappings—there are almost countless pins and badges which Daughters proudly wear and jealously guard. Delegates have been wearing orchids at their Congresses for a long time, but no one seems definitely to have established the origin of this tradition. President-General Gertrude S. Carraway shed some light when she announced in 1956 that the society had discovered a direct connection between their traditional fondness for the exotic flower and their revered first President-General, Mrs. Caroline Scott Harrison.

The apparent connection was discovered by Mr. Frank E. Klapthor, who succeeded Mrs. Broy as curator and who also is the first man to be employed at headquarters in a professional capacity. The new curator noticed a wild orchid design woven in the silk dress which was worn by Mrs. Harrison in the portrait which was being restored for display purposes. Was it possible, thought Mr. Klapthor, that Mrs. Harrison had a penchant for orchids and may therefore have initiated the orchid tradition?

Mr. Klapthor followed his clue to the Benjamin Harrison home in Indianapolis, a museum of relics of the Harrison family and administration. There he found evidence that Mrs. Harrison had been fond of orchids, that she had been an amateur artist of some ability in water color and china painting, and that orchids were prominent in a collection of her water colors. Moreover, Mr. Klapthor learned that a white orchid water color, done by her in 1890, was lithographed a year later and distributed from the White House "in dedication to the mothers, wives and daughters of America." Reporting Klapthor discoveries, Miss Carraway added that three delicate pink orchids are pictured on a hand-painted plaque owned by Mrs. Marthena Harrison Williams of Washington, D. C., granddaughter of President and Mrs. Harrison.

Apparently the connection between Mrs. Harrison and their orchid corsages was news to the Daughters, but Mrs. Carraway liked the idea and felt inspired to authorize new and beautiful orchid note paper. This paper features four reproductions of orchid designs from Mrs. Harrison's water color collections and china paintings and was attractively boxed and labelled "A First Lady's Floral Notes." In 1956, 5000 of these boxes were put on sale at the Congress, with proceeds going to the Museum fund.

To publicize the Klapthor theory, Miss Carraway held a press conference and told reporters that Mrs. Harrison was responsible for introducing orchids in White House greenhouses, that she wore them to official meetings of Cabinet wives and at DAR functions, and: "The Daughters have worn them ever since." Miss Carraway provided the reporters with a good quote. There is a story, she remarked, that "if a lady wears one orchid it means she has a genuine admirer; if she wears two orchids, she has a generous husband; if she wears three orchids, she has a boy friend; if she wears four or more, she's a DAR."

A Washington florist, Granville Gude, has supported the Klapthor theory. Mr. Gude says he can recall that as far back as 1919 and 1921 the Daughters were wearing orchids. "They wore more orchids in the 1920's than in the 40's and 50's, and not because orchids were cheap, either," he said. "They were more expensive in the 20's than in the 50's."

A well known Washington newspaperwoman, who is herself a Daughter and has covered more annual Congresses and known more prominent DAR figures than any of her colleagues, Mrs. Vylla Poe Wilson, long-time reporter for the old *Washington Post*, and the later women's editor for the *Washington Times Herald*, does not recall that the Daughters wore orchids before 1920 and adds, from her recollection, that before World War I violet corsages were popular particularly at Easter time, which roughly coincides with the Daughters' annual gathering.

A search of newspapers dating back to the early 1900's seems to support Mrs. Wilson's recollection. When pretty Mrs. Story ran for President-General in 1909, she entered Memorial Continental Hall carrying a huge bunch of flowers. In the same year a great bouquet of roses was presented to Mrs. McLean, retiring President-General, by adoring Kentucky Daughters. At a luncheon given by her admirers after her election as President-General in 1913, Mrs. Story, whose first name was Daisy, carried a bouquet of daisies. Going back to the Daughters of Mrs. Harrison's day, a picture of the founders shows the ladies in long-sleeved, high-necked sober black dresses, without a flower.

In the 1920's however, DAR orchids started making news. The press mentioned, for example, a bouquet of white orchids which was presented to Mrs. Anthony Wayne Cook, President-General, in 1925, at a luncheon given in her honor by Daughters from her home state of Pennsylvania. In the 1930's and 1940's, the orchid trend apparently was even more impressive, and Mrs. William A. Becker, 1935-38 President-General, led with seven orchids in a bouquet and an orchid shoulder corsage, worn on one occasion, and with a corsage of fifteen orchids worn on another. In 1947, at an official DAR reception, newspapers reported that ladies in the receiving line wore two to five orchids each. In 1941 Mrs. William H. Pouch, wealthy New York Daughter, wore a spray of orchids at one function and carried a large bouquet of orchids at another.

Since World War II the Daughters have fairly bloomed with orchids. At the 1955 banquet ending that year's Congress, the National Broadcasting Company's Grand Old Op'ry star, Minnie Pearl, gave up an engagement in New York to fly to Washington and entertain the banqueters. Miss Pearl was surprised when Mrs. E. Ernest Woollen of Baltimore, banquet chairman, presented her with an orchid. "But I already have one," said the entertainer. President-General Carraway—wearing three herself

—chided almost seriously: "What's wrong with wearing two?"

In one recent year the Washington florist who has the exclusive concession to sell flowers at the annual Congress estimated he would sell 300 corsages—chiefly orchids—a day during Congress week. That same year the *Washington Daily News* predicted that Daughters would buy $5000 worth of corsages during their visit to the national capital.

Fond as they are of orchids, members are no less fond of their Society's insignia. Founding Daughters gave time and thought to the selection of a design for the insignia and also for the Society's seal, both effectively featuring the old-fashioned spinning wheel. Their official membership pin is a beautiful small emblem.

The story of the origin of the insignia has been told by Mrs. Mary S. Lockwood and her collaborator, Mrs. Emily Sherwood Regan. Their account, however, differs in several details from the offically adopted record which appears in the DAR pamphlet *Early History, Daughters of the American Revolution*. The Lockwood-Regan account gives credit to Edward Robey, son of charter member Mrs. Edward Robey of Chicago. The official story credits it to G. Brown Goode, once head of the Smithsonian Institution, whose wife was second chairman of the Insignia Committee. Mr. Goode, a member of the DAR Advisory Committee, secured a patent for his design and transferred the patent to the Society; his claim was not disputed before the Patent Office by Mrs. Robey or her son.

Both accounts agree that the first Insignia Committee was headed in 1891 by Miss Sophronia P. Breckenridge of Washington and that she left for a European trip before any design had been approved. A number of designs were solicited by Miss Breckenridge's committee, principally from jewelers, but everything submitted was too elaborate or inappropriate. Mrs. Lockwood's book says that at this point Mrs. Robey, who was a heraldry expert, suggested the spinning wheel as a symbol, and then her son drew a design based on her idea. The official account, quoting a letter from Mr. Goode, says that the design was drawn at the

Smithsonian by Mr. Goode, assisted by Paul Brockett, and that he had not seen any design by "a Mr. Robey (*sic*)".

An 1891 issue of the *Adams Magazine* reported that the leading jeweler asked to submit designs was Tiffany and Company but that they offered such ornate suggestions that they were turned down. Daughters agreed, the magazine said, that whatever design was adopted should be simple, in keeping with the frugal living of Revolutionary days.

In Mrs. Lockwood's account, Mrs. Robey is represented as going to a Philadelphia jeweler, Joseph K. Davidson, and asking him to work up some designs based on her son's idea. "The Society is small and would appreciate liberal terms," she wrote Davidson. The latter apparently submitted three designs embodying the spinning wheel motif. No action had been taken on them at the time Miss Breckenridge left, to be replaced by Mrs. Goode, and there is no evidence that the Davidson designs were made available to Mr. Goode before he drew the design which was finally accepted and patented.

J. E. Caldwell & Company of Philadelphia offered to assume the expense of making dies for any design chosen by the society. This offer meant a saving of several hundred dollars. The firm became the official jewelers of the Daughters of the American Revolution." It still holds that position; it has to date sold insignia to nearly 500,000 members.

The spinning wheel, symbolic of home, is also the central theme of the DAR seal. The seal pictures a woman seated at a spinning wheel, above which are 13 stars representing the thirteen original states; below is the DAR motto "Home and Country" and the dates "1776-1890" circled around the seated figure.

The design for the insignia was officially adopted by the board of management on May 26, 1891; it is a golden spinning wheel 7/8" in diameter, with 1½" distaff of platinum, the rim of the wheel blue enamel and stars around the circumference representing the thirteen original states. Patented September 22, 1891, this insignia design is DAR property and no manufacturing jeweler may use it without written consent of the organization. Caldwell and Company, exclusive manufacturer, pays the society 50c royalty on every insignia pin sold to the members; and keeping a tight curb on this property, the society allows the jeweler to sell insignia pins only on permits issued by headquarters to properly certified members.

The manager of Caldwell's insignia department, Mr. Frank Kulp, has served the Daughters through many administrations but says not even he can recall the complete history of the society's insignia. Through the years, it has added pin after pin. There must be at least 200, Kulp estimates.

With the official insignia goes the characteristic blue and white ribbon which is pinned to the wearer's left shoulder and from which the insignia is suspended when worn officially. A gold loop hooks over a tiny pin sewn to the reverse side of the ribbon, making the insignia a pendant, and folds back to hide itself when the insignia is worn as a pin. With it goes the member's ancestor bar pin, which is attached to the upper end of the ribbon and affixes the whole to the wearer's shoulder.

The price of the unadorned insignia was $17.75 in 1957. Varied to suit the purse of the buyer, a diamond set in the hub of the spinning wheel raises the price of the pin to $200; and with other jewels added it could go up to $3,000. The most ornate variation is a pin set with precious or semi-precious stones mined in the original thirteen states—moonstones from Delaware, amethyst from Pennsylvana, willemite from New Jersey, laxulite from Georgia, tourmaline from Connecticut, rubellite from Massachusetts, serpentine or gold quartz from Maryland, chatoyant or garnet from South Carolina, aquamarine from New Hampshire, spessartite or amazon stone from Virginia, quartz crystal from New York, pyrope, emerald or fleches d'Amour from North Carolina and thesis hair stone from Rhode Island.

Each new member is entitled to buy and wear the spinning wheel insignia, one ancestral bar and the official ribbon. Made on hand looms and specially dyed to get the right shade of Colonial blue, the ribbon is inch-wide heavy watered silk, with blue center and white edges, ends folded and sewn to a point. DAR rules say the ribbon must be worn over the left breast and must not be longer than twelve inches—no matter how many official DAR decorations or ancestral bars a Daughter may collect (and some collect ancestral bars literally by the dozen). It is not hard for a member who really works at it to accumulate more official pins than can be spaced on a twelve inch ribbon. She may, for example, have been a chapter regent, state officer in four different capacities, a member for twenty-five years, a committee member for the annual Congress and chairman of a special committee, thus earning eight pins or badges, the maximum for a twelve inch ribbon. If she earns more, she buys another ribbon.

Not all DAR's are wealthy women and some members delay buying and others do not buy the official insignia at all. Headquarters sends lists of new members to the jeweler's, which promptly mails these ladies printed folders listing the insignia with their prices. It may be six months or a year before orders come in, the jeweler reports.

When the price of the official insignia was raised to $17.75 in 1947 the Insignia Committee, after inquiry, concluded that the increase was justified because of the higher costs of skilled labor and materials. In 1948, however, the National Board of Management approved a new small-size recognition pin, hoping that this would increase the number of members who "are proud to wear the society's noble emblem" but have felt they could not afford the more expensive, full-size pin. The Insignia Committee chairman reported it was surprising how many members had not bought pins, and with cheaper small pins available she urged them to "make some small sacrifice, give up a few luxuries or pleasures and save for a pin . . . tell their families they would like the emblem of our beloved society for a gift." The cheaper pins—$8.75 for what the Insignia Chairman called a "lovely little miniature" insignia, and $5.50 for a button-type pin—served their purpose.

Each member may buy a chapter bar bearing the name of her chapter in addition to the insignia and original ancestor bar. If members can establish other Revolutionary ancestors through "supplemental" lines, they may buy and wear a bar for every additional ancestor, and this bar is engraved with the name of the ancestor it represents. With a ten dollar charge for verifying a supplemental ancestor's line, and each ancestor's bar costing $7, the strings of ancestral bars worn by some Daughters run into hundreds of dollars.

There are numerous badges for officers and "ex" officers— chapter regents and ex-chapter regents, state officers and ex-state officers, national officers and ex-national officers; pins for officers' clubs—Vice President-Generals' Club, National Officers' and State Regents' Clubs, State Officers' Clubs, ex-state Regents' Clubs, pins for pages, and for twenty-five and fifty year members.

The prize item of all is a magnificent pin handed down from President-General to President-General and worn only by her while holding that office. Designed and ordered about 1900, at a cost of a few hundred dollars, this pin could not be reproduced for less than $2500 at 1958 prices. It is set with diamonds and sapphires in the official blue and white colors and is the finest piece of jewelry ever bought by the organization, except for the four jewelled badges presented to the four official founders in 1898.

Another attractive and expensive pin is a piece of jewelry which probably few rank and file members know is purchased every three years by their society. It is a miniature duplicating the President-General's official pin, set with the same precious stones, and is given to each retiring President-General when her administration ends. The cost of this jeweled emblem is reported to be about $350.

Each of the eleven "Cabinet Officers" elected with the President-General buys and wears a special badge pin, designed to indicate the work of her office, and after her term expires she still may wear the official pin if she adds a supplemental "Past Officer" pin to show her "ex" status. A lamp of knowledge adorns the Librarian-General's badge; a sealed envelope, that of the Corresponding Secretary; for the Registrar-General, crossed swords and a rolled scroll, indicating concern with records of the Revolutionary conflict; a gavel is used for Vice President-General's; crossed quill pens, the Recording Secretary-General's; a replica of the cracked Liberty Bell, the Historian-General's; crossed furled flags the Curator-General's; and a torch of learning, that of the Reporter General to the Smithsonian Institution.

In 1923 standard badges for state officers were adopted throughout the country, the United States possessions and chapters abroad. In the earlier and gaudier days, there was no such uniformity and the results were often somewhat spectacular. For example in 1909 newspapers reported that Kansas Daughters went to the annual Congress in Washington, wearing badges with the state's sunflower on a blue background and insignia pictured in the center of the bright yellow posy. At the same Congress, South Carolina Daughters were decked out with ribbon badges of dark blue, on which the state's official palmetto tree emblem was embroidered in palmetto fibre, with added lettering, "DAR," in white silk.

Staid indeed, by comparison, are the standardized designs for state officers' badges, each somewhat different but all including laurel leaves or sprays of laurel, to indicate leadership and distinction. For the chairmen of the twenty-nine national committees there is a standard badge topped by an eagle and including the name of the committee in prominent lettering. The price of national officers' pins varies from $22 to $24 each, depending on weight, since fourteen karat gold accounts for much of the cost of manufacture. Chapter regent's bars or badges are $13.25 with engraved chapter name, and $20.25 with chapter name in gold on blue enamel. Chapter bars are $7 each, the same as ancestral bars. For pages' bars, plain blue enamel with a silver star for

each year's service up to five years, when the silver stars are replaced with one gold star, the price is $3.75; and for members of
committees which keep the annual DAR Congress running smoothly, a plain round button-type pin is $3.

Each new pin, bar or badge must be authorized by the National
Board of Management. No permit is valid longer than a year after
the time it was issued; if the pin, bar or badge has not been
bought within that period, the permit must be re-issued. The
Registrar-General in addition to other functions, issues permits
for insignia and ancestral bars; the organizing Secretary-General,
whose responsibility has to do with the organization of new chapters and the recruiting of new members, issues permits for chapter, state and national officer pins.

As designer of all official pins, bars and badges, Caldwell
works in careful collaboration with the Daughters and shows much
respect for DAR customs. Describing what happens when the
company is asked, for example, to design the pin for a new DAR
club, Mr. Kulp explains: "Suppose we receive a letter from
Louisiana, telling us Louisiana DAR's want a club pin for a
group of state officers. Maybe it will be a club for ladies who were
state officers twenty years ago. We think of a design including
the state seal, the state flower, or perhaps the pelican (prominent
in Louisiana's state seal) or the geographical outline of the state.
We put the various ideas into rough drafts of designs, digest them
and work until we come up with perhaps two or three suggestions
we think would be right in size and have the proper significance.
We submit these suggestions to the club members for consideration
at their next meeting. If they have suggestions when they see the
submitted designs, they write us and we try to follow their suggestions. Sometimes it takes there or four months to get it boiled
down to an accepted design."

The Daughters do their best to guard against their "beloved
insignia" falling into alien hands or being worn by members who
have resigned or have been dropped from the society's rolls. A
handbook declares: "To wear the insignia proclaims membership.

It should not be worn by former members, either resigned or dropped from the society, as the status of these is as if they had never belonged, although eligible. Non-members wearing the insignia proclaim falsely. Use of the insignia should conform with the dignity and importance of the National Society it represents."

Disposition of the insignia owned by deceased members, as well as by resigned or dropped members, is a source of worry. The handbook even goes so far as to direct how the insignia of deceased or inactive members may be disposed of; it may be buried with the deceased member; the name and number may be erased and the pin re-engraved with another name and number of an active member of the society; another name and number of an active member may be engraved beneath the original name and number; or the pin may be returned to the Treasurer-General as a gift to the society. However, these precautions can not protect the insignia from a danger even more distasteful to the organization—the possibility it may turn up in pawn shops.

In 1949, according to an Insignia Committee report, three official insignia pins were for sale in a Washington D. C. pawnshop for $45. The Insignia Chairman wrote the manager of the pawnshop, asking for the names and national membership numbers on the pins; she thought perhaps they had been lost or stolen, or had been sold by some one who had inherited them, but she could not believe that a "member would dispose of the Society's emblem in this manner." The names and numbers, however, had been erased. To make matters worse, at $45 the pawnshop prices were cheaper than new pins or old ones returned to Caldwell for erasing and replacing names and numbers. What happened to the three pawnshop pins has not been reported, but in another instance the organization used pressure to force a reputable antique dealer, who had a DAR insignia pin in his stock, to sell it for its melting value. The Daughters pointed out to the dealer that his continued display of the pin would cause him to "lose the esteem" of many of his customers.

Further protecting the insignia, the society has set up rigid and numerous rules governing its use. The insignia must always be accorded the "place of honor," which is the top center or left upper corner of stationery, programs, yearbooks, conference reports and so forth. and there must be no wording above it. On covers of chapter yearbooks the insignia is placed a little above the center; on cast bronze tablets, if it is not at the top, sufficient space must be left around the insignia to give it definite prominence.

So many rules govern the wearing and use of the insignia that even the Daughters are confused. In her report to the 1956 DAR Congress, Mrs. Lawrence G. Tinsley, Insignia Chairman, reported some of the questions put to her: Where can twenty-five and fifty-year pins be ordered and at what prices? What to do with the insignia of deceased persons? Where to buy the Handbook on insignia? Can a Daughter use her deceased mother's pin, which she inherited? Should the twenty-five or the fifty year pin come first on the official DAR ribbon?

Reporting that most of these questions were easily answered, Mrs. Tinsley added that some difficult ones had been posed such as whether a member could wear her deceased mother's Regent pin when she became a Regent, though the pin bears the seal of a state other than her own; whether the DAR insignia could be worn only over the left breast, when this seems impossible because the wearer has so many other pins and ancestral bars (to this Mrs. Tinsley replied practically: "Pin the ribbon higher on the shoulder"); whether the official insignia could be cast and erected on top of the tall flagpole in front of a chapter house and DAR museum.

The last question the Insignia Chairman referred to national headquarters, which ruled that the insignia could be placed on the base of the flag pole, provided it was imprinted on a bronze marker and laid flat on the face of the pole's base.

So careful are the Daughters about their own use of the insignia that, during World War II, members who joined the Armed

Forces took steps to find out if they could wear membership pins and badges on their uniforms. Asking Major General J. A. Ulio, Army Adjutant General, for a ruling, they were told DAR membership pins and badges might be worn by service women on their uniforms, along with service decorations and medals of the Armed Forces, while attending meetings, ceremonies and conventions of the society.

Not quite so important as the insignia, because it is worn by fewer members, is the official ribbon. The sight of delegates to a Congress inspired the following lines by one observer:

> *Some of their noses are snub*
> *And some are Roman*
> *But all of them wear a ribbon*
> *Across their abdomen.*

This ribbon is a shoulder sash, that is worn over the right shoulder and under the left arm. Only state and national officers—President-General, Honorary President-General, Vice President-General, Past Vice Presidents-General, elected national officers, past national officers, state regents and past state regents—are entitled to wear the shoulder sashes and may do so only on formal DAR occasions.

There are slight differences in design which probably would escape notice by anybody except a Daughter; the President-General's ribbon, for example, has a blue center with white edge-stripe, and when she takes this off and dons an Honorary President-General's sash, she must buy a new one; the "Honorary" sash has colors reversed—white center and blue edge stripe.

More complicated are the designs for the shoulder sashes of national officers other than the President-General. Members of the President-General's Cabinet wear a ribbon with blue center and white edge stripe, and when they go out of office they substitute a ribbon with blue center, a thin white stripe on either side of the center, then a blue stripe on either side of the white stripe, and a white edge stripe. State regents wear ribbons of the same

design as the official ribbon used for "mounting" ancestral bars—
blue center stripe with white edges; but for past state regents the
ribbon design has a center stripe of blue, a stripe of white on either
side and a blue edge stripe.

While not as rigid as restrictions on official insignia, there also
are hard and fast rules for wearing shoulder sashes. The society "recommends" that a sash shall not be worn while attending a funeral and orders that it must not be placed upon a deceased person. A lady entitled to wear the sash must lay aside
her top coat before she puts it on; but if she appears in a suit,
the sash may properly drape her shoulder. If she is a national
or past national officer, she may wear her ribbon at state meetings
on strictly official occasions and at the invitation of a regent when
she is a chapter guest. Past state regents may wear their ribbons
at all society meetings, and national officers, past national officers,
state regents and past state regents may wear theirs at DAR
dedications.

A special gauze ribbon of official colors and design may be
bought and used for decorative purposes, but the official ribbon
itself is reserved strictly for official wear. Also frowned upon is
commercial or semi-commercial use of DAR insignia, which may
not be imprinted on stickers, napkins, match books, playing cards
or used for decorations or ornamentation, even at DAR functions.
However, the Daughters permit Caldwell & Company to turn out
and sell (to members only, of course) place cards with embossed
DAR insignia; meeting notification cards similarly decorated;
government post cards with blue insignia; unstamped postcards
with blue insignia and insignia embossed or illuminated staton-
ery. Members need no headquarters permit to buy stationery,
but it may be used only for official purposes connected with the
work of the society. Top price is $5.80 for one hundred corres-
pondence cards and envelopes, with insignia embossed on each;
but even more expensive are insignia illuminated place cards,
which cost $9.75 for 100.

The jeweler is also permitted to sell a limited selection of articles to DAR customers—beautiful pink Spode china plates decorated with drawings of Constitution and Memorial Continental Halls; tea and coffee spoons of spinning wheel design; memorandum and address books, silver key chains, silver DAR bracelets, silver baby spoons and forks, silver baby cups, the latter with insignia decoration.

With the Daughters, orchids and insignia have become big business.

CHAPTER XVI

WHAT OF THE FUTURE?

The Daughters understandably resent much of the criticism levelled at their organization and its works. This criticism, they say, is one-sided and emphasizes those things that are not truly representative of the society. "Why don't you write about the good things we do?", President-General Carraway once asked a United Press representative.

Apparently having no confidence that the newspapers would themselves give the DAR a better press, Miss Carraway proceeded to do it herself. She reported to the Congress at the end of her administration in 1956 that she had answered every published criticism of the society during her term of office. She also had spread the word of the society's good works. Miss Carraway wrote the *New York Times* defending the policies of the 1955 Congress described by the *Times* as "antediluvian". She protested to the *Saturday Evening Post* because, in his White House memoirs, one of President Truman's Assistant Secretaries, William Hassett, said the DAR was "obsolete." She wrote a defense of the society challenging a comment by Mrs. Eleanor Roosevelt in *McCall's Magazine* that the DAR's had "a great fear of anything new."

The organization wants the public to know that it is not by contributions from wealthy women, but by nickels, dimes, quarters, even pennies or the price of a two-cent stamp, that the Daughters have raised money for their many worthy projects. A quarter assessment here, and a nickel there, a dime for this and a penny for that, multiplied by many thousands in the DAR membership have added up to large sums which Daughters feel have been spent wisely and well. Only once in their long career has there been any suspicion of mishandling of funds—the case of the missing

$8,000 due their jewelers. Money raised the hard way has gone for a wide range of worthy causes, the society points out, from Americanization programs and educational scholarships to historical restorations.

The DAR's past has been marked by a reverence for the ideals of their forefathers as they interpret them, an almost fierce devotion and loyalty to their society, and a tremendous amount of hard and steady organizational work.

What of the future? If the organization could be satisfied with the role of an exclusive women's club, it might live on pleasantly and indefinitely. Most of its members are housewives from Maine to California, many without too much money; in fact it used to be a standing joke that when they came to annual meetings three would sleep in a hotel room and share one evening dress, and Washington cabbies still give them the prize for the record numbers of ladies they can pack in taxicabs. The leadership, however has always been in the hands of wealthy women; and apparently the members feel this is as it should be.

In thousands of home towns, the DAR is an exclusive club to which everyone's next door neighbor cannot belong. At national level it serves the same purpose for well-to-do delegates who come each year to the Congress, meet old friends, make hotel reservations six months or a year in advance for the next Congress, and take pride in the number of annual meetings they have attended. On a more homespun level, two busloads of Missouri Daughters had a pleasant and clublike trip to the 1955 and 1956 Congresses. They had the same drivers all the way, made several side trips, christened themselves the "Bluebird Wives," and in general "had a lot of fun."

There has been a marked tendency to perpetuate the same ladies, practically all of them wealthy women, in most offices. On the platform at the 1956 Congress, for example, were Mrs. Henry B. Joy, of Grosse Point, Michigan, whose husband was president of Packard Motor Company in its greatest days, for years chairman of the Resolutions Committee and a power in the society's politics; Miss Katherine Matthies, of Connecticut, donor of thousands of dollars to DAR projects each year, who has been a member of the Resolutions Committee, a teller, a Vice President-General, and undoubtedly would have been President-General were it not, according to some, for her shyness; Mrs. William Sherman Walker of Washington, of controversial National Defense Committee fame, has also been organizing Secretary-General, first Vice President-General, Buildings and Grounds Committee chairman, and more recently Resolutions Committe vice chairman. Mrs. Brosseau began her service as National Transportation Committee chairman went on to chairmanship of the important Ellis Island committee, was elected Treasurer-General and President-General, later was Resolutions Committee chairman and was for three years unpaid magazine editor.

Twelve candidates on the ticket of Mrs. Thomas Henry Lee of Philadelphia, who finished second in the 1956 President-General election, campaigned on an "experience" platform and headed their campaign literature with the boast that the group together had served a total of 63 years on the National Board of Management, whose members are national cabinet officers, Vice Presidents-General, and state regents.

But, regardless of the easy-going social features of the organization, no one who has observed the Daughters in action could entertain the belief that having tried their mettle in national and international affairs they would be satisfied with an inconspicuous club-woman role. Win or lose, the Daughters have moved too far from their earlier, more peaceful paths to make a return journey seem likely. At the same time there is a vast difference between the Daughters of the 1950's and their determined predecessors of thirty years ago. Some of the fire and dedication of the controversial 1920's seems to have disappeared.

At least there is now a realistic acknowledgement of the need for good public relations—a tacit understanding that the over-aggressive and high-handed actions of the past will not boost organizational prestige. Mrs. Throckmorton's 1956 press conference, at which she tried to set reporters straight on the DAR stand with regard to the United Nations, is indicative of this new era.

Almost thirty years earlier, Mrs. Brosseau had adopted no such conciliatory attitude when she was attacked on all sides because of the DAR Black List. Nor is it likely that Mrs. Brosseau, in the 1920's, would have answered criticism as Miss Carraway did from 1953 to 1956.

During the Black List furor, Mrs. Brosseau demonstrated the spirit of the 20's in a letter to Dr. Clarence Cook Little, President of the University of Michigan, who had joined many other public figures in deploring the list. The Brosseaus had lived originally in Michigan and gave the University of Michigan a $115,000 scholarship endowment shortly before Dr. Little made known his position on the list. Promptly, Mrs. Brosseau addressed this letter to Dr. Little:

"From a newspaper report, I learn of a recent diatribe of yours against the Daughters of the American Revolution, part of the attack being based upon an 'alleged blacklist.' Frankly, I would say that the policies of the Daughters of the American Revolution are not any of your particular concern. You are supposed to be an educator and not a censor of organization methods other than the particular organization with which you are connected.

"The DAR has not attacked you. Why should you go out of your way to needlessly criticize it?

"Last, but not least, the National Society, Daughters of the American Revolution, does not issue any such list as you condemn—which fact you might have learned had you done me the courtesy of an inquiry. That would have been quite logical, considering our mutual interests in the University of Michigan, of which you happen at the moment to be President."

Defense through attack was Mrs. Brosseau's technique in those rare instances when she recognized that criticism of the DAR existed at all. It is quite doubtful that she would have written a letter such as Miss Carraway addressed in 1953 to *McCall's Magazine*, challenging a comment made by Mrs. Franklin D.

Roosevelt in a reply to a question as to whether her opinion of the DAR had changed since Marian Anderson was refused the use of Constitution Hall. "When I was in Washington," Mrs. Roosevelt stated in her column, "the DAR's were an extremely narrow and conservative group of people, with a great fear of anything new. They still, I fear, have these same characteristics, but that doesn't prevent them from doing excellent patriotic service in the preservation of historic landmarks throughout the country. This, however does not make them one of the forces for moving forward in the world today."

In her carefully-drawn reply, Miss Carraway wrote: "If being patriotic, with a deep love of country and its welfare and being zealous to maintain our American Way of Life can be considered narrow and conservative, then we plead guilty of such a worthy characteristic. Would that more Americans were 'narrow and conservative' along this line, when it comes to trying to preserve and cherish our Constitutional government."

On a "broad scale," the President-General insisted, the DAR's are not narrow and conservative. "Nor are we afraid of anything new. We have many important 'firsts' to our credit, to disprove this charge: First to build a large headquarters for women anywhere in the world, first to award prizes for anti-aircraft gunnery, first to get women in our Armed Forces, among the first to plead for adequate military preparedness after World War I, first to start occupational therapy in public health hospitals and among the first to aid immigrants on Ellis Island and to start schools for underpriviledged children." On military preparedness," wrote Miss Carraway, "we were proved right . . . among the first to combat Communism, when others were coddling Communists or fellow travellers, again we were vindicated by time."

Listing three primary objectives since 1890—historical appreciation, patriotic service and educational training—Miss Carraway added an inventory of "numerous constructive lines on which we try to be a force moving forward"—student loan funds; Junior American Citizens' Clubs for all races, creeds and classes of school children, with 245,275 members in 1952; awards of 2138 Good Citizenship medals in 1952, to youths of all classes, creeds and races who showed qualities of honor, courage, scholarship, service and leadership; presentation of 23,000 medals to outstanding girl seniors in accredited high schools over the previous three-year period, with substantial prizes to many; distribution of thousands of DAR Manuals for Citizenship; work of Committees for Americanism, Red Cross, Indians, natural and human resources; "and many other worthy undertakings, including the erection of a $500,000 Memorial Bell Tower at Valley Forge."

Miss Carraway then sounded what could only be the last note in the Anderson affair: "Daughters of the American Revolution hold Miss Marian Anderson in highest esteem as a great singer and patriot. She has sung twice in our Continental Hall, and has another engagement for a concert there next March 30."

An incident in February, 1957, furnished additional evidence that the Daughters are increasingly sensitive to public criticism.

On February 10, 1957, the *Denver Post* reported that Mrs. Charlotte Rush, a member of Denver DAR chapter, had refused to let a Mexican boy carry an American flag on a Lincoln's Birthday program to be given at the Colorado State Industrial School, a correctional institution to which are sent all nationalities, races, creeds and colors. The story was reprinted all over the country but Mrs. Frederic Alquin, President-General, learned about it only when she had a query from a Washington newspaper on February 11. Rushing into action, she issued a public statement to all news services, saying the comment quoted was entirely contrary to the policy and practices of the DAR.

Other developments followed swiftly. Mrs. Rush, who had been chairman of the Denver Chapter's patriotic education committee, publicly apologized for the comment, saying she had spoken "carelessly" and that she, not the DAR, was at fault. Mrs. Richard P. Carlson, state regent chapter and spokesman, also said Mrs. Rush was speaking for herself and deplored the comment. On the evening of February 11 the Denver Chapter met and Mrs. Rush's post was "vacated". A month later, the "true story" of the incident was reported by Mrs. Ray L. Erb, National Defense Committee chairman, in a memorandum sent to all chapters; and at approximately the same time, the DAR Press Digest (monthly publication distributed to all chapters) devoted its entire space to a complete report of the incident. It reprinted favorable editorials, reported mail "six to one" in favor of the DAR position; and quoted U. S. veterans of Mexican descent in defense of the organization and its work for foreign-born.

Both Mrs. Erb's memorandum and the Press Digest declared that the incident had been misrepresented—that it actually happened in 1950, not 1957—as Mrs. Rush recalled in talking to a reporter for the *Denver Post*. The dismissed patriotic education chairman also was defended; the official reports said Mrs. Rush, training a number of boys for a 1950 pageant, found that an American youth assigned to carry a flag had not shown ample respect for it, while a Mexican was respectful, enthusiastic and eager to carry it. They reported that Mrs. Rush told the unenthusiastic American boy, "I wouldn't let a Mexican carry Old Glory, would you?" And this, they said, was merely an "appeal to a child to carry his own flag."

In her first annual report as President-General, at the 1957 DAR Congress, Mrs. Groves also made a complete report of the incident and how it had been handled at headquarters. "Telegrams were sent out immediately to members of our national board, state regents, state press chairmen and honorary officers in explanation, with statements for use for local coverage," she said. "In addition, 300 letters were sent to newspapers by our press relations department and every unfavorable editorial was answered. May I again remind you that this is an incident that happened in 1950, not 1957? May I also remind you that we have every reason for pride in the accomplishments of our national society? We have a magnificent record of service."

There was no further reference to the incident at the 1957 Congress, except by Mrs. Groves at a New York luncheon, in which she urged her fellow members to "watch their words." The 1957 President-General, a gentle-voiced lady who interrupted voting on controversial resolutions to remind delegates that "minority opinion" must be accorded every courtesy, gave the Congress dignity, gentility and charm. She wore orchid corsages, a different smart hat every day, and a succession of handsome outfits, but never was overdressed or conspicuous. Obviously no platform personality, Mrs. Groves made few extemporaneous comments, but what she did say was dignified and to the point.

A business woman, the President-General presented a businesslike approach to her responsibilities as head of this great woman's organization. Under her leadership the Society had arranged with a Washington trust company to recommend good investments, "with the hope of having our principal grow and increase," it had employed a team of professional analysts to survey the Society's headquarters operations, "with the hope of insuring maximum efficiency;" it had increased insurance coverage on books, manuscripts and treasures exhibited in the DAR museum and state rooms, for greater protection; it had engaged a nationally known accounting firm to simplify auditing and reporting of cash transactions; and it had reorganized the Registrar-General's office, to increase the flow of work and avoid lost motion in handling lineage papers.

But Mrs. Groves also repeated warnings of previous Presidents-General that the organization had some reason for alarm over its finances. Reporting it had many problems as a result of expanding operational costs she stated "it is quite likely that our Society will have to give serious consideration to increasing our national dues, which have increased only 50c in 1948 and 50c in 1952." This, she said, was a matter not to be handled by the 1957 Congress, but one which would have to be faced. She reported membership increase—185,997 Daughters in 2816 chapters—but warned against optimism because "allowance has to be made for the many deaths reported during each year and other membership losses." And she urged the importance of contributions to the Society's investment trust fund, for maintenance of our "magnificent national headquarters;" a fund which has not increased as the Daughters had hoped. In fact, contributions in the previous twelve months had been discouragingly low; another officer made this report and pleaded with the Society's 185,000 members to give $1 a year to the trust fund.

There were no dissident Daughters at the 1957 Congress, to raise their voices from the floor in protest against a group of resolutions which put the Daughters more belligerently on record than any group adopted in previous recent years. Rising votes, instead of "Yeas" and "Noes", made it difficult for reporters to get a completely accurate count of the few dissenters. Asked the reason for the rising vote, Mrs. Groves referred the inquiry to Mrs. Henry Robert Jr., Honorary President-General and parliamentarian, who replied that it allowed greater delegate participation and lessened fatigue.

Mrs. T. B. Throckmorton of Des Moines, Iowa, resolutions committee chairman, climaxed reading of controversial resolutions with a rising inflection and quickened tempo; in very few cases did she fail to draw applause. But she prefaced the reading with remarks which, reading between the lines, seemed to indicate that ruling Daughters were not entirely sure of the temper of their voting delegates. "I would like to make a statement concerning the resolutions committee," she said. "It is made up of over 50 women who come from all over the United States, every woman proven and able, most of whom have been state or national officers, including some Honorary Presidents-General. Fields of business, law, medicine and education are represented, and I am sure you feel that your resolutions are safe in their hands."

The resolutions proposed by this nation-wide group, all adopted as drawn with the exception of one on water conservation, condemned UNESCO and called for U.S. withdrawal from the United Nations if Red China is admitted to membership; asked the U. S. Congress to nullify the Status of Forces Treaty, which subjects American service personnel to the jurisdiction of laws and courts in countries where they are stationed, for offenses committed while off duty; urged withdrawal of American support from the International Labor Organization, calling ILO an "important aspect" of the world Communist movement; attacked "usurpation of constitutional power by one or another branch of the federal government"; recommended that Congress reject all pending civil rights bills and recognize rights of states to protect their citizens as provided in the Bill of Rights; deplored President Eisenhower's record peace-time budget and called for federal economy and tax reduction, declaring the "present tax take is approaching confiscation"; demanded that the Government abandon all business, professional, commercial, financial or industrial enterprises except as specified in the Constitution; supported the McCarran-Walter Immigration and Nationality Act; opposed legislation to require registration of all citizen-owned firearms, because such registration lists enabled World War II invaders to quickly locate and seize privately owned weapons of citizens in invaded countries; urged Daughters to work for traffic safety; deplored "progressive encroachments" on states' rights, and urged "cessation of these prejudicial practices," opposed President Eisenhower's "atoms for peace" plan because of Russia's reputation for refusing to live up to its treaty obligations; opposed President Eisenhower's plan for federal aid to school construction; demanded "effective programs of fundamental education with particular emphasis on history, English, mathematics, science and languages"; urged members to work through their legislatures to require loyalty oaths for professors, teachers and school administrators; and finally charged Communism in the churches and urged each Daughter to "seriously study the psychology of subversion, in order to distinguish between the word of God and the voice of Moscow."

So despite some indicated concern about public opinion in 1957, the organization continued to follow its traditional line. Its resolutions still made news, but roused no such public interest as in the past.

In earlier and more controversial days it would have been unthinkable to answer press stories such as the *Newsweek Magazine* article of May 2, 1938, which reported that President Roosevelt had "insulted" the Daughters by calling them Daughters of Rebels and of immigrants. The magazine's story began: "Known to irreverent correspondents as the Damned Annual Row, the 47th DAR Congress opened. . . ."

In its early, less complicated years the Daughters had very few occasions for controversies. They were then essentially a national woman's club; their resolutions were of a less world shaking variety and they had a spontaneous, almost rowdy spirit that turned their Congresses into reporters' field days. When, in the early days, boisterous DAR's were ousted from the Union Station in Washington by the station master because their electioneering among arriving delegates created such a turmoil and nuisance, this was news.

And election campaigns were then rowdy and fun, with everyone in there pitching. In 1911, Mrs. Story's supporters, urging their candidate for the second time, charged that defective construction had caused the sinking of the walls of Memorial Continental Hall. Two years later, when Mrs. Matthew T. Scott was ending her administration, an open letter from a group of Daughters charged laxity in financial affairs connected with debt payments on the Hall, and Mrs. Scott replied indignantly in an open Congress session: "That is a libel upon the integrity of your chairman and a libel upon the integrity of the Administration."

In 1913, election judges missed their dinners while they waited for 14 voters who had not shown up at the polls. In 1917 Mrs. Guernsey charged that candidates on her ticket had been "stolen" because they had been allied to the opposing ticket of Mrs. James Hamilton Lewis, wife of the Democratic U.S. Senator from Illinois. On account of this charge there was a five-hour delay in opening the ballot boxes and delegates sat for 13 hours in Memorial Hall auditorium waiting to be called for voting. In the same election, after war had been declared against Germany, there was a rumor that because of the need for unity in the national crisis, delegates would be released from their pledges to support opposing candidates. War or no war, Mrs. Guernsey refused to release her delegates, although Mrs. Lewis declared she was the one "war candidate." The same Congress produced a startling query by Miss Aletha Serpel, Virginia regent, who flat-footedly asked if it was true that Miss Florence Finch of New York, magazine chairman, had misappropriated magazine funds. Miss Finch not only vigorously denied the charge but countercharged that attacks against her, a Story appointee, had so weakened the magazine that it could not get advertisements.

This kind of thing seems impossible now, when campaigning is done in whispers and off limits of DAR property, and with the three-minute debate rule in effect. Today's annual programs move like clockwork and are dressed up with a patriotic fanfare which features pretty young pages, solemn processions, banks of flowers, big name speakers and grave and numerous resolutions. If Congresses are now fancier, they are also a lot less exciting. Daughters frequently listen apathetically and vote automatically —when they do not weary of the proceedings and fail to attend. Today's Daughters wouldn't dare throw their hats in the air or wave handkerchiefs or umbrellas, as their grandmothers did in ovations for Mrs. Story.

A more subtle indication of the society's present standing and prestige is the diminishing frequency with which DAR functions are blessed by the presence of guests of first rate prominence. In earlier days, for example, Mrs. Josephus Daniels, wife of the World War I Secretary of the Navy, received with Mrs. Guernsey at a DAR reception, and Mrs. Thomas R. Marshall, wife of Woodrow Wilson's Vice President, sat in a box at a DAR session. After Mrs. Matthew T. Scott induced President William Howard Taft to address the 1911 Congress. President Taft and President Wilson came year after year, and President Wilson treated the Daughters to some of his best oratory.

Marshall Joffre of France, with his family, attended a DAR

ceremony at Mt. Vernon in 1922. Mrs. Thomas A. Edison was a successful candidate for Chaplain-General in 1923. Mrs. Herbert Hoover attended an Iowa delegation meeting in 1931; Miss Eugenia Lejeune, daughter of Marine Corps Commandant General John A. Lejeune, was a personal page for Mrs. Cook in 1925; and famous wit Will Rogers was a speaker at the 1931 Congress. Presidents Calvin Coolidge and Herbert Hoover made major policy speeches at annual meetings.

But Franklin D. Roosevelt attended a meeting only once, and President Truman not at all.

In 1954 President Eisenhower appeared for a few minutes and then not at one of the big night sessions of the annual Congress. Throughout 1957, Mrs. Eisenhower never attended a meeting, although she had allowed herself to be enrolled in the Society after her husband's first inauguration. Also, teas and receptions given for state delegations by wives of Senators and members of the United States Congress seem to have been abandoned. DAR Congress week features many teas, luncheons, dinners and receptions, but delegations give most of these for themselves; state organizations entertain for candidates; or candidates entertain at vote-getting parties for delegates.

Glamour has been lost by eliminating a Tuesday night reception at which Presidents-General and Cabinet officers entertained all delegates. This reception was held on the stage of Memorial Continental Hall, and later in Constitution Hall. As recently as 1947 newspapers reported the gorgeous gowns and careful coiffures of ladies present, including corsages of two to five orchids each. This function gave way to a Tuesday night session devoted strictly to national defense—with more speeches and another long program.

What the annual Congress has lost in political influence and glamour, it has gained in efficiency and dignity. Garrulous ladies have been restrained since the days of unlimited debate. Also, the annual meetings have been streamlined, with the delegates now working a shorter work week beginning on Monday evening and ending on Friday.   In earlier years the session began on Monday morning and continued through Saturday.   The shorter meetings have the disadvantage of making reports so brief that if delegates really want to know what the Society is doing, they must pay $3.50 for a copy of the Congress proceedings.

Another barometer of the Society's future prospects is membership growth.   Although in 1957 President-General Groves proudly reported an all-time membership high of 185,997, this actually represented a very slow rate of increase over the membership twenty-six years earlier. In 1930 the total was 171,000 even though the organization then was under fire because of recurring bad publicity, with numerous resignations of prominent members. Reduced by the depression to 163,000, members were added very slowly and it was nearly thirty years before Mrs. James B. Patton, 1950-53 President-General, reported it had 3,000 more members than the 171,000 enrolled in 1930.

To reach recent record figures, the Daughters had openly sought new members—for the first time in their long history. They initiated an "Honor Roll" for chapters, awarding stars to those meeting ten Honor Roll requirements, among which was a net membership gain per chapter and the enrollment of at least one new Junior member in a year.   That this had "aided membership," was reported by Mrs. Thomas Burchett of Kentucky, membership chairman in 1956.   A year earlier, in another move to encourage new recruits prizes were awarded to the DAR mother with the most DAR Daughters.   Continued in 1956, this award was won by Mrs. Margaret Clifford Jameson of Cynthiana, Kentucky, with ten DAR daughters. Other states reported impressive runners-up, a South Carolina mother with seven DAR daughters, an Iowa mother with eight, and an Illinois mother with nine. Counteracting factors in membership growth are deaths and dropouts, the former averaging 3,000 a year and the latter apparently an even higher figure, judging by Miss Carraway's 1956 membership report that 27,410 new members were admitted during her administration, while net membership gain for the three years was only 11,542.

Although the Daughters collect and disburse vast sums, finances may be another future problem for the Society. In recent years some top Daughters have admitted that its income is not adequate to maintain the organization's valuable real estate and continue its projects. The Society has inaugurated an "investment trust fund" drive among members. In 1956 Mrs. E. Ernest Woollen of Baltimore, Treasurer-General, said she "earnestly hoped" all DAR chapters would contribute. "I cannot emphasize too strongly the value of this trust fund to the Society," Mrs. Woollen said. "Without this fund, it would be almost impossible for us to carry out our various objectives. Our only definite income is from annual dues, and this will not meet current expenses unless it is augmented by other income." A year later, in 1957, Miss Faustine Dennis, Treasurer-General, deplored the fact that only $11,019 or 6c per member had been subscribed to the trust fund in the previous twelve months.

In 1956 Mrs. Woollen made another suggestion for increasing the society's assets; she proposed that each member add a codicil to her will, leaving the modest sum of ten dollars to the society. The Treasurer-General reported that the Society had had more than 3,200 deaths during the previous year, and "at that rate, if every Daughter left ten dollars to the Society, it would amount to $140,000 in five years and would help give us a more or less permanent fund to continue and increase our work."

A $175,000 renovation of Constitution Hall was done in 1956, but despite the fact that it earns an average of about $82,000 in a season in rentals for concerts and other engagements renovation was paid for by a bookkeeping transfer of money from the magazine fund.

The record shows that in 1942 there was a small real estate maintenance fund created by setting aside $50 from each Constitution Hall rental fee and $100 from each of similar fees for the use of Memorial Continental Hall before it was replaced by the genealogical library. In that year the Constitution Hall fund was only $18,537.83 and the Memorial Continental Hall fund $5,592.

With an estimated 2 million women eligible for membership, the Daughters' future might be unlimited if they could attract even a fraction of these potential members. Irrevocably bound by its past, the Society's policies undoubtedly have alienated some prospects while attracting others. No one can tell why more of the 2 million estimated eligibles have failed to join, any more than it would be possible to predict what future DAR policies will be. Certainly many of the issues for which they have fought most vigorously in past years have lost urgency. Billions are being spent for national defense; the United Nations is almost universally accepted; Communist aggression has been resisted by the democracies; and pacifist organizations are quiescent, if not a thing of the past.

A Daughter with a broad acquaintance among the members has remarked that they miss their great money-raising projects of the past; they as a Society feel at a loss for something to do. Since no more such projects are indicated—unless the organization takes seriously the idea of setting up a really large endowment fund to assure an adequate income for its heavy operating expenses, the proper maintenance of its beautiful buildings, and the more or less routine traditional DAR work—the Daughters' future promises to be less vital and intriguing than their past. It seems too much to hope that their interest in history is sufficient to inspire them to embark on some project as was described by one of the speakers at their 1956 Congress—Dr. Wayne C. Grover, United States Archivist.

Reminding them first that their organization "had much to do" with the construction of the National Archives Building in Washington, through their insistence for many years that the government should establish a national historical depository, Dr. Grover reported some highly interesting developments.

In view of their past policies concerning textbooks and education, the Daughters might well take to heart these words by Dr. Grover:

"It has been said that written history is an act of faith. This may or may not be so, but I know I have faith in American history. All historical facts are acceptable, whether good or bad, so long as they are sought truthfully and used honestly. That is how we learn. The only thing we cannot accept is ignorance and indifference. If we are to continue the forward progress of what George Washington called 'the experiment entrusted to the hand of the American people', our great experiment in self-government, we must continue to know ourselves. And this knowledge is the knowledge of history."

The theme of the Daughters' 1956 Congress was "Protect America's Future Through Patriotic Education." Dr. Grover opened the session by an attempt to educate the DAR educators. If they could be inspired to make the future theme of their society at least a partial dedication to the sort of ideal Dr. Grover described, then indeed they might wear the mantle of their founding forefathers as leaders in a changing world.

Unfortunately, however, Dr. Grover's words seemed to fall on deaf ears. The Daughters were not inspired. In 1957 their resolutions made no reference to history at all, except to demand "effective programs of fundamental education with particular emphasis on history, English, mathematics, science and languages." The National Defense Committee Chairman, Mrs. Ray L. Erb, reported that 915 chapters had members who were reading and "evaluating" school textbooks, and 746 chapters were aware of "subversive activities in their communities or states." Mrs. Erb suggested that chapters seek information as to whether their teachers were required to take loyalty oaths and if there was a committee to investigate un-American activities in their states. Nothing had changed. Not really.

INDEX